A NOVEL BY

JEFF KIRBY

THE HEART OF THE PANTHERS

www.jeffkirbybooks.com

Published by Sycamore Publishing Co., LLC.

Book design by Andy Hayes.

Andy@HucklebuckDesign.com

Executive consultant, Scott Hull

Scott Hull Associates

www.ScottHull.com

Library of Congress Cataloging-in-Publication Data applied for.

ISBN (10) 0-9796185-0-9

ISBN (13) 978-0-9796185-0-9

Printed in the United States of America

October 2007

First Edition

With good milkshakes and great burgers, the K & W was a place to eat. But more than that, it was the place to hang out – during the summer, after school, and especially after a ball game.

To my teachers and coaches, for the loving
Guidance and correction I needed...

To my childhood friends, who showed
Me the value of laughter...

To my brothers John and Joe and my sisters
Jenny and Julie, for putting up with me
All these years...

To my parents, for the very same reason...

To my children, Chloe and Adam, for
Reminding me of how fun it can be to be a kid...

And to Kim, for love and support, and being
The girl I always dreamed I would have.

PREFACE

And now... for Springboro,
starting at guard, a six-three
senior, number 34...
-- The dream

A TYPICAL WORKDAY

Present Day

One hot summer morning, not too long ago, I was driving through our subdivision on my way to work. I had a busy day planned, with two court hearings and several appointments, with countless urgent phone calls to answer in between. In other words, it was a typical day in my adult life as an attorney.

My friends joke that my job is to charge outrageous fees to do nothing. I must have missed the class they taught that in law school then. Before walking out the door, I put on my "work face," as my wife calls it, and kissed her without saying anything more. My mind was already at the office, playing out the various problems I was going to wrestle with. I hate when this happens.

I looked in the rearview mirror and was struck by how old I looked. When did that happen? When did life get so complicated? Where are those carefree days I had as a kid when I played Wiffle ball all day? They certainly aren't found at my office. Nor are they found sitting in my den paying bills. Why did we ever *want* to grow up anyway? Life would have been just fine always wearing jeans and tennis shoes and dribbling a basketball all over town.

Turning my attention back to the road ahead of me, I turned left at the stop sign and made my way out the main road. Those glorious childhood days would never come back.

PREFACE

As I neared the end of our subdivision, I drove by one of the newer houses in our area, though that is hardly a unique sight anymore since there are so many newer houses around here. Everywhere I look, a developer is throwing up another house, and it's at such a rate that there soon won't be any countryside. But this newer house was different than the others. It's a split-level home with a nice side yard and an Ohio State flag hanging from the garage. The yard is flat and well groomed. And it has a brilliant array of flowers around the front door. But that's not what made it different. What immediately caught my attention was something near the driveway, standing tall and proud, just ready to be used -- a basketball court. The driveway was large and flat, perfect for a court, with lines painted in all the appropriate positions. The Goal-Rilla erected on the south side added the extra touch. This was the workshop of a budding star.

And that's when I saw him, a twelve year-old boy, alone to his own thoughts, shooting corner jump shots. One after another, he fired the jumpers, paying as much attention to his form as he did to the result. His shirt was already soaked, and his hair so wet it looked like he had just gotten out of the shower. He was so focused he didn't notice me or any of the other people who passed by. It was on *The Game.*

I smiled. The scene happily reminded me of similar days a long time ago, when it was me shooting those jump shots, pretending I was a starter on the varsity. I remembered those great times when I never wore a suit and tie, and I didn't have any worries. That thought led me to a thousand wonderful memories, which for a moment caused the work face to temporarily disappear. As I drove on down the road, my past came back to me.

At the office, my morning went fairly smoothly, but it still had its tough moments. I had a heated discussion with another lawyer on one case and an emotional session with a grieving client on another. By noon, the work face was again back in place, and I needed to break free to regain my sanity. I called my wife Kim and headed home for lunch, which can often be the necessary retreat in the middle of a hectic day. We'd have hot sandwiches and cold lemonade on the back porch, with my young daughter Chloe running around the yard with her friends, which is always fun to watch. Meanwhile, my stepson Adam would be working on his car, his new prized possession, so seemingly awesome that it was the only thing in the world that seemed to matter to him. When experts argue whether life begins at birth or conception, I say it begins at age sixteen when a kid gets his driver's license. I think I've only seen Adam four times in the four years since he started driving.

I pulled into the subdivision, turning towards home. I was talking on my cell phone with another client who had an emergency. As I talked, I looked over at the house with the basketball court. The boy was still there, only now he was in the middle of a pick-up game against his friends Jeremiah and Devyn and others from around town. He took a pass near the corner, took two dribbles and fired the corner jumper. It connected. And I drove on by.

With a smile. *Man, those were some good days. Do these kids know how good they have it?*

He was a better player at noon than he had been at eight o'clock in the morning. He would be even better at eight o'clock that night. Who knew how far his dreams would take him? I thought about that the rest of the day.

Turns out I needed the diversion. I had more heated phone calls and more emotional meetings. But my day ended with my brain still intact, and I came home a little tired but content. For another day, I had done my part to resolve the conflict that eternally exists in our world. Kim had chicken and rice ready, and Chloe and her friends had turned the dining room set into a fort of some sort, with blankets on top of chairs and pillows underneath. Adam, meanwhile, had long since hit the road, never to return. We had dinner, cleaned the dishes and I let Kim retire to the serenity often found in a nice warm bath. Our typical day was ending.

That evening, I walked through the neighborhood listening to the Reds game on my Walkman. I took my typical route, up one street and back down another, then over to still another street. I ultimately ended up at the edge of our subdivision, past the boy and the house with the perfect basketball court for a final time that day. The sun was setting and the skyline was a brilliant orange, picture-perfect for Ohio in the summertime. The boy was still out, but once again by himself and this time shooting free throws. He'd changed clothes, presumably having stopped long enough to eat a little dinner, and maybe sit down for a few minutes to rest. But the drive and energy inside him no doubt was endless *(was I really ever like that? I almost can't believe it)* and he was moved to play and practice some more. The free throws were all game-winners, I was sure, with only seconds on the clock and his team down by two in snake-pit gyms like Fenwick or Lebanon or Franklin, Springboro's top league rivals at the time, and he was practicing for the real moment one day. Been there, done that.

He took two dribbles, spun the ball in his hands and followed through with his arms extended, just like he had been taught by his dad. Boom! The shot was good. The make-believe crowd was going wild, the scoreboard changed numbers to reflect the close score of the game, and a timeout was being called to psyche him out. The game's biggest shot would come next, and everything rode on his shoulders.

PREFACE

I recognized the scene so vividly. Austin was at an age when nothing mattered but the game. His goals and dreams were all about that. Not excellent grades. Not girls. Not anything but playing for the varsity someday. Austin's dream, like mine so many years earlier, was to follow in the footsteps of famous names and great players and be a Panther someday. He dreamed of Friday nights and clutch plays and being carried off the court after a big victory. Such is the life when you're twelve.

* * *

When I was twelve, it seemed like every day was a warm sunny afternoon with a Creedence Clearwater Revival song on the radio. I didn't have to worry about anything. Almost magically, a home-cooked meal was on my dinner table every night at five-thirty. I had electricity to watch TV by and water to shower by, and a dollar a day bought my lunch and gave me all the leftover spending money I could ever need. School was one big social event. And when there was no school, I would leave home sometime in the morning and be free to go to all ends of the Earth and back, so long as I was home for dinner. I could practically do anything as long as I was home by then.

I went *everywhere* around my small town, sometimes on foot and many times on my bike, and it was easy because almost everything was within ten minutes of my front door. There was always something to do, guys to see and places to hang out. A blanket over a clothes-line was a make-shift tent perfect for a campout. The hills at the gravel pit were dangerous challenges that only the most sophisticated of us would dare try to navigate. And there was basketball and football, too, not to mention Wiffle ball, which was a sport that we elevated to an Olympic event.

We would play Wiffle ball for hours, and we were particular about it. If I was the Atlanta Braves that day, I had to know their batting order, and I had to know that Darrel Evans hit left-handed and Davey Johnson hit right-handed. If Felix Milan was up, I couldn't hit a home run – instead, it had to be a bloop single, just like he would hit. And Phil Niekro threw knuckleballs, not fastballs, as everyone knew. Breaking character was as much of an out as a fly ball, and all of us knew better.

We stopped for two things and two things only -- Kool-Aid and the ice cream man. When our ball was either lost of beaten beyond any value, we suspended the game and scoured the town for empty pop bottles so we could get the nineteen cents it cost to buy another one. And then we would get right back to our game.

Then there were the varsity games on Friday nights. Those were a focal point of our week, and the players we watched were our heroes. Our television had only three channels and none of them were devoted to televising ball games, like today. We watched one baseball and basketball game a week, because that was the "Game of the Week." Maybe there were a few more football games, but nothing like it is today. We didn't have video games or computers. There were no cell phones or iPods. And despite all those seemingly horrible travesties, as my kids see it, I never remember a kid sitting around saying he was bored. We always found something to do. And our innocence allowed us to hope for a better day in the future. We followed the varsity teams like they were some sort of heavenly presence.

Kids today feel pretty much the same way, despite the influx of computers and cell phones. On a cold January Friday night in 2007, thirty-five years after I was a twelve-year-old kid, I went to Springboro's basketball game against Xenia, and the place was packed. What lay ahead was a big showdown for supremacy in the Great Western Ohio Conference south division, Springboro's newest conference.

Before the game started, though, there was a lot of commotion near the Panther locker room. Kids were making their way there in droves, like a rock star was in town or something.

Turned out it was something bigger, at least in the eyes of these kids. Jake Ballard, a recent Springboro graduate who has since gone on to play tight end for Ohio State, had come home for the weekend to watch the game. What he wore was nothing special – blue jeans, tennis shoes and a white long-sleeved T-shirt. But to these kids he was their hero, and they clamored to be near him and perhaps get an autograph. One little guy, Ryan Little, had been writing letters to Jake for almost a year, and recently was thrilled to receive a long letter in return. He managed to get Jake to sign an Ohio State football and an Ohio State jersey with number 86 on it, Jake's number.

Little Ryan would not have been more thrilled if Michael Jordan or Tiger Woods had been at the game.

It showed me something. Even today, kids have dreams to be like their high school sports heroes, just like me and my friends used to do.

* * *

I returned from my walk to find Kim sitting on the living room sofa, talking to her mother in the telephone. She waved at me and then breathed a heavy sigh. She then went on to tell her mother the very same things she had told her an hour earlier. Kim was patient, though this was happening with a frustrating degree of frequency. More than once we wondered, why is there such a thing as Alzheimer's? It seemed so cruel to have a healthy body but a mind that couldn't remember anything more than a few minutes ago.

I took a seat on the sofa across from her, propping my feet up and flipping on the television. I knew we had tons of housework to do since we had Adam's graduation party coming up. Flower beds had weeds, and some trees needed trimming. Then there was the broken closet door in the den and the broken boards on the deck behind our house. Isn't it always something with a house? But it had been such a long day, and I was tired. Surely there would be no harm if I sat for a moment and rested my tired eyes, at least as long as Kim was on the phone.

I flipped the channel past all the news shows and instead found what interested me the most, a *Seinfeld* re-run. After a day in the middle of intense emotional conflict, I didn't want to hear about anymore problems anywhere else in the world. Give me neurotic George and crazy Kramer, and give me a reason to laugh, which I have always found by watching this show. Laughter has become my means to escape the responsibility and pressures of my adult life. I silently calculated the number of years I had to work until I could retire and watch *Seinfeld* all day long.

In a short time the sounds around me faded away. My thoughts then returned to Austin and his shoot-around sessions on his driveway. Wasn't life so much fun back then? Was I ever afraid of anything? I don't think so. And now, years later, when I see my nephews, Connor and Chase, or the kids in my neighborhood like Jeremiah and Elijiah and Barret outside playing ball, pretending, dreaming the dreams that all young boys have, I often put in some classic rock music and I let my mind go back. I can see the games and the players, and I remember the dreams. For a while, I'm a carefree kid again.

It's the final seconds in a Springboro basketball game against Mason, a team that had beaten the mighty Panthers three straight times, making the Comets a more hated rival than they had been before. Jim Hough, a senior guard who would be on everyone's all-star team in 1973, dribbled up-court to set up the game-winning shot. Coach Harry Hall was off the bench, raising his right index finger to show which play he wanted his team to run. Underneath the basket, Jeff Howard and Gordy Gregg shifted their spot near center Chuck Mockabee.

The shooting guard, Gary Patton, swung to the outside to take Jimmy's pass.

The capacity crowd was on its feet. I was in the front row, my fingers crossed, standing next to all of my friends…

Wanna' go back with me?

Good. But you'll need a pair of bell-bottoms. You'll also need some longish hair and a vocabulary that uses words like "groovy" and "right on." Plus you have to embrace AM radio, too.

And one more thing.

Tag, you're it.

PART 1

The heart of a small town rests in its diners and churches, and in the kids who play ball in the parks, but it mainly rests in the excitement found on a Friday night in football season...under the lights.

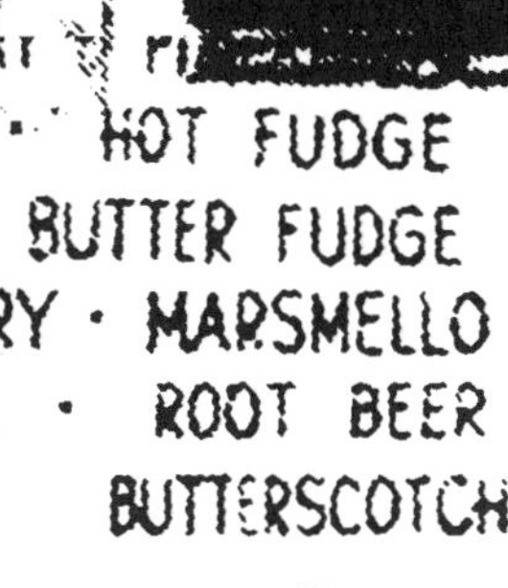

CHAPTER 1

The lights, the camaraderie and the game,
And being black and blue the whole next day.
It's great, and as Kenny Chesney sings, but
"I'm never gonna' feel that way again."
-- Friday night memories

FOOTBALL FRIDAY NIGHT

AUGUST 26, 2005

With his massive arms and thick chest, Coach had always been so strong and seemingly invincible, like a concrete wall on a cold winter day. He used to mix it up during football practice with big, burly linemen, and even though they wore pads and he didn't, he could knock them flat. In basketball practice he would post up against the biggest guys in town, some nearly a foot taller, and still he could muscle his way to the basket. He was Superman.

But now he was approaching seventy. He looked good for a man his age – a thick head of powdery hair, a chiseled jaw and a trim waist – but there were obvious signs that he was aging nonetheless. Maybe it was the glasses, or perhaps it was the way he walked, which was more of a shuffle than a stride. But he was no longer the rock I remembered him to be, thirty-five years ago, back when I was but a kid and he was a legendary junior high coach.

We were side-by-side at our high school football field, a place where we had spent so much time together through the years. Our designated spot is an area just beyond the home bench, behind a chain link fence. It's closer to the field than the bleachers are, and it's to the side of where the players stand. Many of us men stand there so we can feel more connected to the game, where we can not only see the action, but also feel it – which was probably more important, since we are more than just fans. We are former players and/or their fathers and we have to hear pads popping and coaches yelling in order to fully experience a football game. In our book, blood and mud go together.

For Coach, this area is now his coaches' box. It's where he is once again in control, watching the entire field and analyzing every play and every situation. It's amazing the things he sees. "Watch this," he'll say. "We used to run it right up the gut in this situation. Have Dave Dillon go right overtop John Mockabee and we'd score every time. Boom! Let's see what they do here." About all I notice is whether I need more salt for my popcorn; Coach, on the other hand, acts like he should be wearing a headset.

"Take it outside! Take it outside! Did you see that? He cut inside and got clobbered, when all he had to do take it outside and he could have run forever. Dang it!"

I imagined he still dreamed about football in his sleep.

He is Harold "Brutey" Baker and he is the biggest Panther fan since Lowell Hayes and Myrtle Reedy. He's has been around Springboro his entire life, watching it grow from a small town to a fledging city. He's seen all the great players play, and he remembers every important game Springboro has ever been in, starting in the late forties when he was a kid, to the fifties when he actually played in them, then into the sixties and seventies when he was a coach.

Name a player and he could instantly tell you when he played and what his greatest quality was. Name a game and he'll remember who won and what impact the game had on the Panther season. He would do this and his wife Norma would chuckle and shake her head. The man could remember all those details, but never their anniversary. "November 4th," he would say.

"The second," she would add.

"See, I was close."

Brutey was never a head coach, so his name was never seen in print. He was never quoted in the newspaper, either. To the many fans who attended the games, he was some unnamed assistant coach whose role they never appreciated. But to those who participated in the games, from fifth grade on up to the varsity, he was both known and valued, and for that he was as famous as anyone whose name was in headlines.

That's how I knew Brutey. Way back when, his influence was as important to me as anything done by the varsity coaches. I wanted to someday quarterback for football coach Don Ross, and play point for basketball coach Harry Hall, but until then I had Brutey showing me what to do. Sometimes those unnamed junior high coaches do more to develop players than do the head coaches who later get the credit.

"No, no, no! You can't call that kind of defense in that situation. C'mon, fellas, stay with it!" His face turned beet red and he had to wipe sweat from his brow. I was tempted to offer him a drink of my Pepsi, but I'd put too much salt on my popcorn. We all have our game time pressures.

His coaching days were long since gone, but the memories remained, as vivid as if they had just happened. As he stood and watched and cheered, something would inevitably happen that reminded him of a story from years ago. And then his eyes lit up.

"I can still see Jerry Raffel breaking through for a fifty-five yard touchdown run. Man, could he run. Or Al Wight practically breaking some kid in half. Boy, could he hit. I see any game -- football, basketball, baseball -- and I think back to the boys I coached. Great kids. They did so much for this town. If only I could go back to live in a certain place and time, I'd go back to when I coached those boys."

Still, he stayed current. Every year, he assessed the current crop of talent and evaluated its chances of a championship season. He read press clippings on the teams Springboro played and kept up on the changing tactics that developed over the years. He cheered for the undefeated Panthers in '82 and for Sam Little in '84 and Todd Worthington in '91. He thought Jason Anderson and his tenacious cohorts were fun to watch in '99, and he enjoyed Jake Ballard, everybody's All-American, in the same way everyone else in Springboro appreciated him, in '04 and '05. He hoped to still be watching many years after that.

"I see the Cottingim kid isn't playing tonight. They say he has a *bruised* shoulder. Can you believe that? The doctors won't let him play. You know what Jeff Kees would have done in a situation like that? He would have played through it. Tough kid, that Jeff. Toughest kid I ever saw. I remember a home game we had with Waynesville back in '69. Jeff got banged up when he crashed into Steve Pressel during practice. Remember him? Big, big boy, the biggest in Ohio at the time. Anyway, he had a bruised shoulder. Doc Swope put a bandage on him and sent him in. Kids aren't tough anymore."

He was just getting started. He would go on and tell another story from 1972 with Dave Dillon playing with a broken collarbone, one he had repeated no less than a thousand times. There would be a dozen other stories after that, some of them actually new ones.

Since the game on this night had not yet reached halftime, Brutey would tell a lot more stories before the night was over.

"Good hit! Way to go, there!" He would then look over with a grin. "Reminds me of a time when Jay Hopkins knocked the breath out of some kid. Remember Jay? *Good, good* player."

Another play reminded him of Dan Wade. Still another of Ernie Melton. Or Brad Lamb, Craig Dudley or Adam Dillon.

In Brutey's mind, they were all good players.

Good, good players.

Brutey turned around to see the bleachers packed with fans, all wearing Panther blue. Parents of players sat in the reserved seats at the fifty-yard line. The band and student sections were on the far end. Other fans from the community sat on the near end, waving spirit towels. On the field, Springboro's marching band finished up its halftime show, and as usual it was excellent. The Springboro football team gathered in the area just to our left, waiting its turn to get back on the field and warm up for the second half.

"Sometimes I hate standing here," Brutey commented as he removed his glasses to clean them. "Can't they let some of us stand in the end zone like everybody used to? Remember that? You weren't just *at* the game. You were *in* the game. Everyone stood along the sidelines and back lines circling the field. Man, the kids loved that. Now, I need binoculars to see the game."

A lot of things are different than they used to be, I said. Brutey looked at the gray hair around my ears, and crow's feet around my eyes. Then he gave me the once over head-to-toe, and chuckled. "Tell me about it," he joked. I didn't think he was nearly as funny as he did.

The second half started with Springboro kicking off. With a two-touchdown lead, the Panther faithful was hopeful that the second half would be a formality, an easy stretch on the way to a certain victory. But the opponent was Kings Mills, a rival of Springboro's for more than forty years, and the rivalry had produced many epic battles, including some come-from-behind victories. So the coaches knew better than to take anything for granted.

Brutey knew the history well. In the fifties and sixties, Springboro and Kings fought for the Warren County basketball championship. Later, both fought for championships in the Fort Ancient Valley Conference, which was a collection of smaller schools in and around Warren County – Mason, Little Miami, Blanchester, Waynesville and Clinton-Massie. Some of their games defined the term "barnburner," since Kings Mills literally played its basketball games in a renovated barn. Though Springboro left the FAVC for the bigger Mid-Miami League in the nineties, and then the even bigger Greater Western Ohio Conference in 2006, its battles with Kings are still intense, even though a conference championship may not hang in the balance.

Brutey remembered how the '91 football team lost only one game, and it was to Kings Mills. The loss kept that team from going to the state playoffs. It was a painful moment for head coach Dave Stuckey. Brutey watched that game from the sidelines and it easily reminded him of a similar tragedy that happened back in his coaching days.

In 1971, at the height of Brutey's coaching career, Kings Mills (now known only as Kings) beat Springboro in the final conference game of the season, forcing a tie between the two school for the FAVC championship. "I remember that game like it was yesterday," he told me. "We went down there with all the momentum in the world, winning five games in a row. But those Testerman boys sliced us up and spit us out. So we dropped down into a tie for the championship with them, which in a way was okay because we'd never won a football championship before, but we always felt like we left something unfinished. For the next three hundred sixty-five days we had one date circled on our calendar – the return match with Kings Mills at our place. We owed 'em big time."

"You guys hated Kings Mills about as much as you hated Mason," I offered, making sure to speak loud enough so Brutey could hear me.

"Nah, we could never hate anybody more than we hated Mason. But it was close."

As we talked, my daughter Chloe fluttered back and forth from the concession stand with her little fifth grade friends. My stepson Adam huddled near the student section with some of his buddies. Off to our right I saw kids in their blue football jerseys watching the game, doing as I once did, idolizing the varsity players on the field. Max Webb was a running back on the seventh grade team, and Jake Pfahl was a quarterback on one of the fifth grade teams. They were both surrounded by their teammates, and they hung on every play. If junior linebacker Spencer Vanover broke a shoelace, these guys would know it first.

I also noticed a couple walk by and do a double-take. I wasn't sure if it was directed at me or at Brutey, but I suspected it was at me. I'm now a lawyer, and also magistrate in the Springboro court, and that means some people think I'm the worst person alive. People do that when you don't support their position in a disagreement, and I've reluctantly gotten used to it. For that reason alone, I figured it had to be me they didn't like. Besides, who wouldn't like Brutey? The guy was practically a saint.

He kept talking. "You know, thirty-five years ago, when these two teams played, you'd only see old pick-up trucks and banged up cars in the parking lot. I'll bet if you added up the value of all the cars at the '71 championship game, they wouldn't equal the value of that one BMW sitting right there. Nobody in this town had any money, except Doc Swope and Dr. Garland maybe. Nobody in South Lebanon had any money, that's for sure. The same was true for Mason, and now look at it. It's crazy."

I would have repeated my comment about how a lot of things were different now, but I didn't want another visual inspection by Brutey. I know I need to lose a few pounds, and I didn't need to hear it from him.

The bleacher crowd cheered as Springboro's Shawn Carnes, whose father, Mike, had played in that '71 championship game, stepped in front of a Kings receiver and intercepted a pass. The Panthers took over, first and ten on their own forty-three. The band tore into a rousing rendition of Bon Jovi's *You Give Love A Bad Name*, and the offense broke huddle and raced to the line of scrimmage. I figured this was a good time to throw a bomb and try to break the game wide open. Now that my popcorn was gone, my perspective of the game seemed to improve.

Meanwhile, Brutey kept complaining. "And no way would you find a student whose car was worth more than any of the adults. Back then the kids took whatever was handed down to them. Ever hear what Jimmy Hough drove? Or Gary Patton? Best basketball players around, and all they were looking for was something with four wheels. Nothing like it is now. Now it's more like a car show out there."

"You're in one of your moods, aren't you?" I asked.

I already knew the answer.

"Burns me up sometimes. Tell me, what's a kid got to look forward to when he gets a $50,000 car to drive to school? How's he being prepared for anything in life? You wait and see, we've got big problems coming someday."

"You done?" I asked, turning to face him.

"Maybe."

We both knew he was lying through his teeth. He had an opinion about everything, and he never hesitated expressing how he felt. Bush had better be more convincing about the war in Iraq. The oil companies ripped us off when they jacked up prices for no apparent reason at all. And Jim Tressel was the messiah because of the work he had done to renovate the Ohio State football team. Just about all of his conversations turned to Ohio State football eventually.

I noticed the hateful couple staring down in our direction from their spot in the bleachers. What was their deal? The game was playing out on the opposite side of the field, yet they were looking right at us, deep in a discussion. The guy seemed to be more upset than the woman, but it was impossible to tell what they were talking about. Neither of them looked familiar, but that didn't mean anything. Our paths could have crossed in some courtroom years ago and I would never remember it. I figured maybe it would come to me eventually.

On the field, Springboro scored again to take an even bigger lead. The ensuing kickoff sailed high and a Kings player took it at the one. He ran ten yards before being swarmed in a sea of Springboro Panthers. The whistle blew and the players celebrated like they had just won the Super Bowl, causing the cheering section to roar. Brutey watched this intently. "I've been watching that for forty years," Brutey said quietly, "and it gives me chills every time. When I die I want them to spread my ashes right here on the field."

This field? I asked. What about the other field, the old football field, the one that is now used only for soccer? It seemed to me he would rather have his ashes thrown onto the field where he had spent so much time years ago. He said he'd have to think about that. But that reminded him of other opinions he wanted to share.

"You know, they should name this track after Larry Hefflin, for all that he did for the track program, and they should name this field 'Smith Field,'" he said. "E.B. Smith is a great man, and was a great coach. Helped start the football program, you know. Then his teams dominated. And Bruce coached – what? -- fifteen years and won eighty percent of his games. At least that, maybe more. Seems like they should do something to remember both of them. You don't see that very much around here, pictures of old coaches or teams. I'll bet there ain't a player out there who's ever heard of Bill Crocker or Gavin Dillon or Wayne Kemper. Those guys put this town on the map. Kids nowadays need to know who paved the way for the tradition this athletic program has."

"Maybe you should lead that movement," I said. "You've been around a long time, you know people."

Brutey kept talking. "They ought to name a gym or something after Don Ross, too. Coached practically everything and did it well. Think anyone here knows who Don Ross was to this athletic department?"

"Some do."

"Yeah, but everybody needs to," He said. Brutey loved his town, and its heritage.

"So tell them."

He turned towards me and scoffed. "Nah, they won't listen to me. Not anymore, anyway. This town's full of so many people who've come in from everywhere – Cincinnati, Dayton, everywhere – and an old fogy like me is an outsider now. Ain't nobody I know around here anymore."

Kings eventually punted, and Springboro took over on its own thirty-seven. Just then, a band of teenagers walked by, all talking on their cell phones, and I knew exactly what was coming next. Brutey rolled his eyes. "Did you have a cell phone when you were a kid?" he asked. "Don't answer that. I know good and well you didn't, and you got along just fine. I didn't have one either. How many people do I want to talk to anyway? Whatever happened to just hooking up at the K & W? Kids think they're too good for that anymore."

I decided to change the subject, for fear he'd work himself into a heart attack. Sometimes the distraction stopped him and moved him into a different direction, sometimes it didn't. It was worth a try, I figured.

"So why did you stop coaching anyway?" I asked. "You were pretty good. You helped all the great coaches way back when – Coach Hall, Coach Ross. You kicked butt in the lower leagues, too. And, man, you were a motivator."

Brutey looked at me with a twisted expression like I had just asked him his name. He didn't say anything, making me wonder if I'd said the wrong thing. There was a pause for more than a minute. The game went on and suddenly Brutey wasn't paying attention.

"Seriously, you never heard?" he said finally. "You've been around here forever; I thought everybody knew."

I almost apologized. Had I been told something and forgotten it? Had I brought up something that I knew I should never bring up? "Remember, I left Springboro and didn't come back for a few years," I said.

Brutey lowered his head. He had a story to tell and it obviously was a tough one. "Does it have anything to do with those two people up there in the stands? They've been staring a hole in this direction for the last half-hour," I said.

He looked over casually, then groaned. Clearly, he recognized the couple, and not for anything good. There was a history, a story he wanted to tell, but not right there. The game was ending and he was getting tired. Besides, the longer he stuck around, the more chance there was for the couple to come up to him and act on the dirty looks it was throwing his way. Springboro won its season opener easily, 33-13, in what was its first win in a perfect regular season.

Would I mind meeting him the next day, at the old football field where now the Springboro soccer teams play? He would be there to watch his grandson, and we could talk then.

I told him I'd be there. I loved every chance to go to that old field, even if it was for a soccer game. Brutey had something he needed to talk about, and I was going to listen. Whatever the reason Brutey quit coaching, and whatever the reason the couple seemed to dislike him, it couldn't have been that bad. Brutey was too good a guy for any of that. Right?

PHOTO COURTESY OF RON ALVEY

Today, Springboro celebrates massive growth with beautiful subdivisions and gorgeous homes. And native son Jake Ballard plays tight end at Ohio State. It's a far cry from the small-town days many years ago, back when a three-bedroom ranch was a model home and Lonnie Norris was its head football coach

CHAPTER 2

Some grass is sacred – the greens at Augusta; the green, green grass of home, and the one hundred twenty yards of the high school football field
-- Holy ground

A SATURDAY AFTERNOON
RALPH E. WADE FIELD

AUGUST 27, 2005

Years ago, my trip to the field was on a bicycle, with a baseball card fastened to the spokes to make it sound like a motorcycle. My buddies were with me, with our baseball caps turned backwards, and we blew bubbles with our chewing gum. We would cheerfully wind our way through the streets of the Royal Oaks subdivision while listening to The Grass Roots on a transistor radio. Sooner or later, I was promised by one of their songs, love was gonna' get me. I wondered if that was really true.

Now, years later, I drive a Jeep Cherokee that has my daughter's shoes in the back seat and bags of mulch in the trunk. The road to the field takes me past the dangerous curve near The Lovely Farm on St. Rt. 73. There's a new market there owned by Robyn Lovely, who was one of my classmates, and it has become one of the biggest attractions in town. Thanks to the oldies' stations, I still have the likes of The Grass Roots, Grand Funk Railroad and the Eagles on the radio. My wedding ring proves that love did in fact get me after all, which is a good thing.

I arrived at Ralph E. Wade Field midway through the first period of the soccer game, with Springboro and Centerville still locked in a scoreless tie. The sun was warm as it etched its way behind the trees on the other side, and there was a cool breeze out of the south. The bleachers on both sides were full, and other spectators lined the edges of the field, showing just how popular soccer had become since it first came to Springboro in the early eighties.

I found Brutey standing along the fence to the right of the home bench, wearing the same Springboro windbreaker he wore the night before. Did the man ever sit down during a ballgame? He was there to watch his grandson, who was a goalie for the Panthers. Brutey never missed a game. And though he never played or coached soccer, he still coached the game from his perch because, in his eyes, the principles of team competition were the same in every sport.

"Get back! Get back!" he shouted. "Take him to his left, Caleb! To his left!" When the ball went out of bounds, there was a break in the action. Brutey took his handkerchief from his back pocket and wiped his forehead. "You gotta' stay on 'em all the time," he said. "If you don't, they drift off into doing their own thing."

Larry Baker, Brutey's oldest son, sat in the stands behind us with his wife Carmen. They had two children, Caleb – who was their soccer and baseball star – and Lauren, who was a cheerleader. When Larry and Carmen had difficulty getting any of the children to any of their activities, they often asked Brutey to help them. He never once said he couldn't do it.

Ricky Baker, Brutey's youngest son, sat behind Larry, and next to their mother, Norma. Ricky's son, Adam, was also on the soccer team, but didn't play as much since he was only a sophomore. They'd all invited Brutey to sit in the stands with them, but he wouldn't have any of that. Like at the football games, he needed to be down by the field, near the action.

"Say, did you hear the news about Jake Ballard?" Brutey asked me. "He's gonna' be a Buckeye. People say Jim Tressel has been to his house a thousand times, and has called him even more than that. Won't that be something? A kid from little Springboro playing in the 'Shoe."

Brutey looked like a father who's just learned he'd had a son. Cigars for everybody. He had plans for Jake to be one of the best tight ends in the country, and lead the Bucks to a national championship. Then maybe one day play in the pros. He'd watched Jake's mom, Debbie Burson, play girls basketball for the Panthers back in the seventies. He then followed Jake from his peewee days all the way through his high school career, and knew by the time Jake was thirteen that he had a big future. The conversation about Jake distracted him from the soccer game for a while.

CHAPTER 2

"Watch his right side, Caleb! Watch him go right!" he shouted. Then he told the same thing to Jake Eisenhut, one of the other Panther starters. Brutey had the right to yell like that, because he knew what he was talking about. Some of the parents, on the other hand, didn't have a clue.

"I'm going to be hoarse by the end of this game," he said, rubbing his eyes.

I saw that as an open door for a jab. "You never had to do that with me," I joked. "I did everything I was supposed to do all the time."

Brutey chuckled. "Ha, you about gave me a heart attack. You were just like all the rest of 'em. O.J. Powers and I had to ride you like a dog when it came to running the wishbone. You were always so dang nice to running backs that you'd never just hang onto the ball and run up field yourself. Remember that? If we hadn't gotten in your face that one game you'd have never run sixty yards for a touchdown."

"You remember that?" I asked.

"Sure, I do. I remember everything." *Sure, tell that to Norma.*

"Feels weird to watch soccer here, doesn't it?" I said, looking around.

"I say that every time I come to a soccer game. I was here the day back in '64 when they graded the land to build this football field, and then I was here the day a year or so later when the Boosters got everyone together to build the press box and concession stand. This place used to just wreak football. I tell you, every inch of the ground was made for it. The band was over there, and players ran through the goal-posts over there. We saw some good players run up and down this field through the years. I feel like Springboro lost a big part of its history when they took football up to the high school. They coulda' made improvements and kept the game right here."

It was a stretch to think that could have happened, but it was the thought of so many who have followed the program. Fenway Park and Wrigley Field also show their age, with poor parking and antiquated facilities, but no one would ever think of replacing them. Even Ohio Stadium got a facelift when it probably could have been replaced. But years ago Springboro decided to move football from its original birthplace, and it would never return again. A lot of things are different nowadays.

"Remember Wayne Kemper?" Brutey said. He'd asked me this same question a thousand times. I knew he remembered Wayne because he loved the way he played.

"I never saw him play," I said. Wayne was a senior when I was only six years old, too young to go to the football games. But I've always known Wayne and his family because they lived two doors down from me on Redbud.

"Big, strong halfback. Greg Baker was a lot like that. I remember watching Wayne run around right end and lifting a linebacker clean off his feet, he hit him so hard. Happened right there, as a matter of fact." Brutey pointed to a spot around where the twenty-yard line used to be. "Later he came running off the field and I was the first one to meet him with a big bear hug. I loved that style of football."

"Didn't you love Dave Collins, too?" I asked. Of course, I knew the answer because Brutey mentioned him about as much as he did Wayne Kemper. Dave was a three sport star who graduated in 1973. His tenacious play earned him a spot in the Naval Academy after graduation. I always followed Dave's play in every sport since he lived on Walnut right behind my house.

"Aw, man, I did, but for a different reason. Dave was just a little guy – a guard in basketball and an infielder in baseball – but when he played football he played with heart. Not many guys his size would go across the middle the way he did. And he took some hits there. But he always kept coming back. I really respected that about him.

"One night back in '72 when we had that big game with Kings, the grudge match because of what happened the year before, Rod Dillon hit him over the middle – right about there – and Dave just got clobbered. I thought for sure he would have dropped the ball. Hell, a lot of other guys would have come out of the game. But Dave held on and came back for more."

As he told that story, the memory of those days didn't seem like all that long ago. But it was, actually, and a lot had changed. I had moved away, went to college, got a law degree and had since spent twenty years in courtrooms. Brutey had quit coaching, developed a thriving business and officially gone into being the best grandfather he could be. "I missed so much when my boys were growing up," he'd told me. "I thought I was doing the best that I could, but I know differently now." I was now even more curious about why he wanted to meet me. What was the story he wanted to tell me? What could have happened to ever make a great coach like him give it up?

Then it hit me. "That couple last night, did they have something to do with you getting out of coaching? What was their deal?" I asked.

The soccer game we were watching went into halftime. Brutey sighed and scratched the back of his neck. This was going to be a long story, and the couple apparently played a role in why he left coaching. I just never would have dreamed it would have been that big. I was thinking they were disgruntled parents, people who called the house a few too many times or maybe wrote a letter to the editor. Some parents drive hard-working coaches out of their profession because of those kinds of hassles.

CHAPTER 2

But it was worse than that. Much worse.

* * *

When Brutey was a kid, one of his favorite pastimes was riding his bike. Having been born in 1937, Brutey was a grade-schooler in the forties. Springboro was nothing more than a collection of homes on two primary streets back then, and Brutey would ride all the way up Main Street, which was known as "Front Street" back then, and then cruise down East Street, which was otherwise known as "Back Street." He often rode with no hands, something a lot of the other kids couldn't do, so Brutey regarded himself as a magician on the bike. When his family sat around at night listening to the Reds games or George Burns on the radio, Brutey dreamed of one day playing big league baseball in the summer and riding for the circus during the winter. He would do it all.

By the time he was sixteen, he was showing off in his father's car, a 1949 Dodge. There were late-night drag races at the airport north of town. There were also evening cruises to Middletown and back, with Brutey fiddling with the radio and drinking a bottle of Coca-Cola. He steered the vehicle with his left knee. No one else could do that.

The nickname Brutey came in the summer before his junior year. One warm Saturday afternoon just before school started, he went to an Ohio State football game, and the Buckeyes won easily. Brutey watched the game from the tenth row in the north end zone. He was awestruck by the school's tradition and the magnificence of the stadium known affectionately as "The Shoe." He had listened to Ohio State games on the radio, but the game accounts never prepared him for something so spectacular.

He became the Buckeyes' number one fan that day, hanging Buckeye memorabilia in his car and in his bedroom, and memorizing the OSU football schedule six months before the season started. Woody Hayes was his hero and Hopalong Cassady, who won the Heisman Trophy in 1955, was his idol.

After listening to him carry on for six months about Buckeye championships and Buckeye players, his coach, Jim Hough Sr. gave him the nickname Brutey, which is short for Brutus the OSU Buckeye. The name stuck. Brutey spent the next two weeks singing the Ohio State fight song as he drove around town.

With no hands.

He loved everything about sports from the time he was a kid. He played football and baseball on the field behind the school. He played basketball on a dirt court near the Methodist Church. While in high school, Brutey played on Springboro's basketball team for three years, starting in his junior and senior years. He also played third base on the baseball team, hitting seven home runs his junior year and eight more his senior year, earning him comparisons to big Ted Kluszewski, the first baseman for the Cincinnati Reds at the time. He also ran the 440 on the track team.

Among his teammates were Sam Fish and Gil Burson, good guys who have stuck around Springboro their entire lives. Sam dated Barb Arnold, and Gil went out with Sarah Bishop, and when Brutey started dating Norma they all often went on dates together.

Brutey loved football, and always wished Springboro would have had a team he could play on. He spent his Saturdays watching the Buckeyes and Sunday watching the Browns, and secretly he harbored a hope of going to Ohio State as a walk-on. But college wasn't an option for many people in those days. It was too expensive, but more than that, it didn't seem necessary. His father encouraged him to go work at Armco, just as he did, and then settle down and have a family. Initially Brutey wanted something more than that, but eventually he followed in his father's footsteps.

After a stint in the military, he and Norma married and settled down in their brand-home on Market Street, which cost $11,000 and was a Home-A-Rama home of sorts back in 1962. Brutey got a job at Frigidaire and soon his two boys were born. On Friday nights he snuck away to go to the varsity basketball games, and summer afternoons he walked the boys to the nearby park to watch Little League baseball. He had his own car by this time, a 1959 Eldorado, and he would often prop his boys up on his lap as they rode around town in it.

Brutey would hold Ricky in his hands, and drive with his knees. Larry meanwhile, jumped on the front seat.

Brutey had a wife, two sons, a beautiful house and nice car. When he watched the commercials on television, he was told he was living the American dream. He had it all. But while watching a Bob Hope Special one night, Brutey announced to Norma what he had thinking about for quite a while. He needed the intensity of competition again, something that gave him the same thrill and satisfaction that he'd always had as a player.

"So why don't you coach?" she responded. "You know the game and you have the desire. I think you would be an excellent coach."

He looked up from the newspaper, smiling. He'd had the same thought, but he worried about the time commitment. Could she handle the extra time with the boys?

CHAPTER 2

There might be times when she wouldn't see him much at all.

Norma smiled back, knowing full well there was only one answer. "There's a baseball meeting tonight at the school. If you hurry, you won't be late."

That summer Brutey coached the Springboro IGA team in Little League. Then he talked to Ralph Wade about helping out with the Peewee football program. While doing that he met Lonnie Norris, Springboro's first head football coach, and Gerald Saunders, the basketball coach at the time. One thing led to another, and before long Brutey was involved in just about every program there was.

I was a skinny little kid when I first met Brutey. He was one of my baseball coaches the summer Neil Armstrong landed on the moon. In that 1969 season, I didn't know a thing about baseball. I couldn't hit and couldn't throw, and I often got confused about what to do when I was on base. Kind of like the Cincinnati Reds of today. Anyway, Brutey took me under his wing, and slowly showed me what I needed to know. I began to understand, and I got better. By the time I had him again in football in the fall of 1972, I was a much more confident and skilled athlete than I had been. Brutey was a big reason for that.

I remembered a time just before that '72 football season began. We were at the field being fitted for helmets and uniforms. It was a brutally hot August afternoon, probably close to a hundred degrees in the shade. While standing in line, a couple of the other guys slipped into the concession stand for a cup of Pepsi. They didn't pay for it, and frankly didn't see the harm in it. It was just a little something to help cool them off.

Brutey saw them come out and went ballistic. This was stealing, he said. And then he went into a short tirade about the responsibility each of us had to our families and our community. "You're football players! You stand for something! We work hard and we do things as a team! If just one or two of you do something wrong, it makes all of us look bad! You got that! Now get back in line and quit horsing around."

On his way past me Brutey punched me on the shoulder and said something about how proud he was of me. It was a huge compliment, and some of the other guys looked at me like they were impressed.

Brutey's lesson was one of responsibility, and before that I'm not sure I felt a responsibility to anyone except myself. I hoped to always be a positive role model like Brutey said.

And I really hoped no one told Brutey that I'd been in the concession just before the two he caught.

* * *

To this day, I still don't believe Brutey ever found out what I had done. So don't tell him. Our conversation continued well into the fourth quarter, and Springboro had taken a 2-0 lead, which seemed commanding. Jake Eisenhut had one of the goals; Brutey's grandson Caleb had made two goal-saving stops. If the Panthers could hold on and beat Centerville, there would certainly be a celebration.

Telling the story was harder than he had imagined it would be. It was as if he were opening a box of emotions that he had long since put away, hoping they would all die a slow death and disappear forever, and instead finding they were as alive as ever.

Thirty-five years later. How could that be? Was it really that long ago?

"I remember the start of the '72 football season, when the whole football program was in excellent shape. The varsity was coming off a championship season, and the lower programs were feeding off that success. I was working and my kids were doing okay, and I was having as much fun coaching as I'd ever dreamed I could have.

"The football team was loaded with good seniors. And then the basketball team looked even better than the football team. I was right there in the middle of everything. Right there. And then, because I was so stupid, I let it all get away from me."

His voice trickled off as he spoke. I wondered if it was really necessary to delve into the past like that, if all it was going to do was resurrect some awful memories. I had merely made a passing comment about the staring couple at the game the night before. I didn't really need to know about them. I also didn't really need to get into the reason he was no longer a coach. But he seemed determined to do so.

"I'd like to get past it somehow," he told me. "Maybe I could still be a coach." Without the full context of his statement, I didn't know what he meant.

He began his story in late August of 1972, a time I remembered very well. He was a coach and I was a player. I had a lot of great friends, guys like Mitch Leisz, Chris Hill, Lance Penwell and Roger Woolery, and we'd play ball games all day long with Donny Wilburn and Shane Hatfield and other guys from the neighborhood.

As he spoke, I was reminded of how peace and turmoil can sometimes co-exist. I had the carefree life of a twelve-year-old while he encountered the massive struggles that come from being an adult.

We often stood side-by-side. Yet we were worlds apart.

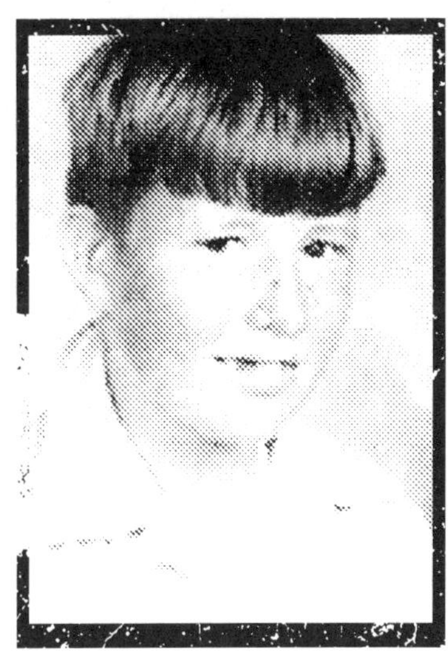

The Heart of the Panthers … halftime entertainment with Debbie Deardoff and Gina Duffy and the rest of the drill team … P.B. Stockman, Lowell Hayes, Bill Crocker and Ralph Wade on the school board … Jeff Howard leaping higher than guys much taller … and a post-game celebration … good friends like Chris Hill …

CHAPTER 3

> ***"Ladies and gentlemen, your attention please. Let's give a warm welcome to the best band in the land, the Springboro Panther marching band!"***
> ***-- Our legendary announcer, P.B. Stockman***

SATURDAY, AUGUST 26, 1972

I couldn't decide who I should be more like. Was I Jack Tatum, the ferocious safety for the Radiers? Or was I Jake Scott, the quick and tenacious free safety for the Dolphins?

It was crunch time, and I just knew the outcome of this game would be up to me. So I had to rise to the occasion, the same way a pro would, even though I was only in the seventh grade. I was a twelve-year-old phenom, which meant I was as capable as anybody.

The Springboro cheering section was on its feet. The beautiful cheerleaders could hardly watch, because they were so nervous. Our opponents, the Kings Mills Knights, were driving towards a game-winning touchdown as time was running out. And I was sure the game-winning play would come in my direction. I anticipated a fake handoff to their big running back, Don Testerman, and then a play-action pass to their tight end over the middle, right at me, the kid who was a foot shorter and weighed a hundred pounds less. But I was ready.

The coaches pulled me aside just before the final drive and told me what to watch for. Men who were icons to me – head coach Don Ross, assistants Bruce Smith, Larry Hefflin, Brutey Baker and Scott Reddick – each had advice for me. When the season began, I was nothing but a squirrelly little kid tossing a football around while the varsity games were played. But the coaches heard reports about me all throughout the peewee season. Dozens of interceptions. Thousands of tackles. The injury-riddled defensive secondary needed help for the big showdown against Kings Mills, and Coach Ross made the gutsy decision to call me up. I was the first seventh-grader in the history of Ohio sports to ever start a varsity football game. And already I had fifteen tackles and two interceptions. Woody Hayes flew in to watch me play.

There must have been a million other people watching. My buddies were right behind me just beyond the north end zone, cheering me on. I was covered in mud, so much so that my number 25 could barely be seen. I had a bandage on my right cheek because of a vicious hit I had made, and my right wrist was heavily taped. One time, midway through the game, I dove for a ball over near our cheering section, and I could hear two girls sigh and say I was the cutest thing they had ever seen.

As we broke the defensive huddle, Kings Mills broke into formation. I could hear our coaches screaming on one side of the field, and the Kings Mills coaches screaming on the other. I couldn't make out a single word from either side. I just did as I was told and stared down the tight end. The guy wasn't going to the bathroom without me.

With time ticking away, the Kings Mills quarterback called the cadence. Mike Colvin called an audible and changed our defensive scheme. The snap came on the second hut. Sure enough, the quarterback's first move was towards Testerman, who'd already run for almost two hundred yards and all three Knight touchdowns. A sea of white muddy jerseys collapsed on him immediately, smothering him to the point I could no longer see his light blue jersey. For a second, I didn't know where the ball was.

"Watch the tight end, Jeff," I remembered Brutey telling me. "If he comes your way, you own him. If he comes into your territory, you need to show him who's boss."

I gritted my teeth. I didn't care about the height disadvantage. I also didn't mind that he could probably flick me like a fly on a dog's hind end. My teammates were counting on me. And my coaches had trained me properly.

The ball sailed deep into the end zone. The predictions had all come true. The nudge towards Testerman had been a fake, and the play called for a pass to the tight end coming right at me. I backpedaled quickly, keeping the big man in my sight the whole time. He huffed and puffed ever closer, and his eyes were on fire. The whole game and the entire season came down to this.

CHAPTER 3

We met midway through the end zone, right in front of the goal posts. He jumped up to catch it, but he couldn't believe that I could jump that much higher. The time clock clicked down.

Three…get it, Jeff!

Two…watch out!

One…he did it again!

And as I came to the ground, ball in hand, I could hear the thunder of people coming in my direction. We'd won! Flashbulbs went off everywhere, and the band played louder than ever! And then, the most amazing thing happened right after that.

The most amazing thing…

The most –

Bzzzzzzzzzzzzzzzzzzzzzzzzzzzzzzzzzzzzzzzzzzzzzzzzzzzzzzzzzzzzz.

Huh?

"Good morning, you're listening to WSAI in Cincinnati, and you've been listening to Don McClean and 'American Pie.' I'm Jim Scott and I hope you're having a super day. If you've just woken up, then here's the Doobie Brothers to start your day in a crazy mood."

What?

I tried to get myself back to the football field, where everyone was celebrating my game-saving interception. I was being lifted up on the shoulders of my teammates. The girls were all trying to get a chance to talk to me. I wanted to go back to sleep.

Then the music played and I could hear the Doobies tell me that Jesus was just all right with me. And then it hit me; I had been dreaming. It was a Saturday morning, and I was not a varsity player and had no hope of being one. In fact, if I didn't hurry up, I wouldn't even have the team I was on. I was going to be late for football practice.

The dream would continue later.

* * *

My baseball equipment was put away, tucked in the back of the bedroom closet to gather dust for another winter. The hat was sweat-stained, the cleats caked in mud, and my glove had the well-worn smoothness of an old shoe. It had been a great season, filled with the full range of events – many thrilling moments, a few laughs, and a season-ending heartbreak that took me days to get over. But all of that was history now, and it was time for football.

My football equipment was in another corner, back behind my baseball card collection. One by one I brought out the items and inspected them – a football that needed air, an old jersey with grass stains on the sleeves, and a different pair of cleats, white in color, which made me look like Joe Willie Namath. All were in good shape, and I was more than ready to go. The summer heat was giving way to chilly evenings, which meant that football was in the air.

Being twelve can be difficult. I had lingering doubts about Santa Claus and how Superman could leap tall buildings in a single bound, but I still believed both might be true. I was in love with Marcia Brady and my favorite singer was Jim Croce. I couldn't see very far into the future, and I couldn't imagine a life without living with my parents, down the hall from my brothers and sisters. Shoot, being fourteen sounded *really old.*

At the same time, however, the world was changing for me in ways I didn't understand fully. By that I mean Saturday morning cartoons no longer held my attention and girls didn't seem so creepy. I actually went out of my way to be around some of them and I found myself wanting to take a bath. The bath thing was probably the scariest change of all.

I got to the practice field at a quarter to nine, early enough to find my coaches in a meeting. Gary "O.J." Powers was our head coach. Brutey Baker, meanwhile, was an assistant coach because his son Ricky was a linebacker on our team. Bill Hammock and Reverend Dill also had boys on our team. All of the coaches were excited about our team, and they said we had the potential to win a championship, which they told us many times. By ten-thirty, when practice was finished, though, my only goal was to live long enough to see lunchtime. This was a conditioning practice, where we ran drills and then wind sprints. So far five wind sprints – sometimes known as suicides – had been run. Practice wouldn't be finished until we ran five more.

Beep.

Ugh. They were killers. But our coaches didn't seem to care. Our center was Pepper Dill, a guy with a name I could never make up in a million years. He hated wind sprints as much as he probably hated broccoli. Practice had been hard enough, but now the suicides just about made us want to quit football and go join the band or something. All of us grumbled. Two guys fell over in exhaustion. Had Pepper not been a preacher's son, he may have been tempted to cuss.

CHAPTER 3

"Let's go! Let's go," Coach O.J. shouted. "Games are won in the fourth quarter by the team that's in the best shape. So let's go! Pepper, you're my main man, the key to the offensive line. Keep it going, bud."

Pepper didn't even acknowledge the comment. All of us pushed onward. My brother John, a linebacker, led the way. Donny, Chris and Tim, my running backs, were not far behind. Then there was Lance, my wingback, and James and Billy and Pepper and the rest of the linemen. A month earlier our summer had been full of sleeping late and goofing off, with little or nothing to think about. Football was what we looked forward to, but now the reality was here, and it hurt like nothing we'd ever experienced before. I doubt I was the only one who wondered if all this was really worth it.

"You can bet Shane Hatfield is working his butt off right now!" Coach O.J. shouted. "He knows what it takes and he's doing it right now. Now let's go!" Most of us would have sold a kidney to beat Shane, our archenemy who was arguably the best player in the league. Shane was quick and strong and cocky. He was good and he knew it, and he bragged about it. And that made us want to beat him all the more. We played his team near the end of the season in late October.

"Mitch Leisz is running his tail off right now. And Brad Swope, Danny Kruer, Roger Woolery. If you guys want to beat these guys, you gotta' work right now. Two more."

And the whistle blew.

Despite his apparent desire to murder us, we liked O.J. He both pushed us and befriended us, which made us want to work hard for him.

"O.J." was the nickname Gary earned while he was a high school sophomore in 1968. He was the leading rusher on the reserve team because he was the biggest running back they had. "It sure wasn't because of talent or speed," he often quipped. That was the year O.J. Simpson ran his way to the Heisman Trophy, so O.J.'s Springboro teammates gave Gary the same name. He later ran the ball for varsity coach Don Ross, enjoying mild success, and after graduation he turned to coaching, which he fell in love with almost immediately.

We were his first team. I was his first quarterback. When we suited up in two weeks against The Lion's Club, that game would be his coaching debut.

"All right, almost done, let's go!" And the whistle blew. I didn't like my coach very much at that moment.

O.J. focused on thorough preparation and proper attitude. Those were the keys to success in both football and life, he'd say. Do both and you'll win, he said. So get used to being pushed. Get used to coaches expecting the best out of us. Only wimps whined about it being too hard.

So I whined in silence. He was killing us.

Coach O.J. had been a kid like us not too long ago. He grew up in on Factory Road, moving there in the mid-sixties when the houses were new. Like us, he walked to school, played pick-up games all over town, hung out at the K & W and went to varsity games. "I had the most incredible childhood anyone could ever have," he often told us. "So appreciate what you have right now, fellas, because you'll never experience this again. You've got a roof over your head, you're healthy, and you get this one-in-a-lifetime chance to play football. I can tell you right now how much you're going to miss this when you're older and you have real jobs and won't be able to play anymore."

We needed his perspective on things because our season would be full of challenges. We were a new team in an established league that had solid teams and hard-nosed coaches like E.B. Smith. We were a hodgepodge of players who came from the other league teams to create this new team to accommodate the expanding number of teams. Ray Rottellini Realty sponsored us, but to everyone we were known simply as "the white team." Shane Hatfield's K of P team was "the orange team." Mr. E.B. Smith's Lion's Club team, which was our first opponent two weeks later, was "the red team." And so on.

Finally, the last wind sprint was finished and we collapsed to the ground. I was exhausted, wondering still if the hard work was going to be worth it. Pepper, with the sweat dripping into his eyes and his shirt soaked like he'd walked through a rainstorm, was breathing harder than anybody. Even Donny Wilburn, one of my halfbacks, a guy who was probably the best all-around athlete in my grade, looked winded – and that said something because he was in great shape. And he was gutsy, too, which made him both Shane Hatfield's friend and archenemy. No one loved Shane more than Donny. Or tortured him as much.

O.J. huddled us together for a final word. We formed a semi-circle in front of him, pulling off pads and sweaty shirts in the process. Only a few weeks earlier, we had been swimming in Clear Creek on hot days like this one. Now we were on the brink of heat stroke.

"Good job today, fellas. We've got two weeks before our season starts, and I think we're making good progress. Jeff, make your reads quicker on the option play. Chris, you gotta' hit that line like you mean it. And on defense, you ends have to really work on containment. Keep them inside where there's help. That's the most important thing you can do."

We were dismissed to the dream of being drenched in ice water. "Everyone in here, on three. Ready? One, two, three, defense!" Within minutes, our supposedly exhausted team was racing to the K & W.

* * *

As we raced to the K, the Springboro marching band practiced its routine at the football field behind the high school. Its music could be heard all over town. Men listened while cleaning out their garages and women looked up while tending to their backyard gardens. We heard the opening strands of the school fight song as we sat out front of the K, gulping our ice water. The sounds of the band were a reminder that football was on its way as much as anything. I wiped the sweat off my brow and took in a cool breeze from the south.

Across town, on the part of Market Street that bordered the Springboro Park, Brutey and Norma stepped into the backyard of their next-door neighbors, the Richmonds, whose daughter Janet was back home visiting. Janet was on the back porch talking with her mother, Hazel. Nearby, Janet's two young daughters played on the swing set. Brutey and Norma had known Janet since she was a little girl, and they regarded her as the daughter they never had.

"Hey, hey, hey," Brutey announced. "Someone told me there was a new cook in town. I'd like a couple of cheeseburgers, medium well, please. And a beer!"

Janet got up from her chair. She hugged Norma first, then looked over and punched Brutey in the arm. "You old coot, it's about time you cooked for me for a change. Beer's in the fridge. Help yourself."

"I'm going."

Janet turned back to Norma. "You're looking so good. How do you stay so fit, Norma?"

"Mainly by chasing these boys around all day long."

"You mean your children, and Brutey?"

"Yeah, the big boy."

Norma couldn't believe how much Janet's children had grown. She joined in with Janet and Hazel about the activities they were in, and when school would be starting. Janet also had a new decorating idea for her kitchen, and both women had ideas for that. If given the chance, the three of them could talk for hours.

Brutey interrupted them when he opened the screen door to the porch. "Hazel, all you guys have is this rot gut beer? Isn't it about time you get some real beer?"

"Still a Wiedeman man, Brutey? If you don't like what we have, then don't drink it."

"I'll drink anything on a day like today. Must've been a hundred degrees out there in practice today. This'll hit the spot, no matter what it is."

Janet sipped from her glass of lemonade. "Has the varsity started already?" Janet asked. Since she had once been a Springboro cheerleader, she had fond memories of the game.

"Regular season doesn't start for a couple of weeks. But last night we went to Lebanon for a scrimmage and we whipped up on 'em pretty good."

"Lebanon?"

"Yeah. Of course Van DeGrift downplayed it, like he always does. He said they'd probably win two or three games all year. We came out smoking. First play of the game, Mike Butts took the snap from Gary Zambon, and our guys plowed through like there was a thousand of 'em. The defense played like that all night. Rod Dillon threw a couple of touchdown passes, and Dave Dillon ran for one more. I'm telling you, we looked good."

Janet had been a cheerleader for Springboro during high school. She loved all the sights and sounds of football, and the band was a big part of that. As Brutey talked, she looked off in the distance, in the direction of the band, and listened to its music. "We've always had the most incredible band," she said. "And P.B. Stockman has always been the perfect announcer for them. What a wonderful man. And that voice! Goodness, he could melt butter with that voice. Those are such magical sounds, you know?"

She settled back in her chair with a smile. "Boy, I miss my high school days."

"We miss you too, girl," Brutey said. "You need to come around more often. These girls will be grown before you know it."

The four of them sat back and enjoyed the summer day. Though it was hot, the breeze cooled everyone down. The band was practicing the Star Spangled Banner. In a community full of front porches and screen doors and tree-lined streets, it was only fitting that the football field was tucked in the middle of a small subdivision. It was nestled in amid the maple trees that banked against it on two sides. When the school was constructed in the late 1920s, it was the only building south of downtown. There was nothing anywhere near it. Through time, though, a small neighborhood went up around it, and when the football field was developed for the school's inaugural season in 1965, neighbors were given a front-row seat. They could literally sit in their backyards and watch the game.

"Sometimes I wonder why I moved away from here," Janet said, looking off in the direction of the field.

"I think that all the time," said Hazel, who was crocheting a blanket. "It's small and quiet. A great place for the girls."

"John feels the same way about his hometown, though. And of course there's the plant nearby." John Spencer was Janet's husband. The two had met at Ohio State, where John was on the baseball team. Janet's parents loved John. And Brutey especially loved him because of the football tickets he was able to get him. The only drawback was that he took Janet to a suburb near Cleveland, where he was an engineer at the auto plant, which is why they didn't get to see her as much as they wanted.

Janet knew how much her mother missed her, and she reached over to touch her mother's knee. "But we come back a lot, though, Mom. John has another business trip pretty soon."

"November, right?" she asked, hoping it would come quickly.

"End of October. If there's a football game at home that weekend, I'd love to go. The girls would get a kick out of watching the cheerleaders."

"Is there a home game that night, Brutey?" Hazel asked.

Brutey took a swig of beer and thought for a minute. The last three games were home games, he remembered. Was it the Kings game that night? Or was it Blanchester? "There's a home game, all right, though I'm not sure who we play. But come on over, little lady. The way this team is playing, I'm sure it will be a night everyone will remember."

Hazel looked at her calendar. "Is that October 27, dear?"

Janet didn't need to think about it. She already knew the date in her head. It would be a day they would all look forward to.

There was a day when police officers patrolled the town they lived in. Sometimes an arrest or citation was warranted. But many other times, a stern warning from Charlie Reedy or Jimmy Beavers was enough to correct a wayward resident. The message was clear – don't do this ever again! And it wouldn't.

CHAPTER 4

On TV, we saw Barney Fife act all weak
and goofy, and maybe people thought
all small towns had bad police departments
... but we sure didn't; we had Charlie
-- The thin blue line

Saturday, September 9, 1972
After midnight

From the second he hit the front door, Brutey looked like he owned the place. He knew everybody and they knew him. The football crowd had poured into the new Ron's Pizza – which had long been the town's favorite pizza, only now in its new building back behind the post office -- a little after ten o'clock, and the place was packed by the time Brutey, still dressed in his coaching gear, walked in nearly an hour later. After spending the evening in Xenia scouting Springboro's next opponent, he had been at the high school in the Panther locker room after their 6-6 tie with Carlisle in the season opener. The fans on hand rehashed and analyzed the official opening of the football season, and Brutey offered his insider's comments, too. The tie wasn't what everyone wanted, but it wasn't all that bad.

The restaurant was alive in conversation. Instantly, Brutey was the center of attention.

"Brutey, you're getting uglier as the days go by, you know that?"

"Brutey, you still owe me twenty bucks, you know that?"

"Brutey, get over here and let me buy you a beer."

Brutey made his way around the room, laughing and patting the backs of the guys at each table. The staff hurriedly served pizzas and pitchers of beer until well after midnight, with Brutey eating and drinking the whole time on everyone else's tab. These were times he enjoyed almost as much as coaching, and he drank almost as much as he coached.

"Bartender, another round for my buddy, Brutey."

By one o'clock, most of the crowd had gone home; it had been a big night in town. Brutey sat at a table across from Paul Sowers, a man he hardly knew, but had seen around a few times. The two had little in common – Brutey was a salesman, and Paul a factory worker; Brutey had never been arrested, but Paul had a lengthy criminal record. But the two did share a love of football and draft beer. And on that particular night, that was enough.

"I'm telling you, Brutey, tonight was a glimpse of what we're going to see in the next few games. I know you love these players and I know you've worked with Rod Dillon, but I'm telling you he didn't look as sharp as he has in the past. And if that continues, we're going to have some trouble."

Brutey took a long pull on his frosty mug. He would hear nothing of the kind about any of his players, especially Rod. He'd known the quarterback since he came to Springboro in the seventh grade. "Tonight was just an indication of first-game jitters," he countered. "Everybody has 'em. Joe Willie Namath has 'em. Rod's going to be fine and we're going to win three games in a row before you know it."

"But this was Carlisle tonight, Brutey. You gotta' be able to move the ball against Carlisle. We have Xenia next week and Franklin after that. Those teams are gonna' make Carlisle look like a bunch of peewee players."

"Just you watch."

They jostled some more about football, then they moved on to more diverse topics like politics and which Buddy Holly song they loved the most.

Paul Sowers looked at his watch. "I'm a dead man. Barbara expected me home an hour ago."

"Yeah, you should go."

"You mean, *we* should go. What, your wife doesn't get mad when you get home late like this?"

Brutey didn't answer. There was no need to bring Norma into this because she just didn't understand. He loved shaking hands and slapping backs and re-telling the latest joke he had heard. What guy didn't? Norma, though, didn't even like to drink. And her shy nature kept her from talking to people. Instead, she preferred a quiet night at home. Through the years they fought about this all the time – he wished she would loosen up, and she wished he would stay home with her more often. The war had no resolution in sight.

"There's just some things Norma has learned to live with," Brutey said. "Hey, there are worse things."

They talked a few minutes about basketball, and how Coach Harry Hall already had his players in the gym working out. Then they talked some more about football. Brutey's conversation with Paul Sowers continued into the empty parking lot, where their pick-up trucks were parked side-by-side. Brutey again promised good play out of his football team and Paul again said he wasn't so sure. They agreed to take up their debate again a few nights later after work. Then they drove off in separate directions.

Only seconds later, the radar gun in Charlie Reedy's cruiser lit up. The officer was sitting in the empty parking lot of the Springboro IGA looking over some reports and watching traffic, which was virtually nonexistent at that time of night. The flashing light on the radar gun told him the truck that had just passed was doing fifty-seven miles an hour in a forty-five zone. He flipped on his overhead lights and took off. He expected that in a few seconds he would make a routine traffic stop and issue a routine ticket for speeding.

But it was anything but that. Instead, Charlie was going for a ride.

* * *

Charlie Reedy was one of the newer members of the growing Springboro police department. He was a mountain of a man, pure and simple, and stronger than a team of linebackers. He was six-foot-two and weighed two-seventy, which was big by any standards. But with the leather police jacket and the belt and the gun, not to mention his hat, he seemed three times bigger. His voice was a deep baritone, the kind that penetrated the loudest of situations. Whenever he walked through a crowd, you could hear him about as much as you could see him in the distance. As a result, no one messed with Charlie.

The pick-up truck didn't slow down as it passed by, as most speeders did. Charlie squealed his tires as he pulled out in pursuit of it. The Franklin National Bank was on his right, as was Jerry's Ashland gas station. The main intersection at the center of town was typically quiet, and he ran the red light there. He was gaining ground on the truck as he saw it brake as it approached East Street. "Yeah, pull in there, buddy. I got you if you go there," he said. Charlie blew his siren. The lights flashed off the houses on both sides of the street. He gap between him and the truck grew even closer, but he still couldn't see the make, model, and color, or license plate number. In a few seconds, though, he would be able to.

And when the truck stopped, the driver was going to get it.

Charlie hated people who ran from him. Hated them more than anybody. Thought they were cowards. Wanted more than anything to hunt them down and knock some sense into them. That's how he got when his adrenaline rushed. That was the cop in him, which was different than the gentle side of him, who cared for people, and made friends easily, and was always loyal to them. He was the father of two boys, Jim and Tom, and he followed them in whatever they did. His real passion in life was farming, not police work, and the image most people had of Charlie was in bib overalls, a John Deere hat and a toothpick protruding between his teeth. Everybody knew Charlie.

With two boys of his own, he knew that most teenagers were good, clean kids, with a natural rebellion inside most of them. Their loud music, fast driving and beer drinking was something to be expected – and Charlie pulled over many a car carrying teenagers out partying. He corrected it usually by pouring out the beer and pointing a stern finger, and maybe escorting one of them home. But if it happened again, then Charlie laid down the law.

He wondered if some kid drove the truck. Why would anyone be so stupid as to run from an officer with his lights flashing? The more he followed the truck, the madder he got. If the driver had any sense, he'd pull over right away.

But the simple traffic stop became something far more than that.

The truck never made the turn onto East Street. It slowed down as though initially it was going to turn, but then it sped up instead, taking off down the hill on State Route 73, eastbound to the edge of town. In doing so, the truck overcompensated and dove into the oncoming lane momentarily, directly at an oncoming car. Charlie felt so powerless, for all he could do was watch the action unfold. It all happened so quickly. The truck swerved back into the eastbound lane, but at the same time the oncoming car swerved to its right. Charlie could hear the tires squealing and the blast of a car horn.

The truck kept going. Meanwhile, the oncoming car smashed into a tree at

CHAPTER 4

Home Avenue. Given the speed of the car at impact, Charlie worried that someone was hurt. But he knew the other officers could quickly assess that situation. He was on the tail of a reckless driver, probably drunk, and he decided to chase the truck.

"Dispatch! Send help right away! I just saw a car being run off the road and it hit a tree, going probably forty miles an hour! Somebody's got to be hurt real bad, so send help over to Home Avenue right away."

He floored the gas pedal. "I'm gonna' get the S.O.B. who did it," he said.

State Route 73 has always been hilly, with several difficult curves that eventually made its way all the way to Waynesville five miles away. This was long before any improvements in the road were made. Charlie hit the gas but the truck went even faster, winding through the lonely stretch of road at a dangerous pace. Before long it pulled away and was nearly out of Charlie's sight. Charlie said a cuss word, then repeated it, then repositioned the toothpick in his mouth, and floored the gas pedal even more, with more adrenaline pouring through him than ever. He radioed to the police station.

"I got me a pick-up truck flying along 73 east of town. Notify the state highway patrol, the sheriff's department and Clearcreek P.D. that they're to stop this scumbag. He's already hurt somebody, and I don't want him to hurt anybody else. Over." Charlie thought about how he was going to hurt the scumbag when he got him stopped.

This guy was not going to get away. No, sir.

It's not a teenager, he thought. It's definitely some drunk, soon to be a dead drunk, too.

Charlie sped past the farm owned by Bob Lovely, barely keeping the speeding truck in his sight. The road was not made for fast-pace highway travel. Years ago, it was an old dirt road used for the horses to deliver feed from the town stores to all the farms along the outskirts of town. Now, it at least had blacktop, but it was still treacherous.

"Can I get a cruiser out to Bunnell Hill Road and be on the lookout for this guy? He'll be there any second now and if anyone out there can be in that location, someone needs to shoot his tires. He's running from me, and right now I'd say he's doing ninety. Over."

"Roger that."

But there were no other cruisers in the vicinity. No speeding trucks, either. He kept going, looking in all directions. Then he got lucky and saw a flash of red light off in the distance. It had to be the truck. As he suspected, the truck had turned right onto Bunnell Hill Road, which was a two-lane old country road that connected Springboro and nearby Lebanon. The stop sign there would surely slow it down.

Or maybe not.

Charlie got to the stop sign and lost all sight whatsoever of the truck.

Had the truck kept going south on Bunnell Hill, Charlie would have seen it. The road was straight and went up a steep hill, thus giving Charlie plenty of opportunity to see it. Instead, the truck had squealed and turned left or right on Lower Springboro Road, he wasn't sure which, where visibility wasn't so good. Charlie stopped and turned off his cruiser to listen for sounds in the distance, but that didn't produce anything either, because old man Harrison had his generators going in the house nearby.

Charlie had lost the truck. It was either halfway to Waynesville or halfway back to Springboro, or parked with its lights off any number of spots in between.

He pounded the steering wheel and cussed again.

He heard fellow officer Jimmy Beavers ask over the radio what was going on. "You got that dad gum sumbitch?" he asked. Charlie usually smiled when Jimmy talked, for his West Virginia roots were always evident, no matter how serious the situation. "I'd lay good odds he's on his way back to town," Charlie responded, not smiling this time. "Until he saw my lights, he was going to turn right onto East from Central Avenue. Do we know anyone on that street who has a truck?"

"I know quite a few people who live on East Street," Jimmy replied.

"I'm coming up on the Patton place. I'll be there in just a few minutes. Can you go over to East and start taking a look around? See if any trucks are pulling in there."

"If I see any of 'em parked, I'll check the hood to see if they're warm."

"What about the other car?" Charlie wanted to know. "Anybody hurt?"

Jimmy told him that a couple from Franklin was making their way home from Wilmington, and both of them were shaken up. The husband cracked a rib when he hit the steering wheel, and the wife broke her right hand when she put it up to shield her from the impact. Both were on their way to Middletown Hospital.

"Buddy, they were lucky," Jimmy added. "You oughta' see the damage to the front of their car. You look at it and you'd swear someone was really hurt in that crash."

Charlie flew down Lower Springboro, past Dr. Garland's place and the Springboro Taxidermy, and then turned right onto East Street from the south end. Meanwhile, Jimmy came in the other way. They met at the intersection of East and Factory, just down the street from the fire department and close to the K & W. It was well after midnight and the town was deathly still. All the businesses were closed and the streets were empty. Charlie had never been outrun before. He again slammed his fist against the steering wheel. He got out of the cruiser and kicked away a rock, looking in all directions for signs of a truck on the run. The more he looked the more frustrated he got. It would never happen again.

Meanwhile, in an alley that exists between Main Street and East Street, just around the corner from where Charlie and Jimmy were talking, the driver of the pick-up truck watched the entire scene from behind his truck. The inside of his truck cab reeked of alcohol and the brow of his forehead was soaked in sweat. He couldn't believe he had just taken a police officer on a dangerous trek through the country the way he had.

He'd run from a police officer, and escaped.

And not just any police officer. He considered Charlie a friend.

* * *

Later that same day, as the day broke to warm sunshine and a cool breeze, a bunch of people spent the afternoon at my friend Mitch's house, which – because it sat right behind the high school – was one of the most popular gathering spots in town. Since Brutey was a good friend of Mitch's dad, and his son Ricky ran around with the rest of us who were football players, Brutey was there. We guys played football in the backyard while Brutey and Mr. Leisz sat on the back porch drinking iced tea. The Ohio State game was set to begin at 3:30 on the Dayton ABC station, Channel 22, which had pretty good reception as long as it wasn't windy. Cable was many years away, and some of us only had black and white TVs.

"I'll be Darryl Lamonica," Shane said. "The mad bomber."

"That makes me Freddy Belitnikof," I said.

"I'll be Dick Butkus," Turkey proclaimed. "Anyone coming across the middle will get his head taken off."

Was he serious?

"Then I'll be Jack Tatum," Donny said. "Come my way and watch out."

Lance and Mitch squared off against one another because they were roughly the same size and quickness. I guarded Danny Kruer, who was a funny guy, and a good athlete. We played for a half-hour and no one had his head taken off, and no one was paralyzed. Our jeans were grass stained and our shirts were torn, though, and when Mrs. Leisz hollered that it was three-thirty we dashed inside to watch the game. We'd resume the game during the Prudential Halftime Report.

Watching a football game on television was a big, big deal. In the fall, ABC showed one college football game each Saturday. CBS and NBC each had one professional game on Sunday, and it was a national game, so there was a chance we couldn't watch the Browns or the Bengals.

We also didn't have anything like a VCR that allowed us to tape games. This put a premium on watching the rare occasion that a game was on television. It also forced us to devour the local sports pages. We knew what games were being played, and what games were on the horizon, and all the pertinent statistics about all of them, all from reading them in the paper. This was especially true for the varsity games. If there was an item about the varsity in any of the local daily papers, or the nearby weeklies, *The Franklin Chronicle* or *The Western Star*, we read every word of it.

"Watch the dirt, fellas!" Mrs. Leisz warned as we trouped in. "Don't be dragging those filthy shoes all over my carpet."

Brutey and Mr. Leisz joined us in the living room, continuing their conversation as they walked in. It sounded serious, but I couldn't make out all the details. Mr. Leisz had seen Charlie Reedy at the hardware store, and he heard about a truck that took off on him and never was found. "Charlie's out to get that boy, all right. Said he's going to check out every truck in town 'till he gets a confession."

Brutey listened quietly as Ohio State took the opening kick. Three plays later, Archie Griffin ran sixty-four yards for his first touchdown as a Buckeye. We all jumped up, and Mitch said he couldn't believe a freshman could be so good.

But, oddly enough, Brutey – the ultimate OSU fan -- never said a word.

The game moved on but Brutey sat and still said nothing. The Buckeyes took a commanding lead, putting all of us in the greatest mood as we went back outside to resume our game. Just as I stood up, I saw Brutey look over at Mr. Leisz.

"Ward, I know who Charlie was chasing last night."

Mr. Leisz looked up from the television. "It wasn't you, was it?"

Brutey whispered what had happened the night before. He talked about drinking beers with Paul Sowers. They drank until about one o' clock. Then Brutey got in his truck, while Paul Sowers got in his. And they took off in different directions.

CHAPTER 4

"Which way did Charlie follow that truck?" Brutey asked Mr. Leisz.

"I don't know. He didn't say."

"Cause if it was east, it had to be Paul," he said. "Had to be. And from what I hear, he's known to do that sort of thing."

"Want me to tell Charlie?" Mr. Leisz asked.

"Nah, I'll do it. Just give me a little bit to think about this."

And for the rest of the afternoon the whole bunch of us played football in Mitch's backyard. Meanwhile, just as the sun was setting, Brutey announced that he was off to find Charlie. They definitely needed to talk.

CHAPTER 5

And that's the way it was...
-- The nightly sign-off
by Walter Cronkite,
CBS Evening News

MONDAY, SEPTEMBER 18, 1972

I woke up to the cheery voice of Jim Scott, who told me the people in the Cincinnati area who were celebrating birthdays that day. He also said that the cold, wet, windy weather caused a major accident on I-75 near the Sharonville exit. He then played Heart of Gold, a song by Neil Young that had been number one six months earlier. For me, it was a typical Monday, and I didn't want to get out of bed until someone told me it was Friday. I slowly dressed and grumbled as I fixed a bowl of Cheerios, and I desperately yearned for the freedom of summer. The chilly wind and cold sprinkle of rain outside offered the first hint that fall was fast approaching.

Mom rounded up our jackets and sent my younger brother Joey off to the Jonathan Wright. Meanwhile, the rest of us headed in the opposite direction, with me going to the high school building and John, Jenny and Julie to the Clearcreek Elementary School. It just seemed too early in the year to be so bundled up, and I grumbled with each step. I was walking with Alan Little, my neighbor across the street, when we saw Brutey in his truck tooling along Kesling Drive, taking Ricky to school.

"Lucky dog," I said.

Alan had a hood over his ears and the wind howling around him, so he never heard anything I said the whole way.

CHAPTER 5

The truck rambled off into the distance, past a hundred other kids who cussed it the same way I had. "I wonder if Brutey ever had a chance to talk to Charlie Reedy," I said to no one in particular. And then I realized it was none of my business.

The day was a typical Monday, with typical gripes about having to do typical tasks. Reading class didn't do anything for me, and Math class was a total bore. The lunch break helped a little in part because I could see that the sun had come out. I settled into my seat in fifth period English and looked around at my classmates who walked in together. Linda and Robyn shared a love of horses, and Laura and Connie had been in many classes together through the years. Donny and Shane played all of the sports, and Lance McKinney and Mike Perry were brilliant minds that seemed so much smarter than the rest of us. Each of us had a friendship with at least one other student, and that friendship was just as important in our development as anything we learned in class -- especially anything in Science class, if you ask me.

My Monday morning grumpiness was slowly fading. I thought maybe it could be a good day after all.

Our English teacher was Mr. Ullum, a man who dressed neatly and apparently kept himself in shape. He had spent the whole first week reviewing everything we'd learned in sixth grade, which was completely dull, and then he decided to put our writing skills to the test, which seemed like a monumental task. He wanted a two-page essay as an in-class writing assignment, on friendship. We were to write about something we did over the summer with just one of our friends, our very best friend. What was fun? What was interesting? Why was this person our very best friend? He was checking our style and grammar skills, as much as the content. Like any other assignment, my whole class groaned. I wondered how in the world I could write two whole pages about anything other than football.

I pulled out my paper and a pencil, and for fifteen minutes I stared at the wall. Did Johnny Bench have to write essays? Why do I have to write essays? How will this help me get to the major leagues? Then I decided I just had to suck it up. The road to the major leagues was full of useless activities, evidently. So then I started really concentrating about what I had done that summer. There were baseball games and trips to LeSourdesville Lake. There were great nights at the festival and awesome afternoons playing Wiffle ball. It was hard to pick just one event. And before long I was confronted with yet another problem. I really didn't have *a* best friend. Instead, I had many, many good friends. How was I supposed to pick just one? I don't think I was the only student who thought that that day.

I had friends all around me. Redbud Drive, which was where my house was, was in the center of our subdivision. I had twenty friends within a hundred yards of my house in every direction. I spent a lot of time with Lance Penwell and Chris Hill, who we called Turkey, though I don't know why. Freddy Brown and Keith Crocker also lived on Market Street, but more in the center of it, near the Prasses and Baileys and Richardsons. Todd Thompson, Jeff Rains and Ronny Hart were on Graham Drive, just around the corner from my house and next to Roger Woolery. Mike Hefflin was on Walnut Drive behind our house, and Donny Wilburn and Shane Hatfield were just around the corner from him. And Mitch lived in the house right behind the school, which made for a natural gathering spot for all of us and every other kid in town.

Best friend? Mr. Ullum, you've got to be kidding me. How am I supposed to choose just one? I've done so many things with all of them.

I started my essay three different times – once about Mitch, another time about Roger. Then one about Freddy Brown. Finally, with only twenty minutes left, I wrote about the night Lance Penwell fixed me up to ride the Ferris wheel with a girl at the Springboro festival. Any story that involved me actually in the same zip code with a girl had to be at the top of the list.

I wrote about how and why I was a friend with Lance before I actually got into what happened at the festival. I mainly did that because it helped fill up the two pages.

Lance and I had been through a lot together in the three years we'd been friends. We played ball together, camped out, went to varsity games and hung out at one another's houses, so much so that our mothers came to expect us to stay for dinner or spend the night. We had similar interests and were at the same level athletically, which made our one-on-one games competitive, unlike the ones against Mitch or Donny – who killed us. If there was a big difference between the two of us, it was that Lance was much better at talking to girls. He was a smooth talker with a flair for impressing them. Meanwhile, I was a klutz.

"Just relax and be yourself," he'd say.

"Easy for you to say. I see somebody like Lana Beavers and suddenly I can't remember my name."

"It'll come."

"Yeah, maybe when I'm really old, like forty or something." I was always pretty shortsighted and stupid.

Lance and I started hanging out in fifth grade when, during basketball season, we were put on the same Saturday morning basketball team. Doug Patton, a varsity basketball player, was our head coach, and Jeff Howard, his younger cousin, was the jayvee assistant, and our team won six of its eight games. Lance and I were guards and probably averaged four points and ten turnovers a game, which didn't make anyone forget who Jimmy Hough was. Lance often spent the night before the game at my house, where, if the varsity had an away game, we watched *The Brady Bunch* and *The Partridge Family* and played Nerf basketball until Dad threatened to throw us outside.

Then, as luck would have it, we were put on the same baseball team that summer. Coach Bill McGraw put us in the lineup right away, with Lance at third base and me at either shortstop or, when Nick Powers was pitching, behind the plate. The Springboro IGA, otherwise known as the Phillies, sponsored our team and we were awesome, even if I do say so myself. We could hit and steal, and Dave Whalen was one of the fastest pitchers in the league. My brother John was a relief pitcher and an outfielder. Meanwhile, Lance, Brian Collins, Jeff Walker, Jeff Phipps and Matt Jozwiak – all other guys from the neighborhood – were other top players for us. For three years this team stayed together and won a lot of games.

We played baseball until dark and then we'd camp out in makeshift tents reliving every play until we finally fell asleep. Then the next day we'd play Wiffle ball and ride our bikes all over with baseball cards pinned into the spokes to make the sound of an engine. With all that, who needed girls?

As it turned out, we all did.

On Wednesday night of the weeklong festival, Lance and I arrived late because our baseball game went into extra innings. We probably should have cleaned up and changed clothes, but it was cooler to go in our dirty uniforms instead. Main Street was alive with booths and rides and a Lion's Club stand that sold cotton candy. We arrived just as Brutey and Mike Lambright completed their free-throw shooting contest, in front of a huge crowd standing around School Street, a crowd that reacted to every hit or miss. We watched the two of them make shot after shot on the old hoop attached to the barn that stood there, until, near the end, Brutey missed his final shot and lost the battle.

We hooked up with other guys and immediately mixed right in. We threw baseballs at milk bottles and tossed ping-pong balls into fish bowls. We jumped on the moonwalk and even played bingo, too. In that respect, it was like every other fun-filled night we'd ever had at the festival. But then, out of nowhere, it became very, very different – at least for me anyway. Just as it turned dark, Lance ran into a girl he'd had his eye on for more than a month. She was a cute girl with dark hair and dark eyes who had just moved to town that summer. Rachel was her name, and she'd been looking for Lance all night, and was dying to ride the Ferris wheel with him.

"All right, let's go," Lance said. I was so impressed by his confidence. I'd have fainted.

"Oh, Lance, wait. I have my friend Ronda with me tonight. Who can ride with her?"

There must have been six of us guys standing there, all looking as anxious and pathetic as the other. Ronda was cute! She was a real catch. If Donny Wilburn had been there, I wouldn't have had a chance; Ronda would have lunged at him, as all girls did. I was probably the one who acted the least interested, not because that was the case but because I didn't know how to act. Lance knew that, of course, which is why he asked me to join them. So I actually rode the Ferris wheel with a girl, and a pretty one at that.

I could see all of Springboro from the top of that Ferris wheel. This pretty young girl from Tennessee had me so scared I couldn't say anything, but that was beside the point. I could brag about what I'd done and hope the whole town saw me with her.

That's why Lance was my best friend. I wrote, "There were so many guys he could have chosen from. I wasn't the smartest, or the best looking, or maybe even the most interesting. But he chose me anyway and I enjoyed a special ride with a really nice girl. Lance will be my best friend for life now."

Hey, there were guys who bought baseball cards for me, or blocked so I could score a touchdown, but Lance helped me meet a girl. That's a true best friend.

Mr. Ullum gave me a B-minus on my paper, though. Said I had a long way to go if I ever wanted to be a writer, which didn't bother me any. Who wanted to spend all that time in front of a typewriter when there was baseball to be played anyway?

* * *

Later that night, after a killer football practice, we were all in a world of hurting. We did up-downs and grass drills, and Coach O.J. killed us again with wind sprints as practice came to an end. We'd have given anything for a ride home.

"I can't walk another foot," Tom Brown said. He was one of many of the guys who felt that way.

"Yeah, well, I think I'll just sleep right here. My parents might come look for me sometime," I said.

"Ha. Don't count on it," Lance quipped.

Ricky was fortunate because he had Brutey right there at practice. Surely his dad would drive him home, he thought. Wouldn't take but a few minutes.

"Hey, Dad. How about a ride home?"

Brutey was talking with Bill Qvick, a parent of a player on another team. He either didn't hear Ricky, or heard him and decided not to listen to him.

"Dad."

Still no answer.

We watched the scene for a second, and then took off on our bikes. Tired of waiting, Ricky interrupted Brutey, who clearly didn't appreciate the intrusion. I couldn't hear what was said, but if gestures and tone of voice meant anything, Ricky was getting a good butt chewing.

Ricky made his way slowly back towards his bike. We slowed down a little so he could catch up. Evidently, he wasn't getting a ride from Brutey.

I rode along with Lance and Donny Wilburn, and we grunted with each push of the pedal. Ricky caught up with us as we reached the Springboro Christian Church, which was next to the elementary school and across the street from the high school.

"Gonna' ride with us, are you?" I asked.

"Yeah, Dad's got a meeting. Said he'll be tied up for a while, so he couldn't take me home."

Just then we heard Brutey toot the horn and pass us by. He was gone in a flash, evidently running late for his very important meeting. Ricky didn't acknowledge his dad at all, which seemed strange since everyone seemed to notice Brutey.

We biked quietly up Main Street and talked about a million things, mostly about who we'd rather go out with, Marcia Brady or Lori Partridge. These were the important issues for twelve-year-olds to debate. Everybody had an opinion, but to me there was nothing to debate. Lori was too quiet, while Marcia was active and smart and pretty as any girl on the planet – even when her nose swelled to the size of a basketball when that football hit her. For my money, the vote was for Marcia every time. Marcia, Marcia, Marcia.

We passed the bus station, which was an old one-story building at the corner of Main and West Mill streets, noteworthy because it had a tunnel underneath it that ran all the way to the Wright House on State Street. I'd heard stories of how it was used in the Civil War days as part of the Underground Railroad. Just north of it was a beautiful two-story whose nicest feature was a large front porch, where Dick Chenault, our new fire chief, often sipped iced tea from a glass.

By that point we were talking about our teachers. We all thought Mr. Nordheim was funny and Mrs. Kuhn was strict. Mr. Ullum seemed okay, provided there were no more pop essays like the one that day. The thought of writing two more pages another time seemed unbearable.

"C'mon, Ricky, I'll buy you milk shake at the K & W," I said.

"Aren't you Mr. Moneybags," Donny joked.

"Hey, that paper route keeps me rich. I made twenty dollars last week."

"Good for you," Donny continued. "Then make mine strawberry."

I chuckled. I almost cracked on Donny a little bit, but then I realized a very important truth – no one cracked on Donny Wilburn. Ever.

"I'll buy one for everybody if you guarantee we beat the red team Saturday."

Ricky had suddenly withdrawn from the conversation. He didn't talk or laugh. He didn't seem to be listening, either.

As we peddled hard past Mr. Chenault's house, we got a good look at his front porch. It was a beautiful front porch that offered a perfect view all the way up Main Street. Mr. Chenault was there laughing it up with several other men. Ralph Wade was one of them, and Lowell Hayes was another.

There was another man we knew, also. When Ricky saw him, he stopped peddling.

It was Brutey, holding a bottle of Weideman beer, which was made in Cincinnati and promoted all the time during Reds' games. He was laughing right along with the other men.

I stopped alongside Ricky to verbalize what he must have been thinking. "I thought you said your dad had an important meeting tonight," I said.

"He has a lot of meetings like this one," Ricky said quietly. "He probably won't get home until midnight." There was a real sadness to his voice. I wondered what he wasn't telling us.

Ricky decided not to stop at the K & W with us. He said he suddenly wasn't very thirsty.

Meanwhile, Brutey kept drinking and having a great time.

The Panther tradition continues... Jerry Raffel (30) set a school rushing record in 1969, thanks in part to the good blocking of Dan Wade (shown above). A few years later, Dave Dillon went after that same record with the help of good blocking by John Mockabee and Ed Sullivan and the rest.

If there was a name that became synonymous with Springboro football through the formative years, it was 'Smith.' E.B. Smith helped start the peewee program, and soon became one of its dominant forces, creating havoc for opposing players like Lance Penwell (#47). Bruce Smith, who was a member of Springboro's first football team, became a legendary varsity coach in the seventies and eighties.

CHAPTER 6

Jim Scott, Robyn Mitchell, Bob Goode,
Buddy Barren, K.C. Patrowski
and Bob "Shotgun" Kelly
-- The top radio station of 1972
AM 1360, WSAI

SATURDAY, SEPTEMBER 16, 1972

At the peewee level, we did not have cheerleaders or marching bands. Nor did we have an ambulance whose lights and sirens went off whenever we scored a touchdown. And the stands were nowhere close to being full, let alone spilling out along the sidelines, like they were for the varsity.

But the sights and smells and sounds of our games were as thrilling for us as the varsity games were, or at least they were in our imaginations anyway. I rode my bike to the field for our first game of the season, and as I approached from a considerable distance away, I stopped and looked at the field ahead just so I could take it all in. The field was lined and there were flags on the end zone corners. The officials were meeting at midfield and the scoreboard lights were on. This wasn't just a backyard pick-up game. Instead, it was real football.

I was in full pads and my adrenaline was pumping. I could feel the excitement of the anticipation. I could imagine the action that was about to be played out.

The rite of passage for all boys to manhood is football. Has been and always will be.

In grade school, we acted big by dressing up in Army gear and playing war with plastic guns and make-believe bombs, choosing sides and then scheming to attack one another and become king of the hill. Then we grew up enough to love the gore of Halloween and spookiness of a dark night on the edge of town. Then came basketball and baseball and riding bikes up the steep hills at the gravel pit.

What defined our masculinity the most, however, was football. When a kid's mom wouldn't let him play, it's like he shriveled up and died. That's because the desire for brutal contact is at the core of every boy's soul. Football doesn't focus on speed and athletic skill. Instead, it focuses on smashing the face of the guy across from you, even though he might be your best friend. The real cheering goes for the player who will stick his head down and make an earth shattering, bone chilling, and mind-boggling hit.

Watch any game and you'll see. Listen to the coaches and hear the crowd. It's like a car race, where drivers use uncanny skill to maneuver a speeding car throughout a race, yet all anyone wants to talk about afterward is the crash on turn three. It's the same with football, when a spectacular touchdown run is often overshadowed by the hit that separates a player's head from his shoulders. When you hit like that, you are considered great.

At some point during his formative years, a boy begins to understand what football means to who he is. He sees the helmet and the pads and the mud and the blood, and he longs to be part of it. And so he will muster up the courage to eventually approach his mother, who in typical fashion has always ridiculed the game as nothing but brute violence for thickheaded bullies. The boy will then take a deep breath and blurt out the news she has been dreading, "Mom, I'm signing up for football."

Behind her, his dad would fist-pump the air.

Just about every athlete in town had played football at one time or another, even if his best sport was something else. Jimmy Hough, one of our best varsity basketball players, loved football. Jeff Howard played it. So did Gordy Gregg and a lot of the other guys walking the halls. When we went to varsity games, the main reason we watched from the north end zone was so we could hear the colliding and the pads popping on plays that were at that end of the field. At its rawest level, there was a combat involved in football that appealed to every guy.

This happened for me when I was in the sixth grade. One day, I had been out in the neighborhood goofing off and hanging out with a bunch of other guys, and the talk turned to how they were all signing up for football. They made it sound so cool, like it was something I had to be part of. I was four-foot-eight and maybe a hundred pounds wringing wet, but I was a pretty good athlete. I'd played football at Mitch's house and on the Jonathan Wright playground and held my own. So I figured it was time to get my nose bloodied a time or two, if that's what it took for me to prove myself.

Just then my mom pulled up in the driveway. I was standing next to Dave Young, who was a year older, not to mention nearly a foot and fifty pounds bigger than me. I think she called me "sweetie" or something when she got out of the car. That's when I blurted out my intentions for the coming fall, and she practically fainted.

But she supported my decision, knowing full well it would've killed me had she said no. She and Dad came to all of our Thursday night games under the lights, which was when our games were played that year. And she was ready for me to play again when my seventh grade season came around, too, which was the year my brother John started playing. She sat in the stands with other mothers, never really understanding the game but enjoying it nonetheless, right up until the one moment that would make her mad. When someone yelled, "Kill the quarterback!" she wanted to do a little killing of her own.

For our season opener, we played the red team, sponsored by The Lion's Club. They were a tough team. Players had been known to have arms and legs broken while playing them. They had Mitch at quarterback, Roger at tailback and Danny Kruer at wingback. More than that, their coach was E.B. Smith, the tenacious legendary coach whose name was synonymous with Springboro football. They had whipped us the year before with a bunch of guys who were now in the eighth grade. Dave Young ran overtop of us, and Mark Rhule ran around us. I think I about broke my neck in that one.

But this was a new year, and we were determined to start strong. As we ran onto the field for our opening game, we were pumped up, ready and focused. Coach O.J. gave us a motivational pre-game pep talk, and Brutey went around to each of us pointing out what we should do against some of the red team's tendencies. "Watch the defensive end, Jeff. If he's on top of you, the pitch to Donny is there. If he overplays the pitch, you can tuck it and run," he told me. Brutey was always so smart with stuff like that.

The whistle blew and the game started. On the first play of the game, Danny Carmack, the opposing defensive end, came charging at me like he'd just been released from prison. I managed to pitch out to Donny so he could go around left end and run for twenty-five yards. But in the process I was knocked flat on my back by a vicious, and probably illegal, tackle, and when I looked up I thought I was in another zip code. Now that's a hit.

Carmack stood overtop of me, pointing and laughing his butt off. After coming to, I had a sharp pain in my side and a ringing in my ear. Had this not been football and my rite of passage into manhood, I probably would have asked to go to the sidelines and play with some Lincoln Logs. But I wasn't allowed to do that. The Code required me to stay in the game. I got back in the huddle and called a play to the other side, away from Godzilla.

Meanwhile, Mr. Smith was congratulating his defensive lineman for such an awesome hit. I looked up and saw one mom giving a high-five to another, obviously enjoying the fact that I was writhing in agony and would be crippled for the rest of my life. But that was football.

Hmmmph. I got ticked, and I vowed to do something to change their tune.

Just as soon as I could feel my feet again.

* * *

Though football was relatively new to Springboro, we were blessed with some really good football coaches, and because of them our program became successful quickly. The varsity program started in 1965 with Lonnie Norris as its head coach, and he was just the man to get the program off the ground correctly because he was a born leader who knew the game. Coach Ross was an assistant on that team. Later, after Coach Ross became head coach, Coach Larry Hefflin joined the staff, as did Coach Bruce Smith. The peewee and junior high ranks had good coaches as well, with men like O.J. and Brutey, Bill Crocker, Jr. and Mr. E.B. Smith, Bruce's dad, who was perhaps the best of all of them.

Perhaps the best? Okay, he was definitely the best.

Mr. E.B. Smith was the best because he pushed his teams hard. They practiced hard and played mean and evidently ate raw meat for dinner. He made that red Lion's Club jersey one of the most feared in all of Springboro.

Away from the football field, Mr. Smith was a cordial, respectful and gentle man. His gruff voice didn't seem so intimidating. He was a man who cared about his family and the community it lived in, so much so that he spent a lot of time and energy to make both of them better. But somehow, the minute he stepped onto a football field, he morphed into a ruthless tiger who utilized every strategy and weapon he could use in order to win a game. By 1972, his coaching status in town was legendary and everybody wanted to play for him.

He was not a Springboro native. He moved the family to Springboro in 1955 to be closer to his work, which was Frigidaire in Dayton. His oldest son Bruce was seven at the time and Brian newly born. A few years later when Bruce played on Ralph Wade's traveling team, Mr. Smith became a coach, something he did until Springboro's peewee program started several years later. From the start, Mr. Smith's teams dominated, and their reputation grew as the program got bigger and bigger. In '72, it got so big that the four-team league expanded to six, in part because of football's gaining popularity and because games were played under the lights.

There was nothing cooler than playing football under the lights. Our games were on Thursday nights, which made Thursday the greatest day of the week.

And for a while, there was literally no expense for the program to turn on the lights. The Dayton Power & Light Company either didn't know the lights were there, or couldn't find the meter to gauge how much electricity was being used. So years went by and DP & L never sent a bill. Sixth-graders felt like varsity stars. We felt like we ran faster and hit harder. Stories were told the next day and more and more kids got excited about football.

But all of that changed as '72 season approached. Sadly, the meter was found. The bill for the usage was staggering, so much there was no way the program could have paid it and still survived. Fortunately, DP & L realized it owned part of the blame, so the expense was waived. But there was no more Thursday night football and our games were moved to Saturday.

Mr. Smith's Lion's Club red team entered the '72 season as defending champions. And though they had lost Mark Rhule and Dave Young, they still had plenty of talent, which Mr. Smith would no doubt mix and mold in order to give Shane Hatfield's team and ours a run for our money.

Meanwhile, Bruce Smith was an assistant coach for the varsity in that '72 season. He'd been on Springboro's very first football team in '65, and was destined for stardom until his varsity career ended before his very first game. In the final scrimmage before the start of the season, Bruce took a handoff from quarterback Ed Wade and sprinted down the sideline. He had room to run and Bruce had the speed to break something open. But just as he hit full stride he was hit and knocked out of bounds. And Bruce went down with the worst pain he'd ever felt.

The sound of broken bone could be heard from fifty yards away. "It was the worst thing I ever heard," Ed Wade recalled later. "I can still hear that pop like it was yesterday."

Bruce missed the entire football and basketball seasons, which was devastating to him, though he did return to run track in the spring. He loved all sports -- especially football -- and showed promise of being one of the best halfbacks in the area until the injury shortened his season.

By far, Bruce received the most recognition by playing basketball, though it was not his best sport. During his junior year, Bruce was a sub on that legendary basketball team that went to the state finals, a fete that put him in the newspaper a lot. He was in a picture when Springboro won the county tournament. Then, in the post-season tournament, it beat Lockland, Mason, College Corner, New Miami and Cincinnati County Day to win the District title, which meant yet another championship picture. Then Springboro won the Regional championship and the subject of yet another picture, this one with Bruce hoisting the championship trophy over his head, his teammates celebrating around him. And then there were pictures of the trip to and games played at the state tournament in Columbus.

It was a magical ride that turned the town upside down.

Bruce didn't play much, but it was a memorable experience for him. He aspired to be a coach someday, much like his father, and that is exactly what he became after graduating from Lee University in 1970. He returned to Springboro and became freshmen coach; then he moved up to be a varsity assistant when the fall of '72 came around, serving as the line coach. His goal was to give other Springboro kids the kind of experience he had enjoyed when he was younger.

Through the years, Mr. E.B. Smith continued to reside in the house on Lookout Street, right behind the high school. Meanwhile, Bruce moved his wife Sherry and their two children, Ronda and Jay, into a home near Red Lion. On Friday nights, Mr. Smith worked the first-down chains and Bruce was calling blocking schemes from the sidelines. Both have since become synonymous with Springboro football.

* * *

Midway through the second quarter, my friend Roger took a handoff from my friend Mitch and raced sixty yards for a touchdown, barely outrunning my brother John. What kind of friends were they? Sheez! We tied the score a little while later when I hit Donny with a five-yard slant pass that he ran fifty yards for a touchdown. But late in the game, Danny Kruer broke the game open with a forty-yard touchdown on a wingback counter. Coach O.J.'s coaching debut was a losing one, but he was nonetheless proud of our effort.

We went to the K & W afterward and commiserated the loss. We ate our burgers and drank our milk shakes, and within minutes we'd forgotten all about losing the game. There'd be another next week and we'd win it for sure.

As we finished up, we saw Brutey standing outside talking to Charlie Reedy. They were far enough away that we couldn't make out everything being said. Charlie was pointing a finger, though, and Brutey was gesturing his hands. We did hear him say "Market Street" and "that way" as he motioned in that direction. Then they started talking louder.

Charlie said he knew what happened late Friday night, and it was either Brutey or Paul Sowers who ran from him. Charlie had talked to the bartender at Ron's and found out they were the last two to leave. Brutey swore it wasn't him. He didn't know if it was Paul, but he had the suspicion that it had been, just like Charlie said. He said he'd check it out and let Charlie know for sure just as soon as he found something out.

Charlie would get to the bottom of it eventually, and at the moment he was violating about ten constitutional amendments in his thorough thrashing of Brutey. Then he said something that was loud enough for people five miles away in Franklin to hear. "I hate it when people run on me. When I find out who it was, he's got hell to pay. Got that? Brutey, I better not hear it was you."

Brutey walked towards his car. He put his ball cap back on and opened the door.

"Did you hear me, Brutey?"

Brutey heard it all right. Everybody heard Charlie.

Don Ross was Springboro's head football coach from 1969 through 1973. Though his style was not like Mike Ditka or Vince Lombardi, he succeeded nonetheless in much the same way Paul Brown did. He utilized crafty strategy and finesse to prepare his team and win football games.

CHAPTER 7

...One nation, under God, indivisible,
with liberty, and justice, for all.
-- The beginning of the school day
Pledge of Allegiance

TUESDAY, OCTOBER 3, 1972

Coach Don Ross awoke with a smile, something he hadn't been able to muster in the past few days. His daughter Jody, who was five, occasioned the smile. Though normally a late sleeper, she had awakened before anyone else in the house, walking to her parents' bedroom and plopping up on her dad's chest, where she lay until her dad woke up.

Then she announced, "Daddy, you need to make me bwekfuss."

He chuckled because it had been the most innocent demand he had heard in a while. "Okay, honey. You go get the milk out of the refrigerator and I'll be right in." His wife Michele and his older son Steve stayed asleep.

The varsity was winless after four games. After the season-opening tie against Carlisle, it had played hard and been beaten by good teams, losing all three by a total of eleven points. It was hard to be too critical of his players, but the zero in the win column was getting more and more difficult to look at. He could hear the grumblings in the stands. He could also sense the frustration around school and around town. For the first time since he started coaching football years earlier, he wondered whether all the time and effort was worth it.

Though no high school coach ever takes a position for the money, the compensation has always been pitiful. For the countless hours at practice and scouting and preparing for games, Coach Ross was paid a mere $600 per year. That averaged out to about seventy-five cents an hour. The assistant coaches made even less money, and guys like Brutey – who had full-time jobs and were not teachers in the school system – did all their work on a voluntary basis. But they all coached because they loved the game and the kids who played them. Still, a little more money would have been nice.

Jody poured the cereal, and Dad and daughter enjoyed a bowl of Cheerios at the kitchen table, discussing life from a five-year-old's perspective. She filled him in on everything Mr. Green Jeans taught her on *The Captain Kangaroo Show* the day before. She also talked about a "fwog" she found in the creek. Her days were an unending series of play land adventures, raised by two good parents. Coach smiled at his little girl, reminding him that life's most enjoyable pleasures were free. He showered and shaved, and made the short drive to the school, just as he did every other day, but on this beautiful morning he had a brightened outlook. Football games would come and go, but the love of his children mattered most. And for that he was always a success.

Coach Ross was a sophomore English teacher in addition to being a coach. He was a quiet but intensely competitive man who chose his words carefully and motivated his team by modeling excellence. He was in his fourth season as head coach, his eighth overall with the program, having been there since it began. His first team in 1969 team went 7-3 with Jeff Kees, Cork Jackson and Jerry Raffel leading the way, and the 1971 team won all five games in October to rebound for a share of the Fort Ancient Valley Conference championship. The stage was set for the '72 team to go where no Panther team had ever gone before, to win eight, nine or maybe all ten of its games and repeat as conference champions.

Coach Ross was as optimistic as anyone about the future of this team because it had both experience and talent. Rod Dillon was at quarterback, with his brother Dave at tailback, and Joe Leach was at fullback. Dale Midkiff was the tight end, and Dave Collins, Dave Vicroy, Russ Chesney and Mike Lambright played wide receiver. Across the front, Rich Miracle was the center, Brian Smith and Steve Rottert were the guards and John "Hog" Mockabee and Mike "Meathead" Colvin were the tackles.

The tie against Carlisle didn't hurt so badly, and the loss against Xenia Woodrow Wilson in week two was still recoverable. But the last two losses against Franklin and Clinton-Massie really stung. The Panthers had been the victims of some bad calls in both of them. First, Dave Dillon had a long touchdown run called back at Franklin, and the coaches and Springboro fans protested the call loudly when it happened. The penalty could not be verified in the film session the next day, either. Then, in the conference opener, our two-point conversion to win the game at Massie came up inches short, though everyone from Springboro was certain Mark Houseman had scored. We lost, 13-12.

Now the Panthers prepared for their game at rival Mason, a team they had never beaten before. If ever we needed a reason to hate Mason, that may have been it. Coach Ross prepared for the game just as hard as he had for all the others, not wanting to think about what another loss would do to his team.

But changes had recently been made that showed some promise. Ed Sullivan was inserted at center and Larry Cash at left guard, moves that allowed Miracle and Rottert to devote their full-time attention to defense. Additionally, Houseman started in place of Leach and suddenly the Panthers seemed like they had the right combination. Only time would tell for sure.

With Jody's happy wake-up call still fresh in his mind, Coach Ross was in good spirits as he arrived at school. Things just seemed to go well all day. In class, he spent his day in the language he loved so much, and he felt connected to each of his students, like there was a clear link between his voice and their ears. He was reminded why he always wanted to be a teacher. But football remained on his mind, too. During his free period, he talked a long time with the principal, Vince Ross, no relation, a man whose opinion and approval he always appreciated. Vince Ross assured Coach Ross that he was coaching the football players properly, that the talent and effort was there, even if the wins weren't.

"The Clinton-Massie game is over. Surely they won't win all of their conference games. You just have to figure that the conference schedule starts this week," Vince Ross said. "It's like you start all over. You're undefeated in the conference right now, so just view the first four games as practice games."

Coach Ross finished the school day refreshed and glad that he had a football team to coach. As he often did between classes, he looked around at his players walking the hallways and appreciated just how much he enjoyed coaching them. They were good kids. They behaved at school and around town, and they were fun to be around. Once or twice a week a prank was played that got the whole team laughing. And he knew in his gut that this team was going to win. It had too much talent not to.

He turned the corner near the coach's room, eager to change clothes and take the practice field. But in the distance, he saw a player's father standing in front of the door. The man's body language said everything -- arms folded and eyes squinted, with his body leaned up against the wall.

Coach Ross' day was about to take a turn for the worse.

* * *

As every high school coach knows, every parent believes his or her child has the potential to be all-state if only used in the proper way. As a result, a coach has to set aside a significant amount of time every week talking to parents either in person or on the telephone, listening to the parental concerns and explaining the decision to use the player in a certain way, if he uses the player at all. For most coaches, it can be the most frustrating and exhausting task of the entire season.

It happens in the best of seasons, but it is particularly apt to happen when a team is struggling. Coach Ross had already had to explain himself to several parents already that season. His refrain was always the same -- the team had talent and it was playing well. It was only a matter of time that the wins would come. He was sure of it, which was why he continued with the lineup he had. There had been some changes here and there, but nothing significant, because he had faith in the one he started the season with.

Usually, by listening to the parent and then carefully offering his explanation, the conversation would end on a positive note. But now, at the end of a seemingly perfect day, with an important practice ready to begin, he wasn't in the mood to have his day ruined.

"A minute of your time, Coach," the man asserted.

"Practice is starting in five minutes," Coach responded respectfully. "Can we talk later?"

"Now's fine. It won't take long."

"You're Mark Robinson's dad."

"Yeah, I played some football when I was a kid, so I think I know football pretty good."

"Uh-huh."

"Seems to me you guys can't throw the football very well, yet you're staying with that Dillon boy. You know, Mark can throw circles around him and you're not giving him a chance. What's wrong with you fellas? Can't you see that? Or do you just like to lose football games all the time?"

Coach Ross was more stunned than anything. Playing Mark Robinson, a sophomore, over Rod Dillon, a senior, was like playing Bill Plummer at catcher instead of Johnny Bench. A coach would have to be crazy to consider it. Coach Ross maintained his patience as he listened, but it was hard. His patience wore thin. "Listen, we can talk about this later. Come back around six o'clock. Better yet, give me your phone number and –"

"What, you want to talk to me so you can fill me up with your crap? I ain't no idiot. I don't need no explanations. I'm pulling Mark off this team and I wanted you to know I'm doing so because of you guys. My boy's got talent and I'm going to take him where he can show it, not stay here where everybody knows everybody and we'll play people just because we owe their daddy a favor."

"You're not serious."

"I've been watching for a month now and I can't see a lick of talent better than my boy. That tells me you don't know how to coach. Anyone can see that. Your record clearly proves that." Then he saw Mark emerging from the team room, laughing with a teammate.

"Mark! Over here!"

The smile on Mark's face quickly disappeared. As Coach Ross walked away, Mark walked over to his dad. He stood nose to nose with his father, shaking his head, pleading to stay. But the dad shouted and Mark relented, limping back to the locker room, embarrassed and frustrated. He just wanted to be part of the team and have fun.

Just then Brutey walked in. From a distance he could hear the words and the tone of voice, and he could see the gesturing. He knew exactly what was going on.

"Walter, my main man! How ya' doing? What do you say we sit down over here for a little while and have a talk? Let Mark suit up. Look at him, he wants to play. You can see the disappointment on his face."

"This goes beyond that, Brutey. You know –"

"I know, I know. You've been upset for a while now. I've seen you and I've heard some of the stuff you've been saying. I should have come to you earlier. That's my fault, my fault entirely. So let's sit down and talk about this."

Walter Robinson was reluctant to sit down because it had taken a lot for him to come in and approach the coaches. But he was willing to listen. Maybe something could work out by talking.

The two sat in the gymnasium, underneath the banner that proclaimed Springboro's football championship just the year before. And Brutey let Walter talk for as long as the man wanted to, even though he thought the man was an idiot.

Mr. Robinson rambled for more than fifteen minutes. Mark could do this and Mark could do that. "It ticks me off to see Mark work so hard and then never get to play," he concluded. "Sure he plays on the reserve, but he deserves some time at varsity."

Brutey let Walter's statements linger in the air for a moment. He knew Walter was relatively new to Springboro, having moved in two years earlier from Eaton because of his new position at NCR. And Brutey knew that Walter's football experience was limited to junior high ball back in his younger days; he never played at the varsity level because he was too small. So the guy didn't have a clue what he was talking about. Most loudmouths didn't.

"Walter, I'm with you. We have kids all over this town who work hard and their number one dream in life is not so much to play in the big leagues, because realistically that's not a goal they can obtain. Instead, they want to play on the varsity. They want to be announced as a starter and stand out there in front of the whole town and do the things they've spent their whole life dreaming about when they're out on the playground practicing."

Walter nodded his agreement. He was listening.

"But, like everybody, Mark has to pay his dues. I've been in this town my whole life, and I've seen all the good ones come and go. But none of them got into the starting lineup because his dad marched into a coach's office and demanded a starting position. It doesn't work that way. It never has. I've seen Rod Dillon out here on summer nights working on his footwork and timing. The same is true for a lot of these guys you see on Friday night. They worked hard all through the ranks and then in the summer. It's their time."

It was exactly the kind of talk Coach Ross would have had with him later that evening. But Brutey saved Coach from having to do it this time.

Walter left by himself that afternoon. Mark, meanwhile, was happy beating on his teammates in a blocking drill.

* * *

Practice ended a little late because the offense was required to learn a new special play, and Coach Ross made them run it ten times until they finally got it right. Their reward for working hard was they did not have to run at the end of practice, which got the biggest cheer of the season. He liked having a team loose for a big game, and the players were in good spirits as they came off the practice field. The Mason game remained the biggest of the year, a game where current records and past experiences could be thrown aside. And we had to win. If we did, there would still be hope. If Mason could be beaten on the road, who knew what else could happen? The conference championship was still within reach.

Afterward, Coach Ross sat in the coach's office with his assistants, Coach Smith, Coach Hefflin and Coach Reddick. They joked at the demand by a seething parent that a sophomore replace an experienced senior. What more could happen?

They also finalized the game plan for the Mason game, thoroughly reviewing the scouting notes that Brutey had provided. As the meeting ended, Coach Ross made a note to call Brutey at home that night to thank him for taking over the discussion with Walter Robinson.

Later that night, when the call came, Norma answered the phone and said what she was so accustomed to saying. Brutey was out, maybe in a meeting, maybe not.

At that moment, Brutey sat in a booth at Ron's Pizza, laughing and carrying on with some other men from town, talking about motorcycles and football. Having settled down Walter Robinson the way he had, the Weideman tasted especially good. Plans were made to meet at the bar again Friday night after the football game.

They'd meet there at 10:30 sharp after the game; Brutey would buy the first round. The guys were happy to agree.

CHAPTER 8

'My Sweet Lord,' 'Jesus Christ Superstar,' & 'Jesus Is Just All Right With Me' --The spiritual revolution, God on the radio in '72

SUNDAY, OCTOBER 8, 1972

The last stanza of *Just As I Am* had been sung and the closing prayer had been said. The two hundred members of the Springboro Christian Church, the newest church in town, began to shuffle out of their makeshift sanctuary in the IOOF Building on Main Street, where they would meet until their new church near the school was completed in less than a year. After church, they greeted Reverend Dawes and then gathered in the commons area for fried chicken and mashed potatoes. Such was the agenda for this and just about every other church in Springboro that Sunday.

Dressed in their Sunday best, one family after another shook Reverend Dawes' hand and complimented him on his sermon. Many confessed that they knew it had been directed at them, and one man thanked the Reverend for not mentioning him specifically by name, which drew a hearty laugh from everyone in earshot. Then the Reverend would ask how the family was doing and offer a word of encouragement about an issue that was of particular concern to the family.

"God bless you," the Reverend would often say. "Mother and I will pray about that this very evening." When he said it, he meant it. That was a big reason why his congregation was growing. There was a genuine sense of concern about him that separated him from some of the other ministers of his day.

Near the back of the sanctuary, one woman did not partake in the post-service greeting line. Instead, she remained firm in her seat, with her head bowed, lost in her thoughts about something that had weighed on her for years. Perhaps not so coincidentally, the problem had been the topic of Reverend Dawes' message that morning, and she was more convinced now than ever that there was something she should do about it. But, like most of life's problems, it worried her more that her problems might get worse before they could ever get better.

She intended to wait until everyone was at dinner, and then slip out the side door unnoticed. But Reverend Dawes noticed her as she sat alone in her silence, and when the last family had been pushed into the lunch line, he sat down beside her. Both were silent for a few moments, then the woman looked up at him with a feign attempt at a smiling. He could tell quickly that she had been crying.

"It's my husband," she offered, wiping away a tear. "He's such a great man who does so much for so many people. People are going to think I'm crazy for ever complaining about him." Norma Baker had never publicly complained about Brutey. Part of her felt guilty about it, yet another part of her was thrilled to finally get it out in the open.

"It's like he's one person to everybody else, and someone completely different around me. They see this guy who's fun and active and so helpful to everybody, but the man who I live with is nothing like that."

"There, there, Norma. Does Brutey know your disappointment?"

She wiped away a tear, and then checked to make sure her mascara hadn't run. "Absolutely. I try so hard to please him. I watch what I eat and I try to keep in shape. I cook and keep the house clean. But it seems like the minute he steps foot in the house, he turns into this unhappy guy who can't stand being around me. I have suspected he's out with other women, but I can't prove anything. I try to draw him into a conversation and he'll just snap at me. He'd rather sit in his chair and read the paper and fall asleep in front of the TV. I go to bed around ten and then he'll come in a few hours later, after he wakes up in his chair. I feel so awful like I've done something to turn him away. Then we go to the football field or uptown somewhere and he turns into this wonderful, friendly person to everyone else around town. I don't get it."

She sobbed again and Reverend Dawes sat patiently, waiting for her to regain her composure. The woman had been in his church only a few times, always sitting in the back row by herself. He would have never dreamed her life was like this. Like everyone else in Springboro, he thought her husband was one of those universal great guys and they had a lasting, sustaining marriage. But Reverend Dawes also was never surprised what really happened behind closed doors.

"Reverend, why does Brutey hate me so much?" She cried once more, this time louder than the others. "It wasn't always like this."

Norma and Brutey had started dating in high school, when he was a senior and she a junior. They were such a cute couple, with him a star basketball player and her a cheerleader. After basketball games they shared a cheeseburger and a chocolate shake at Jerry's Restaurant in Franklin.

They broke up right after graduation since Brutey had intentions of going into the Army, which he did in July. Norma went out with some other guys, but none of them could compare to Brutey. Meanwhile, Brutey wondered if he had made the right decision, about the Army and about Norma, and when he came home for Christmas in 1957 he secretly hoped that he would run into her. His wish came true one snowy day in late December, when both of them happened to be at Lahman's Grocery in the center of town. Norma and some friends had walked uptown from her home on West Mill Street just to kill some time, and when they walked in, Brutey was at the counter buying a gallon of milk.

It was a moment she would never forget. He looked so amazing. Dressed in military fatigues and with his hair buzzed in a crew cut, his face thinner and his shoulders broader than she had ever remembered, her attraction to him was instantaneous. And judging how he turned to watch her, she sensed that he was attracted too.

He called her that night at home, and the next night – New Year's Eve – they went to a party together. At midnight he held Norma close for a slow dance to Auld Lang Syne and whispered in her ear something she never dreamed she would hear from him. "I'm going to marry you, Norma McCullough," he said. "When I get out, I'm coming straight back for you. And I'm never gonna' let you get away from me again."

He wrote her a letter a week for an entire year, and Norma was impressed. Then he wrote two a week, and Norma was smitten. When Brutey was discharged, he came straight back to Springboro like he promised and in front of all her friends he got down on one knee and proposed on the spot. Norma felt like Miss America.

That was in early 1959, and they were married later that year, on November 2, Brutey's birthday. Brutey settled into a job at NCR making a whopping fifteen thousand dollars a year, more than he ever dreamed he'd make. They purchased a new house on Market Street for $10,000, and people couldn't believe that a young man his age had so much money. Unlike any house they'd had before, the stove was electric, and there was a commode in the bathroom, and a refrigerator and a dishwasher. Not to mention running water. The first night there Brutey smoked a big fat cigar on the back porch.

"If you don't mind, Reverend, I'd like to make an appointment to come meet with you, sometime during the week when I'm not taking you away from everyone else."

"Oh, that's all right. I'll just –"

"No, you've had a hard morning and you need to be in there having lunch with everyone else."

The door to the sanctuary opened. "Delbert, your food is getting cold."

"Run along," Norma insisted. "I'll set up an appointment early next week. Thanks for your message. And thanks for listening to me."

"Call me anytime. That's what I'm here for. God's healing is available to everybody, twenty-four hours a day."

She gathered her things quickly and left the church because she had to get home soon. Brutey expected lunch on the table by one o'clock, and she didn't want to think about how he'd be if she was late. If only the world could get a glimpse of the Brutey she lived with.

* * *

Norma left feeling like a terrible burden had been lifted. She knew her mother suspected her unhappiness, but they never dared talk about it. A woman's place was in the home. She cooked and cleaned and raised the kids. Her mother thought the whole women's lib movement was craziness.

Now somebody knew her true feelings. Like an explosive that had been bottled up for way too long, it felt good to get it out. Brutey was always the saint and it just wasn't true. In public, he was always complimentary and fun-loving, and people just laughed when they were around him,. But privately, she saw the other side of him. The darker side. The depressed side. Why couldn't she ever have any of the good moments? What did she do to deserve all the garbage? As good as it was to release one set of emotions, she felt another, stronger set of them rising to the surface.

She loved Reverend Dawes. He was so kind and insightful. She was sure she could trust him to put her in a better frame of mind.

In the short time she had had attended his church, she had been impressed with his loving compassion for people. Life had many pleasant moments, but it was also a struggle, and his messages were laced with insightful anecdotes to help people live through their problems.

Reverend Dawes was our town's Billy Graham. He looked the part and, man, did he ever have a passion for life the way God planned it. He grew up during the Depression the son of a tenant farmer in Highland County, which is southeast of Springboro. His family worked hard and held strong moral values, though it never set foot inside a church. Money was tight, but the family managed. Young Delbert grew up to be a strong hand on the farm.

A turning point in his life came one day when he was fifteen. He fell terribly sick that day, weak and washed out, complaining of pain all through his body. He was put to bed, and the area doctor was called out for a house call. The illness confounded the doctor, and a cure did not seem likely, and as a horrified young Delbert lay in bed he overheard the doctor tell his parents that he didn't know if he was going to live much longer. The house was somber all night, and no one had dinner. Delbert put his head to his pillow and thought that he was going to die that very night.

It had been a beautiful, sunny April day, and it saddened him to think he was going to leave the world amidst such beauty. He cried openly. He was frightened beyond anything he had experienced. And somewhere through the night, he felt this inner voice that asked him to call out to God. He didn't know God, so he knew no formal way to call out to him, but the inner voice assured him and strengthened him, and somehow he found the words.

His prayer was simple. "God, if you let me get well, I'll spend the rest of my life serving you."

This continued throughout the night – his anxious feelings, followed by listening to the inner voice, followed by prayer. He didn't sleep much, but soon something did happen. He began to feel better. He saw the sunrise that next morning, and to him it was as if God had answered his prayer.

This was cause for celebration. "I was hungry, and my mom asked me what I wanted for dinner that day. 'I'll fix you anything,' she said. And I told her I wanted fried chicken, mashed potatoes and white gravy. Daddy carried me to the table and I ate like a pig." There had never been such happiness around the table. In time, he got stronger and better. Though he still didn't go to church, he did what he thought a

Christian should do, so he prayed and vowed to never cuss again. And he continued to work hard and, as a response to his answered prayer, he helped others.

When he was twenty-one, his mother came home one day and told him that a young man his age ought to go to the local delicatessen. She didn't say why, but Delbert knew what she meant. There was a young lady there. So Delbert went, and he immediately fell for the young lady who worked there, whose name was Omalee. He saw her but didn't talk to her, though. He couldn't find the right words. Days later, while Delbert was on a double date, Omalee showed up with some other girls. All of them needed a ride home that night, and Delbert – one of the few around who had a car – agreed to drive them. And he showed how he was a smooth operator. He dropped everybody else off before it was time to drop off Omalee. He asked her out, and she accepted. Less than a year later, on February 25, 1946, they were married.

Though they were married in a church, they still didn't attend church regularly, but Omalee did press him on it. Delbert did a stint in the military, then oldest son James was born. "Can we go to church now?" Omalee asked, and Delbert did not agree. Then came second son Dennis, and again Omalee asked and again Delbert found reasons to stay away.

Their only daughter, Candace, was born a short time later, and this time when Omalee asked, Delbert agreed. On Easter Sunday they attended the Church of Christ in Greenfield, and though Delbert was moved by the service and its message, there was much of it he did not understand. Still, the inner voice moved him enough to go back the next week, and then the week after that. Delbert had no idea how quickly his service to God would begin.

Within five weeks, Delbert was asked to teach a boys' class in the church, which scared him to think about. Six weeks later, he was named a deacon. And then three months later, just five months after he had first set foot in a church and gave himself to God's work, he delivered his first Sunday night message. He prepared it based on the text of 1 John, Chapter 5 and wrapped an entire message around faith in the Son of God. But just before he took the pulpit, the real message he was to deliver came to him.

"Just as I was to stand up, God asked me, 'Delbert, do you remember what you promised me?'" He certainly did remember, and that became his real message that night, as well as the purpose to the rest of his life.

He spent years traveling around to churches, sometimes as a temporary pastor until a full-time pastor was called. He went to Kentucky, then to Ripley, Ohio down near the Ohio River, then to Portsmouth, until one day in 1969 he came to

Miamisburg, which was his first exposure to the Springboro area. He started the Springboro Christian Church on February 13, 1971 in an IOOF building at the corner of Factory and Main Streets. A year later, the church purchased five acres from John Dunaway – my friend Mitch's grandpa – in the area right across from Springboro High School and right next to the Clearcreek Elementary. Construction began midway in 1972 and the building was scheduled for completion in September 1973.

The Reverend Dawes never met a stranger. And there was never a person in need that he turned away.

Norma Baker was the recipient that day of that philosophy.

* * *

The varsity's first win of the season was one of the biggest in the school's short football history. It came against much-hated Mason, on the road, which was monumental for many reasons. We had never beaten Mason before, let alone at their place, and we were magically back in the picture for the conference championship. The town talked of little else for days.

Norma stopped at the IGA after church for some bread, eggs and milk. While there she ran into Homer and Lillian Preston, the storeowners, and they talked small talk – something Norma found difficult to do given her state of mind. She was sure they both sensed that something was wrong, since Norma had known both of them since they came to Springboro in 1958 to open the IGA. Fifteen years was a long time to know somebody, and by then it's harder to put on a false front. But somehow Norma managed, and she was glad the conversation got no deeper than it did.

As she walked out to her car, Charlie Reedy was holding court with four other men in the parking lot. It was a collection of important men, too – like Ralph Wade, Bill Crocker and Lowell Hayes, all members of the school board. They could have discussed some pressing school issues like newer textbooks or better lunches, but instead they talked football. Norma couldn't help but overhear.

"That fake punt in the second quarter changed the whole game around," Mr. Crocker said. "Rod fooled the living daylights out of 'em. It was our game from that point on."

"Yeah, I congratulated Coach Ross on such a great call. Took a lot of guts to do that," Mr. Hayes.

"Yeah, and what did he say?"

"In typical fashion he didn't want any credit. Actually, he said Brutey's the one who deserved the credit. Said he was all excited after scouting them a few weeks ago and pointed out their tendencies on punt formation. Sure enough, they all saw it when watching the film. Had it planned right from the get-go."

"Brutey, huh? Man, he's something."

Norma put her groceries in the car and drove away. Yeah, Brutey was something all right. If they only knew.

CHAPTER 9

No hitting my brothers and sisters,
No playing until the chores were done,
Eat your vegetables, and for goodness
sakes, 'No smacking that gum!'
-- The rules of my house

Thursday, October 12, 1972

Lunch finally arrived at a quarter after eleven, and we were starved. A bunch of us hooked up at Mrs. Kuhn's classroom and made the trek down the hall and around the corner to the cafeteria. Being boys, the conversation did not center on the weather or the new shoes at J.C. Penney. Rather, it involved one put down after another. And no one was immune from the barbs.

If there was one thing we seemed to know instinctively, no matter how young we were, it was how to trash-talk an opponent. We watched Mohammed Ali do this all the time on television, making fun of Joe Frazier, calling him ugly and promising to knock him out after three or four rounds.

We also loved Pete Rose. He played hard and ran to first base on a walk, and there was no opponent he was afraid of. Pete could be oh-for-three against a pitcher and when he ran past him on the way back to the dugout his mantra was always the same – "I'm gonna' get you next time." And he would. He did it just the night before when the Reds beat Pittsburgh in the fifth game of the National League championship series. Pete grounded out against Steve Blass to lead off the game, but two innings later he lined to left center to tie the game up and swing the momentum back to the Reds. They later won, setting up a return trip to the World Series, this time against the Oakland A's. Pete was already talking about how he would murder their pitching, and we soaked in every word.

We hustled like Pete and punished opponents like Dick Butkus, and when game day approached we bragged about the ways to make mince meat out of one another. In the group of guys I ran with, we were all good at this in one way or another, but no one was better – or more entertaining -- than Donny Wilburn and Shane Hatfield. Man, they were cutthroat. Brutal. But they could back it up, too.

These guys were alike in so many ways, like brothers. Both moved to town around 1970, when we were all ten years old, and they quickly became part of our circle of guys who played ball. They could play anything well – football, basketball, baseball – and they were so competitive, especially with one another. One always had his sights on the other. One was always trying to get the edge on the other. When they were on the same team, which they were in baseball, they complimented one another. But then an hour later on the playground and later in another sport when they were on opposite teams, the jabs started right away. It was fun to watch.

Donny and Shane were in rare form at lunch that day. We had a special Thursday night football game that night since the varsity owned the field that Saturday for the Homecoming game. We played the blue team that night and Shane's team played E. B. Smith's red team. Our big game against Shane's team was still a couple of weeks away, and both were sharpening their tongues for that one.

"Hey Shane, let's talk about that basketball game the other night."

"Shut up! Let's don't and say we did."

"Still not over it, are you? It was about the biggest butt-whooping you've gotten in, what, about a week since the last time we played."

"Yeah, your time is coming."

"Maybe when I'm collecting social security checks."

"You know that ball was out of bounds. You know that. That last shot shouldn't have counted."

Donny took a bite of his sandwich and smiled at the rest of us. "Hey, do you know what the difference between a loser and a puppy is?"

Shane looked at him but didn't answer. He didn't want to hear it, but there was no place to go.

"The puppy eventually stops whining."

The rest of us laughed but Shane sat there with no expression on his face.

He'd get him later, somehow. When he least expected it.

"We'll see who laughs last," Shane said. "We've got you in a couple of weeks, and we'll see whether you guys will have game enough to make up for all this talking."

"Yeah, keep talking there, Shane-buddy. If you guys stop me on the pitch, Kirby here will just turn up field and outrun everybody you've got. Focus on him, then I'll run overtop of you all day."

It was Frazier-Ali all throughout lunch, only on a smaller scale. It would continue for the next two weeks. I never laughed so hard in my life.

* * *

With football in our thoughts, the school day trudged along like a rainy Sunday. Our teachers did their best, but there was no way they could compete. The dream of scoring touchdowns or diving headfirst into a pile of mud was just too great. It was Homecoming week and there was something exciting going on every night. That night, before our game, the juniors and seniors would square off in a tug-of-war contest that was no ordinary battle because the loser would be dunked in a six-by-six pit full of muddy water. We couldn't wait to see that one, because all week long, the juniors had been trash-talking the seniors, who weren't taking the bait. And why should they? After all, they had "Hog" Mockabee. Case closed.

I walked into Mr. Wilson's Ohio History class at one o'clock for the next-to-last class of the day. My brain was going in a thousand different directions, and not one of them was towards Ohio History. Reluctantly, I took my seat in the far back right in front of Walt Harrell, a new kid, and right behind Ricky Baker. While the girls talked about boys they thought were cute and what dress they had just bought, Ricky and I talked about the game and our chances of beating Shane Hatfield's team. So much depended on our defense, he said. So much also depended on our offensive line, I said. But then the bell rang, and Mr. Wilson made it clear that our focus for the next fifty minutes would have to be on him.

Rats. Mercury Morris was playing in the NFL and I'll bet he didn't know a thing about Ohio History. Why should I?

Surprisingly, though class was actually pretty interesting. I learned something I'd never known before, in all of my twelve years of living in and around Springboro. I learned the history of my little town.

CHAPTER 9

When the Ordinance of 1787 made settlement in the area later known as Ohio possible, many men from the East explored the area. One was Joel Wright, a surveyor and civil engineer from Pipe Creek, Maryland. He made several trips to the valley near what had come to be known as the Great Miami River. In 1806, he bought a thousand acres in an area that would later come to be known as Waynesville.

A few years later Joel Wright brought his son Jonathan to the Miami Valley and surveyed an area west of the Waynesville property. Jonathan soon purchased that property to the west and incorporated it as a village.

The land was useful because it sloped to the south, providing access and energy from two small streams that flowed into a bigger creek, later known as Clear Creek, which then flowed into the Miami River that served the entire region. In addition to the creeks, the area had a number of springs that kept the land fertile and suitable for farming. Hence, Jonathan Wright named his little village Springboro. That was in 1815.

The original plat consisted of eighty-six lots, all within a square mile. By the time of the Civil War, there were two streets that allowed travel north and south, one being Main Street and the other being East Street. Both ran north into Franklin Pike, a road that went west to the city of Franklin and east to the village of Waynesville, which later became known as St. Rt. 73. The other cross streets were, in descending southward order, North, Market, Factory, State, South and Mill Street.

Jonathan Wright brought with him to Springboro his Society of Friends, a Quaker religion, and through the years the group multiplied and the town grew. But then, as was the case all throughout the country, the Civil War turned Springboro into a critical area. Mr. Wilson told us all about the war and the reasons behind it, and how some Northern states, such as Ohio, became havens for Southern slaves who were trying to escape their bondage.

"Slaves from the South were always on the run. They would run away from their owners, then have to scurry about to keep from being captured. It was one of the more violent times in our country's history. Battles were being fought around people's houses, and on others' farms," he said.

"Being a Union state, Ohio was on the forefront of fighting this battle for freedom. It was one of the first northern states in their migration. And they found it here. Red lanterns were placed outside homes where the slaves were welcome, and some of those homes can be found in Springboro. The Jonathan Wright house on State Street is one of them. It had an underground tunnel that leads to it from where the school bus garage now stands.

"The slaves were looking for freedom. The red lamp became symbolic of that."

I couldn't imagine living such a dangerous life. As Mr. Wilson talked my mind ran wild of the images of events that took place in the very spot that I was sitting. Maybe a part of the Civil War had been fought right here. Maybe a cold and starving slave and her young son had finally reached this point, realizing this was their promised land, and collapsed to the ground in exhaustion. I wondered if someone had died right in the middle of where the football field was.

I could see on the television every night the battle scenes from the Vietnam War, but that was far away and only on my TV. I couldn't imagine living right in the middle of a war zone. We only *played* cowboys and Indians when I was little. Back then kids my age actually lived it.

—"So think about all this the next time you think you have a rough life," Mr. Wilson concluded. "I'll bet most of you have never had a gun pulled on you or been asked to sleep in a tent in the dead of winter. That's a much tougher existence than wishing there was more Pepsi in the refrigerator."

I was definitely given something to think about that afternoon. For a while, it actually took my mind off of football.

By the turn of the century, Springboro had four flourmills, six blacksmiths, one woolen mill, four wagon and carriage shops, and three sawmills. Fathers handed down their trades to their sons, who in turn handed them down to theirs.

I'd seen pictures of a small village, with little traffic and lots of family ancestry. In time the farms grew larger, carrying names like Taylor, Easton, Null, Beck, Fish and Sheehan. The young boys who grew up on those farms would only be seen on Saturdays when their families came to town for supplies.

Through the years, Main Street and East Street were eventually paved. President Eisenhower's commitment to build national freeways brought an exchange for I-75 to within two miles of Springboro. As a result, people who worked in Dayton could move out of the city and enjoy a quieter setting. So Springboro grew even more. The first house in Royal Oaks was constructed in 1959, and more homes went up in the years after that.

Homer's IGA, which in my eyes was practically the nerve center of the whole town, wasn't built until 1958; until then, people did their grocery shopping at Cookie's in Franklin or, for the small things, they could run into Lahman's, a small store on the northeast corner of Main Street and Central Avenue, which was where

CHAPTER 9

Brutey and Norma met during that Christmas break in 1957. Jim Eyler, the real mayor of Springboro, opened his furniture store just north of the IGA late in the sixties. And going further north, there was nothing but farmland until you got to the Dayton Mall, which opened in 1970. Aside from all that, you were in the country.

"Remember all of this when you walk by the bus garage, or any of the older houses downtown. This town is so different now than it was a hundred years ago. It will also be so much different a hundred years from now." Mr. Wilson got me to thinking.

We had one traffic light, the one at the center of Main Street and Central. Many days, when my paper route was finished, I would go to the Party Supply store on the corner there and drink a Mountain Dew as I watched the traffic go by. One time I counted ten cars in an hour, which was the most I'd ever seen.

How long would that be the case? I figured one day Springboro might actually have two stoplights. Now, that would really be something.

* * *

Later that night, we played our football game in the rain. It was a blast. I had mud in my facemask and dirty crud on my hands, and the numbers on our uniforms were barely recognizable. A day at Kings Island wouldn't have compared with this.

In the middle of the third quarter, with our team holding a slight lead, the officials called a timeout because a guy on the other team went down with a leg injury. As the other coaches huddled around seeing if the guy was hurt badly, I huddled my team together. We had a third down play coming, with only three yards to a first down, and we were thirty-five yards from the end zone. We had the ball, we had the momentum, and we had good field position. A touchdown at this stage of the game would almost certainly put the game away.

"Fellas, this is it right here," I said. "Everybody do their jobs and we can ram this down their throats." I tugged on the facemask of Pepper Dill, my massive center. "You guys on the line going to make some room for Donny?"

Before Pepper could answer, Donny interrupted, which he often did when he was mad.

"Hell yes, they're going to block because if they don't I'm going to stick my foot up somebody's butt." We had just run a 46 trap, a play Donny had run for a touchdown several times that season, but this time was tripped up for a gain of only a few yards. Ever the competitor, Donny went ballistic, and as usual he took out his frustration on our line. "You guys are sorry! You make me sick! Next lineman who lets a guy get through has to meet me after the game and I'm gonna' kick your ass! You got that? You hear that? Now we're going to run the same play and this time, block! On two."

Fortunately, our coach called a timeout, which calmed everyone down and gave Donny some time to cool off while our linemen got a chance to get some water. Coach O.J. gave a quick pep talk and the refs told us play would start in another minute. I then stepped out of the huddle and did something I did every so often, though it was never planned: I looked around at where I was standing and considered what exactly I was doing, and I remembered how lucky I was. For years I'd watched the Panthers on Friday nights and dreamed of the chance of one day playing for the varsity, and at that moment I was standing at midfield, under the lights, with mud on my cleats and all over my uniform. I was a quarterback, leading a touchdown march in an important game that would help set up the big game against Shane Hatfield. Surely this was how Rod Dillon felt on Friday nights.

I looked in the stands, I checked out the scoreboard, I listened as the ref blew his whistle and I was thrilled to get back in the huddle and call the next play, an option left to Donny. The line blocked and Donny ran for fifteen yards, giving us a first down. He walked back to the huddle like Pepper Dill was his best friend. Four plays later we scored. We won easily and celebrated with a walk to the K & W for a milk shake.

Shane was waiting near the north goal post to play the last game of the night.

"Nice game," he told us.

"Good luck," Donny said back.

I stopped in my tracks, unsure that I had heard them correctly. Were they actually complimenting one another? Donny kept walking and Shane took the field. Though I'd never seen Ali or Pete be nice to an opponent, I figured they didn't now compete against guys who lived around the corner from them and were in many of the same classes together. So I added a caveat to the trash-talking rule – that in the intense, competitive world of sports, there was always room for a little respect, so long as it was appropriate under the circumstances.

But then that got me to wondering: Would circumstances ever require us to be respectful to anyone from Mason? I hoped not.

I hated Mason. We all did.

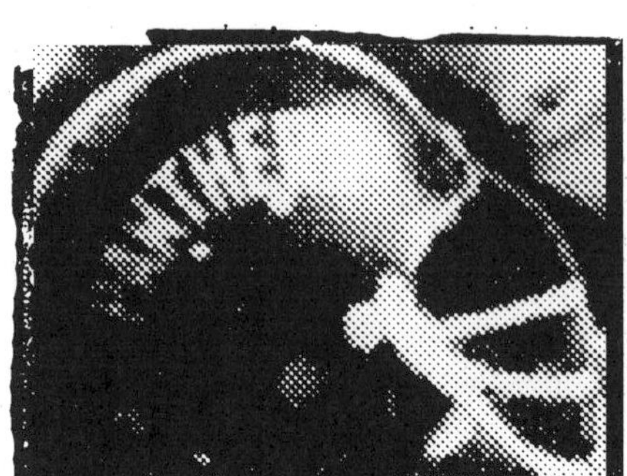

In 1972 Robert McNutt took the Springboro band to a level it had never before seen, making it "the best band in the land," according to announcer P.B. Stockman. It was a sign that Springboro was fast coming of age. Twenty-five years earlier, Peg Dunaway – who later married Ward Leisz -- lived right across the high school, when there was no football field and no marching band. And at that time, there wasn't even a stop light.

CHAPTER 10

> ***"Take your time but hurry," said Mr. C. Gordon in fifth grade and "Do the math and it all adds up," said Mrs. Thompson in sixth. But why did a budding superstar have to go to school?***
>
> ***-- The school dilemma***

FRIDAY, OCTOBER 13, 1972

Two outs. Bottom of the ninth. Game seven of the 1972 World Series.

Riverfront Stadium, home of the Reds, was standing room only, plus a national television audience watched at home on NBC. Cincinnati, winner of the National League pennant for the second time in three years, was tied in the series with the Oakland A's, and now every moment counted.

The fans hung on every pitch. No one was sitting down.

Because it was a Sunday late afternoon in October, the stadium shadows extended just beyond second base into the outfield. It was a crisp sixty-five degrees. Charlie O was in his green blazer in the front row, cheering on his beloved A's.

The Reds trailed by one, 4-3, and manager Sparky Anderson faced a crucial decision. Runners were on second and third and pitcher Gary Nolan was due up next. Yikes! Like most pitchers, Nolan hadn't gotten a hit all year. So Sparky had to go to his bench. He had to bat anybody but Nolan for the Reds to win the title.

But there was another problem.

A mysterious flu bug that had put all of the subs in the hospital had decimated the Reds' bench. So the regular subs weren't down there – McCray, Plummer,

Stewart. Instead, there was only me.

Sparky stepped from the dugout and motioned for a timeout. Nolan knew what was coming. After a few seconds, Pete Rose, then Johnny Bench and Joe Morgan joined them. They huddled close. They took turns talking, nodding when the other was talking. One minute turned into two, and the home plate umpire eventually went over to let them know the game needed to get moving. Rose held up his hand to say they only needed another minute.

Radio announcer Al Michaels looked over at his color analyst, Joe Nuxhall, and their eyes met. This was the second year they had been paired together in the booth, and they were comfortable with one another. Many nights, they called games and the kids who lived in the listening area would listen in as they camped out in makeshift tents or just sat on the back porch looking at the stars. Joe had pitched in the major leagues when he was only fifteen, making him the youngest player in Reds history. No one ever thought that record would be broken. Only now it was going to be.

I was ready. Just give me the chance, I thought. But deep down I wondered, could I really do this?

The stadium announcer played the chant that I had heard my whole life – "Ta-da-da-dant, Ta-Daa! Charge!" He did this several times. It sounded like a million people, not just the sixty thousand who were actually there. It was the most thrilling thing I'd ever seen.

"Let's go, Reds," shouted a guy in the front row.

Finally, the huddle broke up and they all nodded in agreement. Then Pete looked my way. Sparky stood silently, listening to the others. Then Little Joe looked my way.

The crowd was on its feet. It could sense a championship. All that was needed was a two-out line single to right center that would score the tying and winning runs. I was ready. The uniform was a little big, but it fit. It had my name on the back, with my favorite number, 25. I was about to become a most valuable member of the Big Red Machine. It didn't matter that I was only twelve.

"Just give me the chance, Coach," I whispered to myself. "I know I can do it." Just then I heard Pete say my name. I stood up and stepped out of the dugout onto the on-deck circle.

In the TV booth, NBC announcers Curt Gowdy and Tony Kubiak were correctly interpreting the conversation. "Curt, Sparky knows that if Gary Nolan steps up to the plate, this game is over. He's stepped up to tell Nolan that, and you can tell Nolan agrees. So his superstars have stepped up to tell Sparky what deep down he already knew, that he has a kid on the bench who is a phenomenal hitter –"

"You're talking about Kirby?" Curt Gowdy interjected.

"That's right. This kid has just been brought up to the team. He's young, and many within the organization were worried about bringing him up to the big leagues so soon. But in the end they figured that he had such talent that they had to utilize him, particular with so many of their other players being out today. Curt, I saw him in batting practice today. I've played with Mickey Mantle, I've seen all the good ones since then. If Sparky were to bring Kirby up right now, I absolutely think it would be the right thing to do."

"Well, Tony, it looks like Sparky has called for exactly that. And listen to the ovation from this crowd…"

It was deafening. I stepped onto the on deck circle, and when I did the roar got even louder. I put pine tar around the grip of my bat and took a few practice swings. Rollie Fingers was about to go down, I said to myself, and I was going to win it all for the Reds. I took the long walk to home plate for my very first major league at-bat.

Just the day before I was playing Wiffle ball with my brothers in the backyard.

I heard the voice of Paul Summercamp, the legendary Reds announcer, coming through the speakers, "Pinch-hitting, for the pitcher…Jeff Kirby." And the sound of my name resonated throughout the stadium.

And then he did as he always did. He repeated my last name, and the sound of it reverberated throughout the stadium..

"Kirby."

You can do it…

Find your pitch…

Just…just…

"Jeff!"

Just reeeeelaaaaaax…What the –

"Jeff!"

I was busted.

CHAPTER 10

My teacher looked ten feet tall. I was in a room full of about a thousand people, all of them turned and looking straight at me, with a spotlight shining directly in my eyes so that there could be no mistake that I had been caught daydreaming. In class. During an important lecture. Not a good idea. Not a good idea at all.

I was busted all right. Daydreaming in class was a crime right up there with murder.

Mrs. Kuhn, my teacher, had asked me a question. She naturally wanted an answer, immediately. And I would have loved to give her one, but I didn't know the question. For a few seconds, I didn't even know where I was. Then it came to me – science class, seventh period, Springboro Junior High School, October 1972. Oh, yeah, now I remember. Dang it.

I started to sweat as if I were under a hot spotlight. I'd been called out in front of the whole class and revealed as a total goof-off, which I was. Still, I was embarrassed. I turned red and suffered a silent humiliation from which I thought I might never recover. I managed to mumble something about paleontology. And then I used the word "photosynthesis." Neither had anything to do with the subject matter of the day, but at least they were science words. Mrs. Kuhn soon moved on, but she stared at me a lot that day.

It was going to be a long school year with Mrs. Kuhn staring a hole through me all year like that.

It was the longest hour of my life. Every. Minute. Lasted. Forever. It no longer mattered that there was football to be played, and the varsity had a big Homecoming Game the next day, or that a bunch of us were meeting at the K & W after school. Instead, all that mattered was that I somehow make it to the end of class. And then I'd go run away and join the other freaks in the circus.

A few minutes later, Mr. Vince Ross saved me. He made an announcement that we were released to go to the pep assembly in the gym, where I did my best to get lost in the crowd.

I was never so glad to be at a pep rally like that. The football team was introduced. So were all the homecoming candidates and their escorts. I had heard my sisters talk about the Homecoming court all week, like it was something really important. All I knew is we had a chance to look at some pretty girls. Other than that, the whole thing took away from the real attraction of the football game, which of course was most important.

Later that night, there would be a bonfire, where every piece of scrap wood in town was collected and piled twenty feet high, then burned as the cheerleaders led cheers and the band played the school fight song. Then on Saturday morning there was a parade down Main Street, ending at the football field. Enthusiasm around town was at its peak excitement during that week. Everyone was out; everyone was there. There was an electric atmosphere that just wasn't present during the other calmer, softer days around town.

It all made me temporarily forget the horror of Mrs. Kuhn's class. I'd wait until Monday to either jump off a cliff or join the circus.

* * *

Walking home, I turned the corner from Kesling onto Redbud and looked up the street to find a police cruiser in front of my house. Oh great, I thought. First I get busted in Science class and now I get busted by the cops for who knew what. I hadn't done anything, but I just figured with my luck that I was getting nailed for something. I may have thought about letting the air out of Mrs. Kuhn's tires, but I didn't actually do anything.

I trudged up the street like a murderer with a date with the executioner. Big Charlie Reedy was standing outside of his cruiser talking to my mom. As usual, he looked a hundred feet tall. He'd always looked at me suspiciously ever since the night over the summer when he responded to a teeny, tiny fire at the Jonathan Wright Elementary School. Lighter fluid had been poured on all the grass that grew up through the concrete, and then set on fire, creating a glorious scene that looked almost like a war zone. When the police rolled in, everyone took off, and ever since then Charlie had looked at me like I had been in on it.

Don't ask me how I knew so much about the incident. For the record, I wasn't talking. I knew my rights.

Charlie and my mom had been friends for several years, going back to when Charlie had been married to his former wife Betty. Mom was one of her best friends. The marriage didn't last but Mom still talked to Charlie whenever they had the chance. That's the way my mother has always been – friendly and conversational, without a hint of being judgmental. She knew as well as anyone that Charlie wasn't the monster his big frame and big badge sometimes created.

"Did you have a good day at school?" Mom asked.

"Yeah, it was okay. No problems." I think I earned my law degree at that very moment. Man, that was a good lie.

"Looking forward to the big bonfire tonight?" Charlie asked. "Now that'll be some fire, huh?"

Nice try, Charlie. I'm not admitting anything.

"Seems to me we've already had one of those this year, out at the elementary school," he added. Now Charlie was looking right at me. This was worse than military coercion. Didn't something protect me from this? The Geneva Convention maybe? I think I heard something about that while I daydreamed through World History once.

Charlie was a police office by occupation, but his first love was farming. Born to Curtis and Myrtle Reedy in 1930, Charlie was raised on a farm and was taught that hard work, honesty and integrity were the essential qualities a man must possess. He attended Jefferson High School, west of Dayton, playing basketball in the winters and farming during the warmer months. He got his love for basketball from his mother, who had been a player for Springboro back in the 20s. It pleased her to see Charlie also take up the game, and she went to all of his games, just like later she went to all of the Springboro games.

A year after graduating in 1948 Charlie met Betty Bishop of Springboro, and the two were married shortly thereafter. They lived in several places and Charlie held a number of jobs, though he always farmed the land. Nothing came between him and his farming. Pretty soon his sons Jim and Tom were born, and they would acquire that love of farming, too.

Charlie also became active on the Springboro Fire Department and the Life Squad, volunteering for both. Then, after working around Dick Chenault, the fire chief, and Carl Hirschbach, the police chief, he was convinced that he needed to make public service his life's work. That's when he enrolled in the police academy and became a full-time police officer.

The Springboro police department hired him as soon as he graduated, and immediately he made his presence known around town. In 1971 Charlie had a heart attack, and youngest son Tom – who was on the football team – debated whether he should take himself out of the lineup. A prayer vigil was held and Tom spent time at his father's side. Charlie didn't mince words with his son. He wanted him to play. Tom went on to play one of the best games of his career.

Charlie loved Springboro. He loved doing whatever it took to make it a good place to live. I'd see him later at the bonfire, and I knew he'd be looking right at me.

* * *

A few streets over from my house, Brutey closed the door behind Reverend Dawes and quickly turned on his heels. "Now we have the preacher stopping by our house? What was that all about? You been complaining to him now?"

"Uh, I haven't been complaining to anybody, not even him. What he said Sunday just hit me, that's all. He's just checking in on us."

"Us? Why check on *us* if you're the one with the problem?"

"Brutey, I –"

"—you know, you think you have it so hard here, but you don't. I'm the one who has to go to work all day. I'm the one who has to make the money. And if I need some time away to have a few beers to help me relax, that's none of your business. Maybe you should start doing more to take the pressure off me."

"I never said –"

"Next time he drops by we're not answering the door. I don't need anything he has to say. My life is just fine. Ask anyone within a thousand yards of here. If you want to go to his church and listen to him talk, that's fine, but it doesn't need to concern me."

Norma sunk lower in her chair and held her head in her hands. She cried as Brutey left the room to change clothes. It had been a simple little visit by the preacher of a church she had just started attending. Nice preachers did that sort of thing, and he never meant to create the kind of argument that Brutey was starting.

Couldn't she get a break over anything? Was everything her fault? In Brutey's mind, apparently it was.

She was still crying when he left house moments later. He didn't say good-bye when he did.

Moments later, Brutey was the life of the party at the community bonfire and pep rally.

Because everybody loved Brutey.

All week long, the school and the community were in a frenzy because of Homecoming. There were egg-throwing contests, which Dave Dillon enjoyed, plus a bonfire and a parade through the center of town, all culminating in the game on Saturday afternoon, where Mike Colvin (79) smashed opposing rushers and Pam Hepp was named Queen.

CHAPTER 11

I've got a quote for you, Edith.
'A bird that always flies in the
fog is a dingbat.'
--The philosopher of '72
Archie Bunker

Saturday, October 14, 1972

Lance called first thing in the morning with tragic news.

The night before, at the bonfire we had both attended, where the blaze got especially big and the crowd became particularly excited, he'd heard that after we left some of the players were grabbing extra pieces of wood and throwing them on the fire. In the process of doing that, Rod Dillon got too close and burned his right hand, his throwing hand. It was doubtful that he would be able to play that day.

"You're kidding," I said frantically, as if I'd just heard that the entire downtown had burned to the ground.

"Turkey told me this morning," he said. "He just left my house."

"Turkey? He told us last week that Archie Bunker was his uncle. You can't believe a thing Turkey says," I responded. "How does Turkey know what happened?"

"I don't know. He says it's all over town."

"Really? Oh no. This is awful. Today's a big game and we have to have Rod. We can't win without him. I'll meet you at the parade in about an hour. We'll get to the bottom of this," I said. This proved that Mannix had nothing on me.

CHAPTER 11

I quickly made my bed, cleaned my room, straightened the garage, and broke up a fight between my two brothers, and was soon out the door. Mom gave me two dollars, which was more than enough money for the day, and told me to be home by dark.

We had to have Rod at quarterback. There were no two ways about it.

With the parade set to begin in a few minutes, I found a spot along Main Street right in front of the Laundromat. A bunch of girls from school were nearby, and they were giddy at the idea of seeing the homecoming candidates pass by all dressed up in their gowns and fancy hairdos. Just what was it with girls anyway? From what they said, the competition for queen was especially intense this year, with several girls having a legitimate chance to win. I didn't care really, but if any of the cute girls from school ever wanted to discuss the prospects with me, I'd have taken an immediate interest. Debbie Balyo could have convinced me to talk about bows and ribbons, and even to root against the Reds, and that was practically an impossible thought.

I sat next to Keith Crocker and Freddie Brown, two guys who were a year older than me, and then started talking with Robbie Casper, a kid who was two years younger than me, who lived two doors down from Brutey on Market Street. Lance and Turkey were on their way, but until then, I had to know.

"Have you heard anything about Rod Dillon?" I asked.

"No," he said. "Say, what do you know about that Baker family near me? Have you heard what's going on there?"

"One thing at a time," I said. "Did Rod hurt his hand last night like I heard? Have you heard anything?"

"Nah, I haven't heard that he hurt his hand," he told me. "I was by their house this morning collecting for my paper route. I think he was in the garage cleaning out his car. You know, the police were out there the other night."

"Rod's house?"

"No, the Baker house. You sure you don't know what's up there?"

"He looked okay?" I was ready to strangle this kid.

"No, he looked mad. Like he was ready to walk out on the whole family, just like the last time."

"Rod?"

"No, Mr. Baker. Geez, what's the big deal about Rod? He's fine. He'll be in the starting lineup this afternoon, just like always. Now, about the Bakers…."

"I don't know anything about them. Brutey seems like he's a great guy and Ricky seems to love him to death. What else could there be?" Honestly, I was beginning to wonder about everybody's priorities. Another few minutes in this conversation and Robbie Casper would be drinking his milkshakes through his neck.

Just then Lance and Turkey showed up, with Turkey smiling a mile wide like he knew he was busted. Suddenly the conversation about Brutey ended.

"Spreading rumors, are you?" I asked.

"Hey, I don't make them up. I just pass along what I know." Turkey had that confident smile going, like it wasn't his fault at all.

"Yeah, but about the only thing you pass real well is gas," Lance said, spitting into his hands.

"That reminds me."

"No! Not here!" Lance screamed. "You'll kill somebody."

Turkey tried to defend his statements. "I walked up town this morning and they were talking at the Ashland station about the bonfire. I swear someone said Rod was hurt."

"You probably heard that someone threw a metal rod in the fire," I said, rolling up my sweatshirt sleeves.

"Okay, maybe I heard that, too." He smiled again.

"You goober. So Rod's okay?" Lance asked, his eyes intently focused on Turkey's.

"Yeah, he's okay. We just saw him drive through the neighborhood on his way to the parade. He'll be in the starting lineup this afternoon, just like we need."

"Good."

"But let me tell you what I heard about Mike Colvin."

"Shut up, Turkey."

"I don't make them up. I just pass along what I know."

Now I was ready to hurt Turkey.

* * *

CHAPTER 11

The day was cool and crisp, a classic day for October in the heartland, and the trees had blossomed into the proverbial rainbow of colors. Main Street was alive with kids sitting along the curb and older folks in lawn chairs, many wearing Panther blue and waving American flags that had been given out by the police department. The parade started promptly at eleven, beginning at Jonathan Wright Elementary, heading south past Mr. Chenault and his front porch, and ending at the high school. As small as Springboro was, re-routing traffic around the center of town wasn't a problem.

The band was first. It played the school fight song and their version of "Hang On Sloopy," which was a trademark song for the Ohio State Buckeyes, filling the air with a festive spirit. To some football was only a game, but to others it was a reflection of the strength and character of a community. With a win over archrival Mason the week before, the Panthers seemingly had turned their season around. There was still hope. We still had a chance at the conference championship. And aside from all of that the excitement of the Homecoming parade and game was enough to draw our interest.

The Homecoming court was featured next. One by one, the candidates were driven through town in convertible sports cars, first Kathy Manning and then Pam Hepp and then the others. The little girls in town sat on the street curb and admired the candidates as they drove by, waving and smiling. Cheerleaders who were not part of the Homecoming court tossed out candy and chanted Springboro cheers. The fire engines revved up in the distance.

"Blue and white, you're out of sight. Hey, hey, hey. Blue and white, you're out of sight."

After the Homecoming court passed by, the ten men from town who served in World War II waltzed along in their VFW hats. People clapped and put their hands over their hearts as they walked by. And then, finally, the flat bed trailer that carried the football team passed by. All of the players were there, lined up on both sides of the trailer, looking boyish and innocent without their pads and helmets, waving to the crowd and tossing out miniature footballs donated by Ralph Wade Insurance.

"B-O-R-O," the cheerleaders chanted. "B-O-R-O."

The parade wasn't long, but it was powerful. After an entire week of games and festivities, excitement was high as it could ever be, and now it was now time for the game. For a second I actually felt sorry for Little Miami, which was going to be on the receiving end of a butt-whooping.

* * *

I could smell the popcorn from the parking lot.

The marching bands were on both sides of the field, belting out songs so loudly that my feet started to wiggle. As we stood in line with hundreds of other people who wanted in, I soaked in the sounds and the smells of football. I could see players warming up, and coaches were huddled up fine-tuning the game plan. Meanwhile, the bands played on, especially the drums. I loved the drums. As I wiggled and inched forward, I began to get a little impatient. Why wouldn't the line move any faster? Let's go.

The whole town was there. The stands were full fifteen minutes before kick-off, Dads standing in the area just beneath the press box and Moms sitting in the seats just below them. I saw neighbors, customers on my paper route, and Mayor Eyler standing next to some police officers and council members. At ten minutes before kickoff, our team left the field for an outdoor spot just north of the school, an area that was an unofficial locker room, with walls on two sides and large trees shading it. They huddled closely, with their helmets off, and listened intently to the last-minute instructions given by Coach Ross.

"It's been a great week, but now I need to you slow down and get focused," he said. "These guys play good football, and they'd like nothing better than to come in here with all that's going on and wipe the smile off everyone's face. So I need for you to come out strong, play hard, and take the suspense out of this game early. Then we can have some fun."

He didn't have to say anything more.

I was eating popcorn and drinking Pepsi, soaking in the experience, waiting for the game to start, when Lance interrupted me.

"She caught you, didn't she?" Lance asked.

"Who?"

"Mrs. Kuhn." Now Lance had that confident smile that Turkey always showed. He knew something.

Ugh. The name evoked images. Eagle eye. Battie Hattie. I had a dozen of them. And I should've hit Lance for resurrecting such an awful memory.

"She sure did. I know I shouldn't do it," I said, shaking my head.

"Well, if it hadn't been you, it would have been me."

CHAPTER 11

"Yeah? In the World Series?"

"Super Bowl." That would've come later, but not anymore. Not in Mrs. Kuhn's class, where I was going to forever be a model student who paid attention and raised his hand and even volunteered for special assignments. I was going to be a different student in Mrs. Kuhn's until the last day of the year.

Just then the mighty Panthers emerged from their makeshift locker room and ran out single file, with Rod Dillon last as usual, and they stormed onto the field to the sounds of the school fight song. The cheerleaders led everyone in a cheer, and the captains stood at midfield for the coin toss, which we won, giving us the ball first.

"We're going to kill them," Roger said to me.

"Yeah, it'll be a rout," Danny interjected.

Little Miami kicked off and the ball sailed right directly at us, making us feel we were an even bigger part of the game. Russ Chesney received it at the goal line and returned the ball twenty-seven yards, where we started, first and ten.

As the offense took the field, Rod Dillon stayed behind for the play call from Coach Ross. Big number seven took the play, entered the huddle and called the play. The players chanted, "Let's break," and they scattered to their individual positions. Dale Midkiff was split right, and Dave Collins was in the slot. Dave Dillon was the lone setback. "Hog" was on the line ready to blow someone away.

"Here we go, Panthers, here we go! Here we go, Panthers, here we go!"

The game was on. Our perfect Saturday was even more perfect.

We started slow against Little Miami, trailing at halftime, but in the end the afternoon crowd went home happy. Early in the fourth quarter, Rod hit Dave Collins for a 43-yard completion, giving us a first down deep in Little Miami territory. Two plays later Rod rolled right and found Dave wide open for a nine-yard touchdown. Our lead was 16-7 when Rod completed the two-point conversion to Dale Midkiff.

The next score didn't take that long.

Little Miami took over after the kickoff on its own 18-yard line, fully hoping to get back into the game. But, on its first play, quarterback Rick Crain threw a pass that was intercepted by Springboro's Russ Chesney out at the 33.

From there Rod threw a perfect spiral to Russ on a flag route. Russ caught it, escaped the Little Miami defender who was on him, and waltzed in for our second touchdown in less than a minute. We won, 22-7, capping off a great day. The band played louder and the cheerleaders were more enthusiastic. Pam Hepp had been named Homecoming Queen and, afterward, the guys and I started playing football in the area beyond the north end zone.

Afterward, the players were happy and relaxed, and they spread out throughout the shaded area just outside the team room. We saw sweaty but smiling faces. Many of the guys had already taken off their shoulder pads.

"Great job, fellas," Coach Ross said. Coach was always a man of few words, but when he spoke he was to the point and convincing. "That's two in a row now. We have Waynesville next week, which will be a tough one, but if we keep playing solid football we can really turn this season around."

From there they gave out a couple of game balls and then they broke off to hit the showers. That was our cue to finally head home.

"Man, I wish every day could be as great as this one," I said. "No kidding," Lance added.

Looking back now, I think they all were.

CHAPTER 12

Fries and a chocolate shake,
With a stack of baseball cards,
And eight sticks of chewing
gum to chew on
-- The Diner attraction

THURSDAY, OCTOBER 19, 1972

The waitress put a cup of coffee in front of Ralph Wade and returned to the kitchen. He'd ordered the soup and salad, with fat free dressing. "Maybe a few French fries on the side," he said. His heart that was so generous in many ways was failing him physically, so he had to be careful what he ate. Because he was so headstrong, the doctors knew he cheated every now and then, so they built that into his supposedly "strict" diet.

He knew that, too.

Mr. Wade was as smart as he was active in the community. A distinguished man of forty-five whose hair was already silver, Mr. Wade was president of the school board. He had also helped start the peewee football league, the Little League baseball organization, and was also in the Lion's Club. He was in Bennett's Drug Store that day for an afternoon cup of coffee with Ray Perez, the school superintendent, where they would discuss the new land the district purchased far south of town for a new high school, which was still several years away. There were also some personnel issues, and a few budget cuts. And of course the really important stuff, football.

If anything happened in town, it was discussed at the diner in back of the drug store.

Originally known as Wells' Drug Store, the town pharmacy first opened in 1955 facing Main Street, just north of Central Avenue, where the Shell gas station sits today. Six years later, Harold Bennett, who changed the name to Bennett's Drugs and moved the store into the plaza across from the newly built IGA, purchased it. It sat between the hardware store and the Ben Franklin, with two doors – one for incoming traffic and the other for outgoing traffic. The hair salon was at the end of the plaza, and Dutch's Barber Shop was just around the corner. This was our downtown.

If the drug store wasn't already one of the busiest places in town because of all the necessities it sold, it was even more popular because of its diner in the back. It was a restaurant that served home cooked food and great milkshakes. With only four booths, a counter along the far wall, and a small kitchen, it was anything but fine dining.

But it was the place to be.

We knew everyone there. Evalyn Harris had worked behind the counter there for years, and I got to know her well because she lived next door to Mitch. Charlie Reedy and Jimmy Beavers often met there for coffee so they could discuss police business. And we kids often stopped there for a plate of French fries and something cold to drink. While eating the special of the day (or a plate of fries), we could be part of four or five different conversations, all mostly related to the town business. Farmers huddled together to talk about pesticides and yields. Local businessmen would talk about the economy. The politicians talked about policies and school-board matters. But, far and away, most of the conversation was on the varsity football and basketball teams.

Mr. Wade and Mr. Perez occupied a booth across from us. They talked quietly and didn't pay attention to us goof-offs nearby.

Brutey, looking strangely out of character in his dress shirt and tie, walked in around 4:15. Since the varsity had light practices on Thursday afternoons, he wasn't needed at the varsity field. He stayed at work a little later than usual and stopped in The Diner that afternoon for a cup of coffee. As usual, he knew just about everyone in there and quickly entered every conversation going. No one could have guessed that work had been a struggle that day because his sales in NCR's newest division were down. But then again, no one ever saw Brutey down in the dumps.

"Ralph Wade, my man. Say, why don't you get out of that chair and go do something? What's it been, ten minutes since I've heard someone brag about your generosity? You're slipping, man. Better get yourself back out there and go build a building or something. I'm starting to worry about you."

CHAPTER 12

"Thanks for your concern, Brutey."

"And hey there, Mr. Perez. Or should we call you Mr. Superintendent like we do the president? Hey, helluva job calling the game the other night. You finally learned to turn that mike off when talking to everyone in the press box, haven't you? I don't think you've given away a play in three weeks."

"I get carried away sometimes," Mr. Perez said, chuckling. Ordinarily, he loved talking football, but now he wanted to change subjects. "Ralph and I were just talking about the plans for the new high school. We closed today on that land up on the hill south of town."

"Yeah, I heard that. The signs of progress. This town is getting out of control, you know that? It's getting to the point when I worry about my son riding his bike along Central Avenue."

"That's the world we live in, Brutey. Everything's getting bigger. The Reds tear down Crosley, and Springboro gets a new high school."

Brutey took a seat in the booth across the aisle. He took cream and sugar with his coffee. Mr. Wade was dressed impeccably in a dark blue suit and red-and-white striped tie. Mr. Perez wore a gray suit that complemented his graying hair. In another booth three women were talking about a bake sale for the Methodist church.

Brutey was a fan of the Cincinnati Reds as much as he was the Buckeyes. "Oh, I loved Crosley. Must have gone to a thousand games there, sitting in the left field stands –"

"—drinking beer," Mr. Perez interjected.

"Maybe a few. But I'd just marvel at Pete, how he hustles so much. Don't get me wrong, the other guys are awesome. But Pete, man, he was – and still is – the most incredible player. He'd hit a triple and slide head-first into third base, right there in front of us, and I'd swear the ground shook when he did that."

"I understand," Mr. Perez said. "I used to spend a lot of time there myself."

"Hey, that's right. What did you help with, the Spanish-speaking players? Teaching them English or something, right? That's pretty awesome. So you'd spend all this time with guys that we only get to watch from the stands -- Davey Concepcion, Leo Cárdenas, Tony Perez, Caesar Geronimo –".

"We didn't get Caesar until last year."

"Oh, right, the trade with Houston. Say, did I ever tell you that I was at that last game at Crosley? One of the most incredible experiences of my life. We're down one, and I'm sitting there in the left field stands –"

"—drinking beer," Mr. Wade interjected.

"Maybe a few. And I'm thinking, no way we leave here on a losing note. So you know what happens, Lee May and Johnny Bench hit back-to-back home runs so that we win by one. Greatest comeback I ever saw. I swear I thought I was in the middle of an earthquake. Then we stand there and watch the helicopter fly in. They dug up home plate and the helicopter flew off to Riverfront with it. Gave me goose bumps. And, get this, afterward, we were all down near the locker room and I got to hang out with Lee May. Huge guy, big biceps. Nicest guy you'd ever want to meet. Just a normal guy too. I had him talked into coming up here one day over the summer to talk to my Little League team. Next thing I know they trade him."

"The kids would have loved that."

"No kidding. Say, you think maybe you could get Tony Perez up here someday? Are you guys related or something?"

Mr. Perez shrugged off the question. He'd been asked that same question a thousand times. He'd been in education more than thirty years, having been Franklin High School principal for many years – with students who included, among others, Ralph Wade in the class of 1944 – before coming to Springboro, where he was a principal before becoming superintendent in the late sixties. He was fluent in both Spanish and English, which gave him the opportunity to be a translator the way he was.

"Tony may be a little too busy, but I'll see what I can do with some of the other players."

"Far out, as the kids the say."

They then returned to the more mundane talk of school business. Population projections were thrown around, as were budgets. And before long I preferred to return my shake and plate of French fries and re-enter the debate of whether Danny Partridge or Peter Brady was the goofiest kid on television.

I went to The Diner almost every day after I finished my paper route. They had baseball cards and milkshakes, which was about all I needed in life. I'd sit and thumb through my new cards, sipping away, and hear all the opinions and the arguments that inevitably ensued. With that much information filling the air, the town didn't need a newspaper.

The game against Little Miami was dissected there in the days following it, and the unofficial game plan for the upcoming Waynesville game would be formulated there, too. There was never a shortage of opinions, and if one group left the next group jumped right into the conversation. In a few months, they would be discussing basketball opponents and the way each of our varsity players was playing.

I felt like I was in on some inside information. We all went to the games, but these moments were a chance to hear all the locker room talk, which we never got to hear.

"Brutey, how do we stack up against Waynesville?" Mr. Wade asked. I overheard this because it was about football. My mom always said I could hear anything I wanted to, which explained why I never heard her tell me to clean my room. "I know they're not having a great season, but the game is at their place, and in a rivalry like this I think the records can go out the window."

Brutey ordered a refill on his coffee. "That's usually true, but not in this case. Waynesville has too many holes in its defense, and from what I hear and see on film, our offense is almost unstoppable. Rod's really come around. And our defense continues to be awfully stingy. I think you'll see us win by three touchdowns."

"Three?"

"At least."

The men looked at one another and liked what they heard. This was good information for the board meeting that night. They thanked him and excused themselves so they could go home for a while before their meeting. Brutey decided to leave, too, but not so he could go home. Maybe there was a practice he could watch. Or maybe he could find someone else to talk to. There was no sense getting home too early, since that just gave Norma more time to gripe at him.

As they walked to the front counter, Brutey was stopped. The woman looked vaguely familiar, but Brutey couldn't place her.

"The rumors about you were true," she said.

This caused Mr. Wade and Mr. Perez to look at one another. Uh oh. Usually, those were not kind words.

"Rumors?" Brutey asked. "I don't understand."

"You coached my son this past summer."

"Oh, yeah. James. You must be Mrs. Riley." Brutey was still sweating, unsure of where this conversation was going.

"I just wanted you to know that my son always struggled with baseball. Before, he struck out a lot and couldn't catch a ball, and all the other kids made fun of him for it. He told me before last summer that he didn't want to play baseball, but I convinced him to give it another chance."

Mrs. Riley spoke softly. Her voice trembled a little, too. "And I was so pleased that you were his coach. I'd heard about you. I heard you really paid attention to all the boys. What you did with my son this summer was amazing. He hit the ball and did great in the field, and he had a great time. He actually looked forward to his games. That's all because of you. I've been meaning to tell you that for a long time, but the time never really presented itself. "

Brutey's eyes moistened as he took in every word. Mr. Wade and Mr. Perez patted him on the back as they said goodbye. For a full ten minutes after the woman had left, Brutey sat on the bench just outside the door, rubbing his eyes. He did have a gift, he realized. He did really have an effect on the players he coached.

Such was every coach's biggest ambition, to make a difference in the lives of the kids he coached. And this was not the first time Brutey had been told this by a parent. He was a happy man that night.

Until he walked in the front door of his house.

* * *

Two streets over from Brutey's, at the dinner table in my house a few hours later, my family talked about a million different things. Jenny had homework that was driving her crazy, and John wanted his own room because he was tired of sharing one with Joey, who always made fun of his red hair. Julie had heard from Traci Helfinstine that a boy in their class really liked her, but that made another girl in their class mad. She didn't know what to do. Joey, meanwhile, was content to continue blistering John in a never-ending array of put-downs.

Dad listened while Mom piled on the spaghetti and meatballs. Though our lives went in twenty directions every single day, there was one constant for all of us – sitting down to dinner at five-thirty. That happened every night, without exception. Mom never ordered pizza and only occasionally, like when a ball game ran late, did we ever get a burger and fries from Burger Chef, which was way over in Franklin. As a rule, we were required to be home when dinner was on the table, or else we didn't get to eat. That's the way it was at everyone else's house, too.

I went to my room early that night so I could do homework that Mrs. Kuhn had assigned. Jenny had worked through her math problems and sat down with everyone else to watch *The Flip Wilson Show*, which was one of our favorites. I could hear the laughter downstairs, and I knew that I would hear its highlights over and over for the coming week.

The devil made me do it. It was Flip's favorite line.

With the project I was working on spread out in front of me, I listened to the music of WSAI from the small radio behind me. They always played the best songs, and I carried the music and lyrics in my head wherever I went. *Dancin' in the Moonlight* came on around 8:45 and I put down my pencil and looked up at the ceiling. The thought sounded good to me. I'd have given anything to chuck the whole science project and go dance outside and do a little dancing in the moonlight.

Mom checked on me around ten, just before she and dad would watch Dean Martin's show. "You look tired. You gonna' be okay in the morning?" My mom has always been a gentle soul. That was her way of telling me it was time to turn off the lights, and turn off the music and go to bed.

"I'm almost done." I said, rubbing my eyes. She sat down on the bed next to me.

"Everything going okay?" she asked. She was always good at listening to what I had to say. Some nights I didn't feel like anything was going right, and it helped having her ask.

But this was no such night. "Everything's great," I said, closing my book. "School's okay. And football's going well." I didn't mention that had two left feet when it came to be around girls and I was beginning to wonder if I'd stay single my entire life.

"Good. Sleep tight. Your dad and I are so proud of all of you."

I knew that, but I also liked hearing it. I lay awake a while longer looking out my bedroom window, at the stars in the sky. Who knew what life was all about? Who knew where it would ultimately take me? I wasn't entirely sure, but what I knew was life was good at the moment. I had football and my family. I had friends all over town, and I only hoped their lives were as good as mine was.

Health. Comfort. Safety. I had it all.

Dancin' in the Moonlight for sure.

The focus in a small town will fall on the mayor, the chief of police and the president of the school board. But it will also fall on the starting quarterback on the football team. Rod Dillon, who dated and then later married Pam Hepp, the homecoming queen, was a team leader, both in the way he played and in the way he motivated his teammates.

CHAPTER 13

Paul Brown in the NFL, and Woody
Hayes in college, and Coach Don
Ross for the varsity Panthers
-- The coaches of my future
...or so I hoped

WEDNESDAY, OCTOBER 25, 1972

Brutey felt beat up, tied up and horsewhipped by the time he left work. It had been yet another difficult day, which was fast becoming the norm. A sale he'd worked on for months abruptly fell through, which led to a heated lunch meeting with his boss about his sagging numbers. Then he got a call from Norma to tell him that the water heater had busted. Should she call a plumber? Then that will be another hundred dollars. How were they supposed to pay for it? He went straight to the coaches' office at the high school and sat in a chair to take a short nap.

Something had to break sooner or later. He'd love to quit selling and instead coach full-time, because the corporate grind was killing him. But he needed the money. There wasn't enough of it as it was, and a teacher made even less, which he always thought was the ultimate crime against society. He couldn't take a lesser-paying job without his problems with Norma getting worse. As it was, they hadn't had a civil conversation in a long time, and it didn't look like improvement was coming anytime soon.

Why did she think he had it made, going off to work and dealing with hard-nosed business managers every day? Why did she think she had it so hard, staying home and sleeping in and cooking dinner for the boys every night? He would trade places with her in a heartbeat.

Thank God he had the players and the games; he didn't know what he'd do if he didn't have that outlet.

No sooner than he had shut his eyes Coach Ross walked in. He set aside a stack of English papers that he would somehow grade later that night, and lit up his pipe. He looked over at Brutey, who cracked his eyelids only slightly to see his intruder. "You look like crap," Coach Ross told him.

"Good. I'd hate to look good when I feel like crap."

"Rough night last night?"

"I don't drink every night," Brutey snapped.

"I didn't say you did. I didn't say you drank last night, either." Coach Ross took a long drag on his pipe and sorted through the mail piled in the center of his desk.

"I don't want to talk about it," Brutey said finally.

"Okay. I've got to be on the field in a few minutes anyway. We have to work especially hard, it seems, since we have to live up to some expectations you've set."

Brutey poked open one eye. "What do you mean?"

Coach Ross repositioned his pipe. "Somebody told me you predicted we'd win by three touchdowns Friday night. Three of them. So now we not only have the pressure to win, but we have to win by three scores."

Brutey rolled his eyes and realized he now had another reason to be frustrated. "You've been talking to Mr. Perez."

"No, I heard it from Junior Dillon. He called me at home last night. The whole town knows."

"It's true, you know."

Coach Ross didn't like that answer one bit. "Brutey, you know as well as I do how much emotion plays in this game. I can't have these kids getting on the bus Friday night thinking they already have this game in the bag. They're good kids, sure, but they're still kids. We're using this role as the underdog to motivate them the rest of the season."

He had never heard Coach Ross use that tone of voice. Not with officials, and not with a player during practice. And certainly never with him.

CHAPTER 13

"Sorry," he said, closing his eyes again. Brutey's day was now complete. His boss was ready to fire him, his house was falling apart, Norma had been giving him the cold shoulder for six months now, and now he had ticked off Coach Ross – a man who was almost impossible to make angry.

"Let's just make sure this is the last time we have this conversation. Come basketball season, Harry won't like it either."

"Oh, don't I know it. He'd be chewing me out right about now. Nobody works the underdog angle better than him, so I probably wouldn't have a job anymore. Sorry, boss. It won't happen again."

"I'm sure it won't."

Brutey shut his eyes again, amazed at how inept he had become. Coach Ross was mad at him now. Coach Ross. The quiet man. He wanted to close his eyes and never wake up.

* * *

Whether he was on the football field or in the classroom, Coach Ross often used the same voice that he used in English class. He spoke softly, yet matter-of-factly, and he made eye contact all the way around so as to emphasize the points he wanted to make. But he had his moments of frustration. When a player had Coach Ross in his face, he really knew he messed up.

Coach Ross had been with the football program ever since it started. After an athletic career at nearby Carlisle, he attended and graduated from Miami University and immediately came to Springboro in 1963, following Lonnie Norris, his college roommate. In the process he joined his father and mother, who had just moved to Springboro. Mr. Robert Ross later became an administrator at the junior high.

In the beginning years, before football, he was the freshmen basketball coach, which put him on the bench as the 1964-65 basketball Panthers fought their way to the state Class A finals. Years later he went back to Columbus as the head coach of the 1977-78 girls basketball team.

In 1965, Coach Ross was an assistant as Springboro launched its first football season, under Lonnie Norris. That inaugural team had heart and talent and as a result fought its way to a very respectable 6-3 record with Ed Wade as quarterback. They played especially well at home because of a distinct home field advantage – a noticeable six foot slope downward from the north side of the field to the south, a by-product of trying to get the field ready on a limited budget.

"If you were going north late in the game, you were at a significant disadvantage," one former player recalled, laughing. "So while at some fields you play to have the wind in the fourth quarter, at our place you play to being going downhill." The slope was eventually eliminated.

After some success, Mr. Norris left after the '68 season, and Coach Ross succeeded him. He was never a Vince Lombardi in-your-face bulldog kind of coach. Instead, he knew how to combine finesse and strategy with the brute force of the game. Often in the coaches' meetings, the assistants fought fiercely for their particular style against a particular team, and Coach Ross, with his calm and deliberate style, often resolved the issue in a firm but fair manner. It wasn't everybody's style, but it worked for him.

Coach Norris' last team in '68 team had been a good one, going 7-3 behind the running of Al Wight. Though solid seniors like Wight had graduated, many starters from that team were returning, giving Coach Ross a strong nucleus to build on. The '69 team also went 7-3, as Jerry Raffel set the school rushing record and Jeff Kees and Cork Jackson earned statewide recognition for their play on defense. By this time the town had fully embraced its new sport. Games were well attended and talked about for days thereafter. Now all the program needed was a conference championship.

The '70 team was a rebuilding year from the start, and it went 2-8. The speedy Jerry Raffel, one of the few returning seniors, was injured early in the season, sending Coach deep into his bench, which included a lot of sophomores. The added experience paid off, too, because the '71 team did what no Panther team had ever done -- tying for the FAVC championship as it won all five of its games in October. Many of the starters on that team returned in '72.

~The coaching staff felt many of the positions were already set when practice began in August. Like everyone else, they had high hopes for this team. Many starters returned. Dave Dillon was now at tailback. And the senior class was one of the best that ever came through the school.

After the slow start to the season, changes were made, and the team had slowly built some momentum. Wins over Mason and Little Miami had gone a long way to redirect the sinking ship, but his team couldn't afford a loss at Waynesville on Friday night. That would be the end of the season. So he needed everything to go perfectly all week – from the implementation of the game plan to the execution in practice sessions, and especially how the coaching staff, Brutey in particular, talked about Waynesville. He needed the kids on edge.

CHAPTER 13

Coach Ross and the assistants evaluated their play daily, always looking for the best player for the moment. Ed Sullivan was installed as the team's center in week five against Mason, a move that proved to be significant. Other changes were made, too. And if the Panthers lost to Waynesville or Blanchester, thus destroying their conference hopes, then more moves were planned.

There was still a chance to repeat as conference champions. A win at Waynesville was the necessary next step. Then there were games with Blanchester and the return match with Kings Mills. And they needed Clinton-Massie to lose somewhere along the way. If all that happened, the season could still be one for the history books after all.

Brutey addressed the team before practice and assured them that Waynesville was a tough team. The Spartans had the home field advantage and they always played tough in their rivalry with Springboro. "Maybe you heard that I was doing some jawing the other night, but put that out of your heads. My mistake. If you take this team lightly, they'll kick your butts. Believe me when I say that."

Practice went well because they players worked hard, and Coach Ross was satisfied. So Brutey at least worked himself out of that pickle.

He didn't know what he was going to do about his other troubles.

Those didn't seem as easy to fix.

* * *

Brutey walked through his front door at a quarter to nine, carrying his work clothes on a hanger strapped over his right shoulder. The darkness of the October sky made it feel closer to midnight, and a cold wind rustled through the thinning trees. Ricky had been home from practice for almost an hour, and had already eaten and showered and was watching the last few minutes of *The Carol Burnett Show*. As Brutey shut the front door, he could hear Ricky and Larry laughing in the back television room. Surely Norma was lurking somewhere.

Brutey rubbed his eyes as he laid his keys on the table by the front door. He dreaded the fight that he knew was about to happen.

He looked at Norma, who was sitting quietly near the boys. She didn't even acknowledge his presence, a sure sign that she was angry. She was balancing the checkbook, which was just perfect, and the mere sight of that task made Brutey want to turn and run. Of course there's not enough money, he wanted to say instantly. I know the electric bill is due in ten days. I'll figure out something. I always do. But what I don't need right now is any smart-aleck comment from you.

But Norma didn't say anything about their finances. "Tough day?" she asked finally.

Brutey analyzed the question. Was she trying to start a fight? He wasn't certain, but he didn't detect a negative tone in the question. Instead, she seemed to be genuinely concerned about his day, and so he breathed a deep sigh of relief, the way a kid who didn't do his homework realizes there is a substitute teacher. The fighting would probably come some other time, but not now, which was all he needed.

"Brutal," he said. "But it helped being around the kids. They give me so much energy to go on. Makes me want to go in tomorrow and do a bang up job. That'll show everybody there. And then I won't have to worry about you struggling with our bills, too."

"We'll be okay. We always are. It would just be nice for it to be easier every month, that's all. I talked to Homer today about working down at the grocery. That'll help."

Brutey sat down and was surprised by his wife's good nature. Lord knows he needed the gentle touch, even though deep down he felt he deserved the punishment. She warmed up the meat loaf and fixed him a glass of iced tea. When the show was over the boys retreated to their rooms. When dinner was finished Brutey took a shower and went to bed. Maybe everything was going to be okay, he thought. Maybe there was hope after all for his career, his coaching, and for his marriage.

What he didn't know was that Norma had an appointment with a divorce lawyer in two days. She was done.

And Brutey was history.

CHAPTER 14

Give me golf clubs, fresh air and a beautiful partner, and you can keep the clubs and the fresh air.

-- The comedy of '72
G-rated and funny
Jack Benny

THURSDAY, OCTOBER 26, 1972

We broke the huddle and I called the cadence. Pepper Dill snapped the ball on the second hut, just as he was supposed to do, and I took seven steps back, just like I'd been taught. I could see Lance wide open in the left flats, having run his pass pattern perfectly. Just before the crash of the oncoming rush I let loose of my pass. It was a tight spiral. It was directly in Lance's direction. But there was a serious problem -- I overthrew him by a mile and the ball sailed into the nearby cornfield. I was thrown to the ground in the process, and as I lay there with my face in the ground I slammed my fist to the ground. Joe Namath would have never missed that pass.

Not again. Why can't I do anything right? Our last practice before the big game against Shane Hatfield's team was a nightmare for me. I missed open receivers and I misjudged my reads. Seven times Coach O.J. challenged me to run a play correctly or else I'd have to run, and seven straight times I blew it. He finally put my backup in and sent me on my way. When I returned, still frustrated and now out of breath, Brutey was waiting for me.

"Come over and sit with me for a minute." Brutey always had an understanding way about him. I knew I'd messed up. So did he. But his manner of dealing with problem situations always made things better instead of worse.

"But practice isn't over," I said.

"For you it is. Come on over."

We took a seat on one of the benches on the nearby baseball field. I took my helmet off and wiped the sweat from my face. Brutey handed me a bottle of water and sat patiently as I downed every last drop. I was buying time really, as I braced myself for a verbal butt whipping about how important it was for the quarterback to be in control of his game so the rest of the team could follow along. I deserved that, I knew. But Brutey surprised me.

"Did I ever tell you about the night I sat in this same spot with Rod Dillon?" Brutey twirled a football as he spoke. We both looked at the ground in front of us. "Coupla' years ago when Rod was a sophomore. With only two games left in the season, a bad season at that, Coach Ross figured to give Rod some more playing time at quarterback so he'd have some experience to build on throughout the summer. Rod had the arm and he had a good head on his shoulders, but I gotta' tell you, he had some tough times. Everything culminated one Thursday night after practice, and Rod was real down on himself. He wasn't sure he had it in him. Everyone else went in for showers and he and I sat in the dugout of the ball diamond over there behind the high school."

I looked up at him. My expression said it all: Rod Dillon had a bad day? *The* Rod Dillon? I didn't think good players like him ever had a bad day.

"It's true. And I told him what I'm about to tell you. You have the talent, so relax and let it shine through. You wouldn't be in this position if everyone didn't think you could do it. Sometimes the harder you try, the worse you get. That's what I saw out there tonight. You're trying too hard, pressing. Instead, go out, be a kid and have fun. When you do that your natural ability will take over."

I squinted my eyes in disbelief. "Believe me," he said. "Just look for yourself at the way Rod has played. Impressive, isn't it?"

"He's the best."

"And you can be, too. Okay? Just relax and have fun. Now get back in there."

Like a doctor prescribing the perfect medicine, Brutey's advice cured me on the spot. For the rest of the practice, I connected on passes and made the correct reads. Practice ended on a high note and I left feeling a whole lot better. Brutey compared me with Rod Dillon! Someday the dream would come true and I would be on the varsity, playing under the lights for my town. From there, the sky was the limit. Ohio State? Then a dual professional career with the Reds and Bengals. The possibilities seemed endless. I was one awesome dude.

Brutey said so.

* * *

The Dillon family moved to Springboro in the spring of 1967 and rented an old farmhouse on Pennyroyal Road, which had virtually no one around it, giving the four Dillon boys little to do. Those early days were not good days. Rod was twelve; Dave was eleven, Mark eight and Scott five. "I hated it," Rod would say later. Though there were organized sports leagues for Mark and Scott to play in, there was nothing in town for the kids who were a little older, like Rod and Dave. As a seventh-grader, Rod loved all kinds of sports, and yearned to play them, but he needed a team to play on.

Over the summer, he learned about Charlie Harris' seventh-grade traveling football team, and he went out for it, making the team and helping it by playing running back and linebacker. He also played basketball in the winter. That made the transition more enjoyable. He quickly became friends with lots of guys around town, and he established himself as a good athlete. In both the eighth and ninth grades, he again played football and basketball, actually enjoying basketball more than football. Then he was one of four players who made the varsity basketball team as a sophomore. It wasn't until Coach Ross saw his potential as a quarterback that football really took hold with him.

The summer between his sophomore and junior years was a difficult one. His parents had recently divorced, and though Rod could see why the divorce may have been necessary, he still loved and respected both his parents and still wished that somehow they could stay together. His dad moved out of town, while his mom stayed in Springboro. Rod spent the early part of that summer debating whether to stay in Springboro or move to his father's residence in Kettering and play for Fairmont East High School, a much bigger school that received more recognition from the Dayton media. To say it was a difficult time for him would be an understatement.

Rod would talk to his dad, then Coach Ross, then his mom, and his dad again, then Coach Ross. By the end of July, he was still undecided.

Just before practice began in August, he made his decision, choosing the smaller town over the big city, in large part because of the teaching and the guidance he received from Coach Ross. He, Mark and Scotty moved with their mom to a house on Paw Paw Street, which was a few streets over from mine. Dave remained in Kettering and did play football there. When two-a-days began in the summer of '71, there was no question who would be Springboro's quarterback. It was Rod, wearing number 15. He assumed that position from the very first day of practice and strived to be one of the best in the school's history.

It wasn't easy, though. There were so many things to learn. He threw to the flats when he should have been looking up field, and he threw into double coverage up field when he should have been looking to the outside. Coach Ross worked with him constantly, always encouraging him to practice more and trust his instincts. As is the case on most football teams, the Coach-Quarterback relationship became a special one.

"I had to learn how to take criticism," he reported about that first year. "In my first start against Carlisle, I was nervous, and Coach Ross told me before the game, 'If you get confused, just throw it on the track.' That way I could avoid throwing an interception.

'"Well, I must have thrown it on the track seven of the ten times I threw the ball. One time, I threw it in that direction and I knocked the hat off of a guy from Carlisle who was working the sidelines. That was kind of funny." But the Panthers lost the game, and Rod learned quickly how much focus is directed at the quarterback position.

He went to school that following Monday morning and first period was math class with Mrs. Hilda Watkins. Along with being a great teacher and a huge supporter of the athletic program, believing it was an integral part of the high school experience, Mrs. Watkins was also very direct. "Geez, Dillon, you were horrible the other night," adding, "but you did knock that guy's hat off. That was funny."

Right then Rod was put under a character test -- either give it back to his teacher or be gracious in handling the criticism. He chose the latter, a tough thing for a high school junior. "Mrs. Watkins, you know what, I didn't play very well, and I'm not proud of it, but if you'll come to Ross (High School, in Hamilton) this Friday night, I'll show you I can play."

He did play better against Ross, and improvement came steadily throughout the rest of the season. We won all five games in October, all conference games, which tied Kings Mills for a share of the Fort Ancient Valley Conference title. Coach Ross' decision to move Rod to quarterback turned out to be a good one.

The home game in the middle of that junior season with Clinton-Massie was one of the more memorable in Springboro's short football history. The game had to be delayed because the visitors' west side bank of lights wasn't working. The field was very dark, and some thought it posed a danger to the players, who were sent back to the locker room until either the problem was fixed or the game was rescheduled. For over two hours, the Clinton Massie players were crammed into the tiny girls' locker room that housed the visiting teams. Meanwhile, Springboro's players stretched out on the gymnasium floor. The wait was excruciating.

After a half-hour, the coaches had an idea. They might as well prepare as if they were going to play with only half the lights working. Coach Ross then turned off the gym lights and had Rod and his wide receivers play catch. Only the lights from outside in the hallway lit the gym. At first they had a terrible time making the adjustment and balls were missed, often hitting guys where it hurt. But they got used to it after a while, so much so that playing in little lighting was much easier. "We learned to concentrate on the white stripes on the ball," Rod says. "After that, we could catch a ball anywhere."

Officials decided it was best to go ahead with the game with only half the lights working. Springboro, now accustomed to the low lighting, had a considerable advantage. When Rod threw a pass, the receivers saw it easily. And they caught just about everything Rod threw. As a result, Rod connected on 18 of his 20 passes, which is still a school record, and the Panthers won easily, allowing their win streak to continue.

When that junior football season ended, basketball season started almost immediately. Rod wasn't a starter on a team that featured some superstars such as Jim Hough, Gary Patton and Jeff Howard, but he did see a lot of action. The varsity went 11-1 in the conference and won the conference championship, returning to our town the kind of excitement it had grown used to having with its basketball team. It was a great time for Rod, but by season's end he had already made a decision regarding basketball: He wouldn't play as a senior. Instead, he would concentrate on football and the other sport he played, which was golf.

When two-a-days began in August for the '72 season, Rod was firmly entrenched as the team's starting quarterback and one of the team leaders. His brother Dave, who had since moved back to Springboro, started at tailback, while Dave Collins, Dave Vicroy and Dale Midkiff played wide receiver. Optimism was as high as ever had been around town about football, and a nine-win season didn't seem out of the question. But then they started slowly. It hit Rod as hard as it hit anybody, because this was *his* team. The game at Mason was the turning point. His fake punt was the spark that created it. Now they'd won three in a row, with more big games on the horizon.

* * *

So even Rod Dillon had tough practices. Who'd have ever thought that? *Man, I feel so much better, because if he can have a bad day, then so can I.* I rode my bike home from practice singing "Jeremiah was a bullfrog." There was indeed Joy To The World, at least for the moment.

I spent the rest of that evening doing homework and watching television with my family. Though the big game was only two days away, I was relaxed and happy until it was time to go to bed. Even a fight between Joey and John didn't bother me.

Brutey, meanwhile, stopped at Ron's Pizza for a couple of beers. Norma went to bed with his cold dinner sitting on the kitchen counter. It was just as well that he didn't come home that night. She wouldn't have been as nice as she had the night before.

One minute he did something great. The next minute … who was he really?

He learned the game of basketball from Jim Hough Sr., shown with high school principal Vince Ross (L) and athletic director Neil Clingman. Larry Hefflin teamed up in high school with Rusty McClanahan to win basketball games, then later returned to Springboro to coach football, basketball, and the sport he ultimately became noted for, track.

CHAPTER 15

> ***'American Pie' was the song to sing during the walk to school, but there was always a serious question about it – just what the heck did it mean?***
>
> ***-- The debate***

FRIDAY, OCTOBER 27, 1972

The sun rose over the historic homes along Main Street, bringing the needed warmth to break the first frost of the season. Mark Harding delivered *The Journal Herald* to his customers along East Street, and the Borden dairyman made his scheduled stop to the Bailey home on Market Street, delivering fresh milk. When Lowell Hayes stopped at the Ashland station for gas, Jerry the owner washed his windows and checked his oil, in addition to filling the tank. The temperature was expected to reach sixty by mid-afternoon, and it would lower to a comfortable fifty-two by kickoff later that evening. It was, in those respects, a typical day in Springboro.

By the time Norma got out of bed, Brutey was showered and out the door. It was better that way, especially today, since it was the day of her appointment. She made oatmeal and toast for the boys, and by seven-fifteen sent them off for their twenty-minute walk to school.

She was to see the lawyer at ten o'clock, and was determined to go. She had had second thoughts all week long, thinking she would give Brutey still another chance. Her life wasn't that bad, she sometimes rationalized. Certainly other women were far worse off than she. She'd heard stories at the supermarket of other men mismanaging money and gambling, and of others who were physically abusive. Her husband was none of those things. He was just never home. And when he was home his mind seemed to be someplace else. All he wanted to do was talk about himself and his accomplishments and all the people who loved him. All she wanted was a little recognition of her own. Why couldn't he see that?

She could imagine other women laughing at her, believing she didn't have a serious predicament at all. "Yeah, honey, you really have it bad," they'd say, then roll their eyes and walk away.

Maybe they were right. On three occasions the day before she picked up the phone to cancel. Two times the line was busy. On the third, something told her to hang up.

But when Brutey didn't come home the night before until after eleven, she was glad she hadn't cancelled the appointment. She had fixed dinner and was prepared to do what Reverend Dawes had counseled her to do – to be pleasant when he walked in the door, and not hit him immediately with all of her problems from the day. When the boys arrived home on their bikes from practice at seven, she expected Brutey a few minutes later. But he never showed and never called. She would confirm it later, but she was sure he had been at Ron's Pizza tossing beers with the gang there, being a regular life of the party. She still wasn't sure whether there was another woman.

Today she would end it. She felt like she was in competition with the town athletic program, and the program had slaughtered her. So it was time for that game to end.

When their problems first began many years earlier, when the boys were little, she would put them down for a nap and reminisce through old photo albums. For a while, it helped to be reminded of the days when Brutey called her frequently and left her little notes.

She had all the letters he sent her while he was away in the Army, back when he was so attentive to everything about her. When he came home and they started dating, he called her every day. He washed her car and ran errands for her. They were married on a beautiful sunny day and drove all the way to Niagara Falls with the music up and the top down. Brutey was everything she ever dreamed of in a man.

It wasn't long until the boys arrived, and things began to change. Norma's days and nights were spent tending to their every need. Brutey did what he could to help out, but his sales job at NCR required more and more of his time. Each quarter meant another sales goal, and he often worked until well past nine o'clock. As a result, the boys were sleeping when he left for work. They'd be asleep again when he got home. Norma understood the pressure that Brutey was under, and she endured the terrible twos without complaint. Soon came kindergarten and grade school, and sales were getting better, but Brutey's mood wasn't. He was cranky, disappointed and depressed.

Something was clearly wrong. They talked about it until after midnight one night, and it was evident that Brutey needed something more in his life -- a change, but not in her or with his work. He needed to get back into sports, the love of his life.

"It's like a huge part of me is missing," he told her. "I need the competition, and the camaraderie. I need to feel the excitement of a game again."

So he began coaching in the mid-sixties. By being back among the games and the players, a part of his soul was restored. And for a while Norma could see Brutey smile and see an improvement in his view on life. He did better at work and was more involved with the boys. The community loved him too, as always. Life was going well for everyone in the Baker house.

He worked with quarterback Ed Wade in Springboro's first-ever football season. Then he worked with Bill Crocker Jr., the year after, and also the younger players. He helped with open gyms in the summer for the basketball program. And he coached baseball, too, finding success everywhere he went.

Parents loved him. He started hanging out with the guys at Ron's and fascinated them with his stories. He loved drinking and laughing long into the night.

But then came November 23, 1968, the day their son Ricky turned eight years old. He had ten of his friends over for a party, and the plan was to play games until it was time for cake and ice cream and for Ricky to open his presents. "Daddy, you'll be home, won't you?" Ricky had asked Brutey the night before. "Absolutely," Brutey responded. "Nothing could keep me away, little buddy."

But Ricky's birthday was the same day as the Ohio State-Michigan football game. Since the party wasn't scheduled to start until after the game finished, Brutey made plans to watch the game at a local pub along with a bunch of other guys. It was a great game, one of the best in Buckeye history. Ohio State crushed Michigan, 50-14, to remain undefeated and stay number one in the nation. By five-thirty when the birthday party started Brutey was passed out under a corner table. When he came to at eleven o'clock, he walked to his house reeking of alcohol and unsure what day it was. Norma was so angry she screamed at him for twenty minutes while he lay in bed trying to sleep. It made his excruciating headache all the worse. And to top it off he had to deal with how he'd blown it big time. Ricky was crushed.

Norma initially said she would never forgive him, but in time her feelings softened. Brutey took the boys to the movies the next day. He stayed home more, and took them to their practices instead of relying on Norma to do it. He said he was sorry and that it would never happen again. Nothing was more important to him that Norma and the boys.

She believed him. He was such a good man and he had made a simple mistake. Surely he was deserving of a second chance.

But, sadly, Norma's optimism slowly faded. Ricky's eighth birthday party was not the last time that Brutey missed a family function. Nor was it the last time he came home drunk. He went through extended periods when he promised to do better, and did, but then he would inevitably go back to drinking and staying out. The episode from the night before was just another example in a series of similar episodes, and as Norma prepared herself for her ten o'clock appointment, she was so ready for the marriage to end. Enough was enough.

She wouldn't play second fiddle anymore.

* * *

Her lawyer was my dad.

She told all of this to him and then listened to the options she had if she were to divorce Brutey. The house would likely have to be sold, she would get custody of the boys and some financial assistance, but money would be tight. Could she get a job? Had she thought about where she and the boys were going to live? Dad knew of Brutey, mostly by his reputation, but his relationship with him was not so close that it prevented him from representing Norma. It happened all the time in small towns, where everyone seemed to know everybody else.

Norma had thought everything over, more than once. "I know living separate will be a struggle," she told Dad. "I've thought this over for a long time. Every night that he doesn't come home, I sit and stare at the clock and I wonder how he can do this to us. What kind of a person sits on a bar stool night after night when there are people at home who need him? Doesn't he see what he's doing to these boys? Maybe not, because no one is going to tell him but me. And he's stopped listening to me."

She was already emotionally divorced. Now all that needed to be done was make it legal.

"I have to tell you," Dad said, "I always thought Brutey did pretty well financially. He drives a nice truck, and you have a nice house."

"Everything's mortgaged to the hilt. We don't have anything. He doesn't make that much more than the man down the street who works in a lumber yard."

Norma signed the divorce papers and Dad made notes to prepare a Complaint for Divorce. Brutey would be served with them by the middle of next week. Once he received the papers, he would have time to get a lawyer of his own. They would then go through a process known as "discovery," where all assets and debts are accounted for. Then the lawyers would write letters back and forth to whittle down the issues and hopefully reach an agreement.

"He'll probably go to Eddie Lawson," Norma said. "He did our wills a few years ago. He also talked to him when Sears wouldn't replace our washing machine last year when it broke down. He's real good."

Dad knew Eddie Lawson well. They had known one another for years, and had worked together in the county prosecutor's office when Jim Ruppert had been the prosecutor. Eddie was the only lawyer in Springboro. His office was in the same building as Don Barton's insurance agency next to the park. And he was good, all right.

"It's time to do this," she said as she signed her name. "Nothing will make me turn back now. Nothing."

* * *

When Norma returned home, she could see next door that Janet Spencer's car was parked in her mother's driveway. Norma and Brutey had known their neighbors for twelve years, and Janet was a pre-teen little girl when they first met her. They'd watched her go from riding her bike everywhere to getting her driver's license, and from being a high school cheerleader to being a grown woman who was married and had children. So seeing her was such a pleasant surprise. As Janet had promised the day after the varsity opened up its season with a scrimmage against Lebanon, she was back for a Springboro football game at the end of October.

More than anything, Norma needed a shoulder to cry on. She was tempted to march on over, and then she reconsidered. Surely they were in the middle of a conversation, and she didn't want to ruin it. She pulled the keys from the ignition and made her way to the front door.

But Janet had been watching for her. Norma took two steps and heard Janet shout from the front door. "Got time for some lunch?" she asked.

Norma made a feign attempt at dismissing the invitation. "I don't mean to intrude."

"Oh, don't be silly. You're like family."

It was just the kind of relaxed atmosphere Norma needed. The meeting at dad's office had felt eerily similar to the meeting at the funeral home after her mother died the year before. She never imagined having to do either one. Both experiences left her feeling cold. The death of a marriage was just as painful as the death of a loved one. Maybe worse.

"John's out of town, so I brought the girls back for a little visit."

"—and football," her mother chimed in.

Janet laughed. "Maybe we can sit next to you, Norma. Where do you sit anyway?"

Oh, boy. She wasn't prepared for the questions. Could she hide the fact she had just filed for divorce? Was it necessary to ruin everyone's day by spilling out all her dirty laundry? "I don't know if I'll go to the game. I'm just not feeling well, and if it gets cold and rainy, I'll feel worse."

"You go to all those games, don't you? You and Brutey are a regular team," Janet said. Norma sipped her coffee and diverted the attention towards the stove.

"Oh, look, dear! I think the soup's ready. I see it boiling from here."

They talked for the next two hours about everything, in a way that only women can. One topic quickly led to another, and sometimes several topics were in the air at the very same time. It was just what Norma needed. She was reassured that she was a good woman with good intentions. If there were problems in her marriage, it wasn't all her fault. Brutey needed to take responsibility for his share, and until that happened, the marriage was as doomed as she thought.

"Norma, you and Brutey will have to come over tomorrow afternoon. We're having a cookout. If John stays away another day, Janet and the girls will be here, too. Bring the boys. It's supposed to be a lovely day."

"Well, there is an Ohio State game," Norma said. There's always an Ohio State something or other.

"We'll watch it here."

"And Ricky has a peewee game," Norma said, wondering how many excuses she could come up with.

"After that. Norma, you have to have dinner." Clearly, they weren't taking no for an answer.

Janet walked Norma to the door. She hugged her. "Do it for me. I haven't seen Brutey in a while and you know I love to talk football with him."

"I know you do, dear. He loves you for it, too."

"Then I'll see you here at 5, as long as John stays away, that is. Otherwise, I'll catch up with him after the game maybe. Before I leave. If I don't see you tonight, you take care of yourself. I love you."

Norma cried the rest of the afternoon, wishing life could be altogether different than it was. What happened to 'happily ever after'? Was she crazy for doing this? Why couldn't Brutey just go back to the kind, considerate man she married? Then there would be nothing to worry about.

CHAPTER 16

Seventh-graders were Springboro's future, and coaches like Mr. Hefflin were part of Springboro's past – through them the town traditions continue

-- The legacy

LATER IN THE DAY

FRIDAY, OCTOBER 27, 1972

Just after lunch, our gym teacher, Mr. Larry Hefflin, made us run in gym class the way O.J. Powers made us run during football practice, only he gave us a specific assignment to run a mile in under eight minutes. Anyone who did got his name plastered on a list that hung proudly in the gym.

For reasons that may seem obvious, I loved gym class. I loved everything about it, especially when we ran or jumped on the trampoline or gave Melvin Blumthaler a wedgie in the locker room. Essentially, gym class came down to getting school credit for running around and playing games like we did all summer. There was a time I thought I wanted to be a gym teacher, if for no other reason I would get to wear shorts and tennis shoes all day long.

Mr. Hefflin was a football, track and basketball coach, and he was the uncle of one of my very best friends, Mike Hefflin, who moved away to Oregon after the sixth grade. I really liked Mr. Hefflin and learned a lot from him. He knew all the proper techniques in all the sports. Plus he taught us about hard work and sportsmanship, the stuff that was probably as valuable as any skill he showed us.

As much as he was concerned on how we played the game, he was equally focused on how we handled ourselves as we played the game. He spent a lot of time on those character issues.

"So let me ask you this question," Danny Kruer pondered one day. This was typical Kruer – insightful, inquisitive, and downright funny. His father was a member of the Springboro athletic hall of fame, and Danny possessed much of that same athletic talent. But he also had a funny bone that was cut from Bill Cosby or George Carlin. Whenever Kruer showed up, a laugh was sure to follow.

"Yes, Danny."

"Some guy jumps on top of me after the play is over, and you say I'm not supposed to hit him because of it?" His facial expression showed how confused he was about this.

"Listen closely to what I said, Danny," Mr. Hefflin responded firmly.

"'Cause I'm gonna' hit him. Nobody can be getting away with that. No sir." There were some chuckles among the guys in the class.

"Danny, I said hitting him would get you a penalty. The refs always see the second hit, never the first, so don't retaliate when someone does that. What I did say was there are other ways you can get back at that guy, like fly right past him on the next play and score a touchdown and make him look bad. You never want to stoop to some other guy's level. Just because he's stupid, don't you be stupid."

Danny listened, but we weren't sure if it sunk in. "I'm not gonna' be stupid, but that guy's getting it one way or another. Maybe next time on the bottom of the pile I could squeeze his weenie or something. You know…."

Even Mr. Hefflin laughed at that. The rest of us were howling.

Only eight guys in the class beat the eight-minute mark, and Ricky Baker was the lowest of all eight. Sometimes, it seemed, he could be incredibly good at everything. It's like he got a burst of energy and just blew everyone away. In those moments, it seemed like something was bothering him, but he never talked about it. So I just let it go, something Brutey couldn't do. He constantly pushed Ricky, and as a result the two of them didn't always get along. I wasn't sure, but maybe that was what frustrated Ricky the most.

The running was over soon, and we sat in the gym relaxing. For the last fifteen minutes of class, Mr. Hefflin gave us a taste of what we would be covering in the weeks ahead, the game of basketball. It was the greatest game, I always thought. Mr. Hefflin planned to teach us many of the fundamentals to the game. He had played for Springboro in the early sixties, leading the team in scoring. He'd been one of Springboro's great players, and he knew all the other ones, too.

"Fellas, we're going to cover everything about basketball. When we're finished, I want to see you shoot like Jimmy Hough, dribble like Gary Patton and rebound like Jeff Howard. Plus I want you to work on setting a pick. If you watch Gordy Gregg on Friday nights this winter, you'll see how this is done very well." Then Coach Hefflin demonstrated how to set a proper pick. No one was able to pass through him.

After a while, Danny Kruer had a question.

"Yes, Danny."

"Say, suppose you set a pick like this and some guy plow into you and practically knocks you down. Can we plow him back? I mean, that ain't right and seems like we gotta' defend our territory, you know?

"We'll discuss this later, Danny."

"Guy knocks me down and I'm knocking him into next week."

"Let's go. Time's up. I'll see you next week." He blew his whistle.

"He won't be doing that to me ever again...."

* * *

That night, amid the fanfare of a home Springboro football game, Blanchester came to play good, hard, rugged football. Their players ran fast and hit hard. And even though our offense moved the ball at will, scoring was especially difficult. Nothing came easy. Early on, after runs by Dave Dillon pushed us deep in Blanchester territory, Rod scored the game's first touchdown with a one-yard sneak right in front of our spot beyond the end zone.

Later, again after long runs by Dave, Rod rolled left and found Dave Collins for a nine-yard touchdown pass, giving us a 14-8 lead, which is where the score stood at halftime. It had been a difficult half, but we were in control. Another half just like it would secure the victory.

After that second touchdown, the offense ran off the field and accepted the congratulations from its teammates. Guys were laughing and happy with the success they had enjoyed. Meanwhile, Coach Hefflin quickly grabbed Rod and the two huddled near the back of the bench. It showed me that even a senior varsity quarterback playing in the eighth game of his last season still needed to be coached. Coach Hefflin was quite animated in what he saying, and occasionally Rod would nod his head. Evidently, the coach had seen something, and his quarterback had no choice but to listen. Little did we know how significant this conversation would be later in the game.

"Try that next time," he offered. Rod nodded his head, reached for his Panther jacket and trotted in to the Panther locker room. Coach Hefflin, the man who had once was a Panther and always would be a Panther, walked briskly behind him.

He moved to Springboro in the spring of 1953 when his mother Myrtle and stepfather bought what is now known as the Null House, the historic old cabin located in the middle of what is now Heatherwoode Golf Course. Larry was a fourth-grader at the time, the third of his mother's five children – brothers Bob and Bill were older, and his sisters Patty and Deborah were younger. From his fourth grade through sophomore year, the family lived in what is generally known as one as one of the oldest log cabins in the area.

Since Coach Hefflin's stepfather worked at Frigidaire in Dayton, the new home was closer to work for him. They were surrounded by farmland, though the family did not farm. Young Larry would often help out the man who did farm the land nearby, Gene Rider. And of course he did his chores around the house. He went to elementary school at The Old Red School, which was later torn down to make way for the present Jonathan Wright Elementary.

He quickly became involved in any sport he could, though there were no organized leagues in Springboro at the time. There was a Tri-County summer baseball league and, when he got a little older, a junior high basketball and track program. Unfortunately, there was no organized football in either the community or the school, something Larry thought was unfortunate. "I always felt that football could have been my best sport," he says.

Upon reaching high school, he played baseball in the fall, basketball in the winter and ran track in the spring. He was excellent at all three. The new gym was built in 1958, giving Larry the benefit all through high school of what he describes as one of the nicest gymnasiums around. "Many places we played were like the old gym we had, cramped and with a seventy-five foot floor with a double time line," he says. He thrived under the coaching of Jim Hough Sr., who coached him as a seventh-grader, a freshman, and for his sophomore and junior seasons. As a senior he was coached by former Franklin standout Johnny Powell, who was as hard-driving at coaching as he had been at playing, giving young Larry yet another example of a coaching style to learn from.

As a senior he teamed with Rusty McClanahan to lead Springboro in just about every offensive category. It was a good year, though the team did not win the county tournament. After games they would hang out at a pool hall on Main Street near Market, or go to Middletown to the Country Kitchen, or go to Red Lion to the Hum-Yum, which is now Mom's Place. The younger kids in town looked up to them.

From there, his road to coaching took several turns and detours. After graduation, he worked for a year at Inland Container in Dayton before going to Georgetown (Ky.) College, where he was on the basketball team. His career there was short-lived, though, because on the first night of practice, Larry went down with painful cramps in his stomach. He required emergency surgery for appendicitis, and his season was finished right then. He dropped out of school, got married to Sandy Pugh, took a job at NCR in Dayton and evaluated what he wanted to do. Completing his education was at the top of the list; continuing to play basketball was a close second. So his brief stint in the work force came to an end.

A year later, he enrolled at Wilmington College, made the basketball team and played three years there while completing his degree in education. When brand-new Herman Court opened his junior year, he initiated the place with an electrifying sixty-foot jumper at the buzzer to tie the game and force it into overtime, which the Quakers eventually won. It was far and away one of the most memorable events of his athletic career.

After graduation, he took a teaching and coaching position at Springboro right away and immediately began coaching Jimmy Hough, the son of his former high school coach. He coached junior high football, then freshmen basketball and then, in 1970, took over what would become his passion and his legacy at Springboro, the varsity track team, a position he would hold for eighteen years. The Class of '73, utilizing many of the players who were on the football field against Blanchester that night in October 1972, won for Springboro its first conference championship that spring.

"They're a special class with a great group of kids," he'd say about them, a refrain often repeated by many others associated with the school.

When the season started, Coach Hefflin was as optimistic as anyone about the team. As offensive backfield coach, his responsibility was Rod at quarterback, his brother Dave at tailback, and the myriad of players around them. It was a strong group, and smart. Rod was a mobile quarterback with a strong arm, and leadership skills to boot, and Dave was a back with fullback strength and tailback speed. Like everyone, he expected a strong start in the beginning. When it didn't come, he kept encouraging the players to turn the season around. He knew that could happen with positive thoughts. "The season isn't over," he'd say. "We still have plenty of time left. Just stay focused and continue to do what you've done and watch. This season can be magical still."

He knew what he was talking about.

* * *

After a scoreless third quarter, the unthinkable happened. Blanchester scored again early in the fourth quarter, giving it a 16-14 lead. We stood in the area beyond the north zone, quiet and concerned, not sure we could believe what we were watching. Suddenly, with less than a quarter left in the game, everything was in jeopardy – this game, our winning streak, and our chances at the conference championship.

"That's okay," Wilburn said finally. "We can come back. There's plenty of time."

I wasn't so sure. Ricky wondered if throwing a bomb was the thing to do next. That would be a quick fix. Mitch, always the coach, reminded us that the running game had been our strength the whole night. Besides, he said, Blanchester may be thinking we would pass. A solid running attack might surprise them.

All I knew was, I was getting nervous. We had to win this game. The win streak had to keep going. We took the Blanchester kickoff and had a first and ten at our own 32. Rod called the play and then stood confidently under center, calling the cadence. With all that had happened and with so few games remaining, it felt like this was the most important series of the entire season. Punt, and the season may be over. Score, and our chances for a championship remained alive.

He took the snap and faded back as if to pass. But he didn't pass. Instead, he handed off to Dave on the draw play. Because Rod sold the fake so perfectly, Blanchester was caught off guard. Dave took the handoff from Rod, cut through a glaring hole created by Big John Mockabee, broke a tackle and broke into the open field and was gone. Touchdown! The sidelines erupted, the band played the fight song, and suddenly we were ahead, 20-14.

Coach Hefflin's advice just before halftime assisted in the touchdown. His instruction to Rod was to keep selling the fake even when he didn't have the ball. "They're watching you all the time," Coach Hefflin had told him. "Sell yourself even when you don't have the ball. You never know when the half-step we can get from that will pay off."

It paid off right then.

Three plays later Blanchester fumbled. We recovered. And then we marched down the field for a final touchdown of the night. We won handily, 26-16, though the game was not nearly the blowout that the final score indicated. We were 4-1 in the conference, with the rematch against Kings Mills on the horizon. There was still a chance at a title.

Several players fell to their knees, exhausted, covered in mud. The game had been a battle. It took everything for us to win. The coaches gathered everyone together in the makeshift locker room just outside the school. Some of the players sat on their helmets, while others leaned back against the brick wall. They were tired, but happy. The mid-season changes that had been implemented were working. They had talent that was clicking, and now the hard work was paying off. They would soon shower and change and enjoy a fun night on the town – when some would drive north to Frisch's, others west to either Jerry's in Franklin or other places in Middletown.

Coach Ross took his position in the middle of them. "That took some guts tonight," he told them. "You came back against a tough football team, so you should be proud of yourselves. Our time is winding down, so we have to make everything count – every play, every practice and every game. So, fellas, I'm asking that you give it everything you've got from here on out. But for now enjoy what you accomplished tonight."

I was leaning against the north goal post, holding the football I had brought to the game, and I dreamed of the day that it would be me out there, wearing number 11, quarterbacking the Panthers to a come-from-behind victory over Mason in the final game of a perfect season, giving us the conference championship in the process.

It was a great dream.

I couldn't wait until the next afternoon to play Shane Hatfield's team in our biggest game of the year. I was ready to play it right then. I knew I wouldn't sleep.

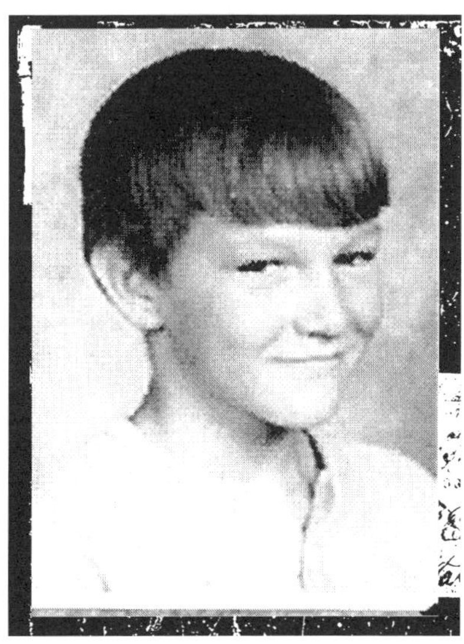

The heart of Springboro rested in people like John Wade and Ralph Wade, who were community-minded, and also through businesses like Springboro IGA and the drug store and hardware store. It also rested in the hopes and dreams of its kids. Danny Kruer was a talented athlete, a good friend, and one funny, funny guy.

CHAPTER 17

Commander Cody sang about a Hot Rod Lincoln and Jan & Dean warned about a Dead Man's Curve...it's why souped-up cars were in the high school parking lot

-- The automotive revolution

NEARING MIDNIGHT

FRIDAY, OCTOBER 27, 1972

In the chill of an autumn night, on a lonely stretch of road east of town, the older of the two little girls first realized that her mother was dead. Maddie had been in the back seat with Jackie, her younger sister, who had just drifted off to sleep for the long ride home. Their mother had just turned on the radio, which softly played a song by Crosby, Stills, Nash & Young. It was late, and they all looked forward to getting home and seeing Dad.

Maddie didn't know what made their car hit that telephone pole. All she knew was it loudest explosion she'd ever heard before. The girls awoke instantly and Jackie started crying hysterically. Maddie looked over to make sure she was okay, and aside from her hysterics she was. The radio seemed to be louder than before. Smoke was everywhere, and some kind of liquid was oozing out onto the ground below. She was reminded of The Wizard of Oz, when Dorothy's house fell out of that tornado.

This was horrible.

Then she realized an eerie silence. Her mother had always been their protector, always there for them whenever there was a sniffle or a boo boo. Now she was lying still, with not so much as a whimper. She called out for her mother several times, and then finally climbed into what was left of the front seat. No answer. She shook her mother, and still got no response. It was only when she turned her mother's head and she saw the gaping gash by her left ear, and all the blood that was gushing out of it, that she realized what no four-year-old should ever have to realize. Mommy was in heaven.

She lost it. No four-year-old is equipped to handle such a sight. While Jackie continued to scream hysterically, Maddie buried her head in her mother's lap and cried like she had never cried before. They needed help.

And fast.

Janet Spencer, the lovable former Springboro cheerleader, the only daughter of John and Hazel Richmond, was dead at the age of 26.

* * *

Twenty minutes before she was killed, Janet had been laughing and smiling in the bleachers as she watched Springboro hold off Blanchester. She had gone to the game with her parents, and with Maddie and Jackie. As Janet expected, the girls spent more time watching the cheerleaders than anything the Dillon boys did with a football.

Janet had forgotten how exciting a high school game could be and she vowed to take the girls more often when they got back home, even if it wasn't a Springboro game. Home now was Amherst, a small town in northeast Ohio, which was where John was from. Surely high school football was just as exciting there. Or at least close.

Just before leaving for the game, she had talked to John on the telephone. He wasn't home yet, but there was good news. His assignment ended early, so he would be home in the morning. Always a little bit of a night owl, Janet had decided to make the trip home after the game rather than wait until morning, knowing full well the girls would fall asleep and she could listen to the radio undisturbed the whole way. Like the girls, she too looked forward to the reunion with him.

As the crowd celebrated a much-needed Panther win, Janet and the girls said their goodbyes. "Grandma, when will we see you again?" little Jackie asked.

CHAPTER 17

"Probably not until Thanksgiving, honey. That's only three weeks. Grandpa and I will be up. Aunt Ruth and her family will be at your house, too, so we'll all have a great time. Here, give me a kiss. I miss you girls already."

Janet's last conversation with her dad was about the bookkeeping she had done for his small appliance repair business. "Now, Dad, if you have any trouble with that program I've given you, just call. Call me anytime. You know I'm never too busy when it comes to you."

"Aw, I'll make do. How much damage can I do anyway?"

Janet laughed. "You don't want me to answer that," she said. Her father laughed with her.

The girls climbed in the back of Janet's 1971 Mercury Cougar. They grabbed pillows and blankets that Grandma had made sure were in place. They'd be asleep before they all got out of town.

"Goodbye, Mom." She hugged her mom and kissed her on the cheek.

"See you, sweetie. I love you, dear."

Then it was her dad's turn. "I love you, Daddy."

Her father hugged and kissed her. "I love you, too. Call us when you get home. You're never too old to be my little girl."

Her parents watched her drive away. When they saw the taillights disappear in the distance as she approached the school bus garage, they began their short walk home. Along the way they talked about the yard work they wanted to get done over the weekend. It was supposed to be sunny and in the mid-sixties on Saturday, making for a perfect day.

And then Brutey and Norma would come over for a cookout. Everything seemed so normal.

* * *

Only four minutes before Janet Spencer was killed, Bob and Sandra Wrenn were driving west on State Route 73 after having dinner that evening at her sister's house in Waynesville. They were relatively new residents of Springboro, with two young boys attending the Jonathan Wright Elementary School, and they lived in one of the newer homes in Royal Oaks, on Catalpa Drive, which connected Paw Paw and Kesling drives. Dinner had been delicious, and afterward they looked through some photo albums and played a game of Monopoly. Around 10 o'clock, they decided it was time to go home and relieve the babysitter from what was certainly a trying night. Their two boys could often be a handful. Besides, *Love, American Style* would be on.

Traffic was light on the two-lane highway that connected Waynesville to Springboro. As they passed Township Line Road, the road was virtually barren. Off in the distance, way ahead of them, there was one vehicle traveling at much the same speed as theirs. They talked about the evening with her sister and about their plans for the next day. She would go to the IGA for the weekly shopping while he stayed home with the boys. Later they would go to the Springboro Park so the boys could swing and slide and play on the monkey bars.

"I'm going to sleep well tonight," Sandra said. "I sure hope the boys are asleep when we get home."

"Oh, I'm sure they've been down for an hour," Bob said.

State Route 73 at that time was a narrow road, with a few twists and turns and hills that gave drivers a feeling of being on a rambunctious roller coaster. One second, a driver was all alone. In the blink of an eye, an oncoming vehicle was right there. As the Wrenns came overtop the hill approaching Lovely's Farm, they saw a vehicle way ahead in the distance. They couldn't tell whether it was a truck or a car, and likewise couldn't tell how fast it was going. They saw it apply its brakes and then drift temporarily out of sight.

What happened next seemed to happen so fast. As the vehicle ahead slammed on its brakes, an oncoming vehicle suddenly appeared. The flash of the headlights drew the attention of the Wrenns, and Bob shouted for Sandra to look out. The oncoming vehicle veered to the side of the road, then snapped back onto the roadway and careened into the westbound lane. The vehicle tried to hang on but its speed was too great. The vehicle crashed into a telephone pole at a high rate of speed. The sound it of was chilling. And the vehicle came to rest with a plume of smoke rising from the engine.

Sandra was horrified. Bob sped up to reach the scene.

Once there, they found the driver slumped over the wheel, her lifeless body bleeding from her head and torso, and the two girls were screaming. The oldest was sitting in her mother's lap. Sandra Wrenn said later it was the worst scene she had ever witnessed in her life.

CHAPTER 17

Bob Wrenn could see that a vehicle stopped way off in the distance. His wife was screaming and the kids were crying, and they all felt so alone on this abandoned stretch of road east of Springboro. He still couldn't tell whether the vehicle was a car or a truck, so he couldn't possibly see the license plate or who was driving. But Bob Wrenn figured that the driver knew what had happened, and knew he was responsible for it. He took three steps in the direction of the vehicle and then watched it abruptly speed away.

"Get back here, you coward!" he yelled.

Sandra quietly confirmed that Janet Spencer was dead, but she didn't tell the girls. She got them out of the car and took them as far away from the car as possible, assuring them all the while their mom was okay and everything was going to be okay. "Mommy, wake up! Mommy, wake up!" the older one yelled. With all the houses way off the street and pitch black, the Wrenns decided that it would be best to take the girls to the Springboro Police Department and report what they saw.

Jimmy Beavers was in the station house filling out a report when the Wrenns arrived with the two little girls. The girls were still hysterical and Sandra was still in shock, but Bob tried to piece together what he had seen. An oncoming vehicle had run left of center, running poor Janet Spencer off the road and killing her.

"You sure she's dead?" Jimmy asked.

"I couldn't find a pulse," Bob Wrenn said.

Dispatch immediately sent out a code red, which sent word to Dr. Scott Swope and the rescue squad, plus the fire department and any available officer. Officer Charlie Reedy was the first officer on the scene and he confirmed what Bob and Sandra Wrenn had already reported – the driver of the car was dead. Soon, Dr. Swope arrived and attempted to revive Janet Spencer, but nothing worked. Her skull was fractured, and the steering wheel had crushed her lungs. At twenty minutes to midnight, not two hours after she left the Springboro football game, he officially pronounced her dead. Charlie Reedy covered her body in a white sheet.

Before long, cruisers from all surrounding jurisdictions had arrived. The life squad carted off Janet Spencer's body. The fire trucks made sure the vehicle didn't burst into flames. Other cars stopped to see what had happened. Everyone had a question. Many had something to say. Stories were shared, and before long the case was mounting. A jerk had run Janet Spencer off the road, killing her, and he didn't even stop to see if she was okay. What's more, he was still on the loose.

Charlie was in the middle of all of it. Jimmy interviewed anyone who had any connection to the scene, but the only real witnesses were Bob and Sandra Wrenn, and it was unclear what they saw in the moments leading up to the crash. As the final rescue truck pulled away, Charlie and Jimmy looked at one another in the stillness of the night on that lonely stretch of road.

"Damnedest thing," Jimmy moaned. "Two little girls have to go through life without their mom. And somebody out there is responsible for a homicide. We need to be finding some guy driving like a crazy man, and fast."

Instantly, one thing was clear. There was absolutely no evidence to go on. No tire marks. No collision damage. No definitive eyewitnesses.

Because John Spencer didn't arrive home until the next day, police attempts to contact him went unanswered. But when Janet's father didn't get the late-night phone call he was expected, he became worried. He called the house repeatedly, never getting an answer. It was around three in the morning that he finally called the Springboro police, and that's when he got the news no parent wishes to get.

They spent the remainder of a sleepless night caring for the girls and waiting for John to call.

And crying.

* * *

It shouldn't have happened. There was no intention for anything like that to happen. The driver of the vehicle that ran Janet Spencer off the road knew immediately what had happened, and knew immediately that the accident was a bad one. He just didn't know who was driving the other car, or how bad the accident was.

He saw the crash in his rear-view mirror, just as he passed a car that was about to pull out onto St. Rt. 73. He wanted to stop, but knew he couldn't. He wanted to go help but he knew he shouldn't. Someone else would come along, and they could do the very thing that he could, and there would be no exposure to even more problems. Because going back there would have created just that, more problems.

Criminal charges. Jail time. A divorce. Public humiliation.

Why risk all of that if no one had to know? It was better this way. And the police didn't always catch the cars that ran from them,

He turned left onto East Street and drove halfway down before turning right. He found the alley that ran between Main Street and East Street, and he sat there like he had so many times over the years. He turned off the ignition and the headlights and sat there waiting for the sirens. Please let everyone be okay! Please let it be nothing more than a bloody nose that hit the steering wheel. He sat there, with sweat pouring down his brow, anguished about the still of the night and the images his mind was conjuring up.

How could he let this happen? This was the second episode of running from the police in just over a month, and surely Charlie Reedy would be madder than hell. He had no intention of causing an accident. That's why he drove the speed limit. That's why he kept his car in his lane of travel. If he hadn't been trying to reach into the backseat, this never would have happened. Why did he have to do that? Why did he regard what was back there as so damn important?

He deserved to be punished. But then again he couldn't risk the consequences that he would have received. Instead, he had to lay low. Wait it out. Hope for the better. And never, ever put himself in a position to let something like this happen again.

Sure enough, the sirens came within minutes. He could see one cruiser whiz by on Main Street. Another one flew by on East Street. Then he saw what he dreaded the most, the life squad, with lights flashing, flying past him. That meant the other driver was at least injured in some way, and he hoped to God it was something minor. He would sit and wait it out, and if the life squad took off in a hurry then that would tell him something. If it didn't go anywhere at all, that would tell him something else – something he didn't even want to think about.

He had to keep himself together!

No one could know about this. There had been no crash, no tire marks, and as far as he could tell, no witnesses. He passed the one car that was turning onto St. Rt. 73, but it kept on going once it reached downtown. It was probably headed for the Interstate and had no idea what had happened back up the road. Instead, it was his secret, one he was determined to keep, since coming forward wouldn't change what had just happened.

Coming forward would only make a bad situation worse. Why have more innocent people affected by his mistake? He ran through the scenarios over and over in his mind, All of them supported the conclusion he had already reached. Soon he would make the short trip home, and go home and go to bed like nothing ever happened. Then he would get up in the morning, and go about his regular activity, again like nothing ever happened.

Surely he could do that, couldn't he?

Maybe yes, and maybe no.

Soon he saw the life squad returning to the station house. Its lights weren't flashing. No one seemed to be in a hurry to get any help.

His mission was now entrenched, to act like nothing ever happened – even though he had apparently killed somebody.

* * *

The case officially became the jurisdiction of the Ohio State Patrol. The Warren County Sheriff's Office and Clearcreek Township Police were also involved, because they were on the scene. But Springboro P.D. was most involved because the crash occurred in the village limits. By morning a county assistant prosecutor would be assigned to lead the investigation.

Charlie Reedy and Jimmy Beavers would keep their ears open for as long as it took. Neither could remember a scene so horrible in all of their years. "I was at the car crash that killed that Mockabee boy, and it was so sad that day when Andy Garland was killed on his bike," Charlie offered. "You never get used to seeing these things."

A grim reality sank in. "The guy could be anywhere," Charlie said. "Taking a right on 741 would take him to Dayton. A left would take him to Cincinnati. He could be as far north as Columbus or as far south as Louisville by now, or at any point in between."

"And no physical evidence to tie him to the crash. The witnesses said there was no contact between the cars. And from what I saw, there weren't any tire marks. And no one has a license plate, and no one knows the make and model of that vehicle."

"So the guy who did it could be anywhere. And it could be anybody," Jimmy said. This would be a tough case in more ways than one.

Bob Wrenn thought the vehicle was a truck. He couldn't be sure. Maybe it was an El Camino. Maybe it was a van. He racked his brain but never came up with a definitive description.

"Must be a thousand trucks in Springboro alone," Charlie told Jimmy.

CHAPTER 17

Both of them remembered the runaway truck from a few weeks earlier. Charlie still believed it belonged to Paul Sowers on East Street, and he made a note to go there right away.

Jimmy, meanwhile, would check the local bars. They found no one. The streets of Springboro had settled down by midnight; those who had walked to the game had long since arrived home, and anyone who drove had been to their post-game hangouts and was also tucked in bed. Charlie and Jimmy cruised around town anyway in the off-chance that they would stumble on something, anything, a mysterious truck that had broken down and the wayward stranger would confess to what he had done. With the chase from a few weeks earlier still fresh in their minds, they also checked and re-checked every truck on East Street, finding only three and all of them in cool condition like they'd been parked the whole night.

They met again in the Lawson's Market parking lot around 4.

"Nothing," Jimmy said.

"Me, either."

"That guy's long gone."

"Maybe so. But there's no way we'd know even if he wasn't." Charlie's adrenaline was still pumping; he'd cruise around all night if the Chief would let him.

"I'll see you tomorrow."

"Yeah, maybe something will develop then."

The crash and the death of Janet Spencer, as tragic as it was, would not be a headline in the Saturday Dayton Daily News, nor was it an item on the Channel 7 eleven o'clock news. Word of it spread around town among the adults, but none of us kids knew anything about it. Aside from the horror that existed inside the home of her parents and immediately family, the death of Janet Spencer became another statistic and unsolved case in their files.

This can't be, Jimmy thought. Surely there was some lead, some piece of evidence, some witness who could point them in the right direction. Idiots like that driver always screw up in a big way, so something will turn up. It had to, eventually.

On his way home, Jimmy drove by the house owned by Janet Spencer's parents. It was only two doors up from his, catty-corner from Brutey's. He stopped and reflected on what must be going on inside it. The shape, size, front door and window frames all looked the same as his house and about a hundred others in the subdivision, but the conversations going inside were in a completely different world.

Someone needed to be held accountable for this, Jimmy reasoned. He and Charlie Reedy would see to it that someone was.

Donny Wilburn (#46) was one of the most talented and competitive players in the whole seventh grade. He later went on to join the 1,000 point club as a player on the varsity basketball team. In 1972, Coach Gary (O.J. Powers) used him as a primary weapon throughout the football season, especially in the big game against Shane Hatfield's team – which had a tragic ending.

CHAPTER 18

In our minds, we could make a seventh-grade game as important as the Super Bowl, or OSU-Michigan, or even a Springboro-Kings varsity game
-- The hype

Saturday, October 28, 1972

As the sun crept over the maple trees along Main Street, there was a quiet peace once again. But it was misleading. All over town people were waking up to phone calls about the accident. Details were sketchy, but rumors were flying. There was a lot of speculation over what happened, but one thing was unfortunately certain. Janet Spencer was dead, and her family was going through a living hell. Having heard the news just after breakfast, Reverend Dawes said a prayer for healing and comfort.

To the old-timers around town, the scene was eerily similar to the one in July of '65 when Bob Mockabee, a basketball star, had been killed. Or a few years later when Andy Garland had been run over by a drunk driver while riding his bike home from football practice.

I heard my parents talking about the accident a little, but I didn't pay much attention. In typical fashion, I was focused on football from the time I woke up until the time I left the house. Such is the mind of a twelve-year-old boy. Had I truly digested the story, I'm sure I would have been sad, at least for a little while. But football was all I cared about. My sisters would never understand this.

Five hours before game time, I was already dressed. My football pants were fresh out of the dryer, and my jersey slipped loosely over the sweatshirt I would need for such a chilly day. The helmet and shoulder pads would come later, but I didn't want to wait. I had been so psyched up since the varsity game the night before that I found it hard to sleep, and all morning I wondered how Dave Collins or Dave Vicroy or Mike Colvin calmed himself down before such a big game. I had two bowls of Cheerios, cleaned my room, straightened out the garage and started two loads of laundry, and it wasn't yet nine o'clock. How in the world did the varsity players make it to seven-thirty at night?! Yikes, I was ready to play already.

Our mission was to beat Shane Hatfield. His was the team to beat for the league championship. He was the most explosive player in the league, besides Donny of course. He was also responsible for more touchdowns than anybody, some by running for them and others by throwing. And he had a will to win that was as strong as anyone we knew. I figured he'd be playing in the NFL by the time he was a sophomore.

While I waited, I played the game over and over in my mind. I imagined certain plays in certain situations. There were great runs and saving tackles. I would throw touchdowns like Rod Dillon and run the ball like Dave, and on defense I would play free safety just like Russ Chesney. Every time I imagined the game, we won. So after a while I figured it was time to go do it. I got to the field early. Way early. When I got there, the field was alive as the yellow team played the blue team in some useless late-season game that had no effect on the league standings.

I stood with Donny and Lance and Turkey in our traditional spot just beyond the north end zone. Turkey, who wasn't on our team, was chomping on some popcorn. Donny, Lance and I tossed a football.

"We can beat them just like we can beat anybody," Donny said. "We've got everything they've got and then some. As long as our line blocks." Some of our linemen nearby ran for cover.

"You can beat them," Turkey said, "but you won't."

For a second, I was stunned. Surely he didn't say what I think he said. I've got a helmet right here I could hit him with. Or the three of us could sit on him and squish him like a bug.

"Shane always finds a way to win," he said. "You watch, something will happen. He'll find a way to win. He did it to me in baseball all summer."

"Yeah, like the time he hit it over the C & C Trophy sign on you," Lance said. When home runs were hit at the ball park throughout the summer, their impressiveness was measured by which advertising sign that hung on the outfield wall they went over.

"It wasn't that sign. It was the IGA sign."

"Oh, yeah, five feet to the left of it. Big difference. Either way, he hit to the moon. Looked like something Ernie Melton used to do."

Atta' boy, Lance.

"The trick will be to get so far ahead he can't do something on his own," I said, slipping on my shoulder pads and jersey. "He can't do a miracle late in the game if we're up three scores."

"I wouldn't be so sure about that."

"Three scores? Late in the game? There's no one who can overcome that."

"I wouldn't bet on it," Turkey said, showing that confident smile again.

"You watch," I said, wanting desperately to wipe it off his face.

"Yeah, we'll see."

We started our pre-game warm-ups as the game before us eventually came to a merciful end. There was a slight post-game celebration, probably because both teams were one more game away from putting an end to such a miserable season. Coach Powers huddled us together for some last-minute instructions, and Tim Campbell and Chris Mills were named team captains for the coin toss. Brutey assured us that we were the right team to beat this team, and everyone was as pumped up and loose as I had seen them all year.

"Hustle!" we shouted, and our defense took the field. The big game had finally arrived.

* * *

Nearly two hours later, after a lot of hard hits and big plays, the big game was over and I was lying flat on my stomach at our thirty-yard line, having lunged and landed there after missing Shane Hatfield. I had the last chance to catch him. I had the chance to save the game. Instead, Shane faked me inside and then ran around me, something that hadn't happened all season. As I lay there I pounded the turf, taking out my frustrations on the few blades of grass that had made it through the long season. All around me, Shane and his teammates were celebrating. They'd won the game and championship on an unthinkable touchdown run in the final moments of the game, with Shane running sixty-three yards around and between every player we had, including my last-ditch grab. I watched him run the last thirty-five yards untouched, and there was nothing any of us could do. It was over. And it was awful.

I hated Shane Hatfield. I hated his team. I hated the way he carried the ball and the way he shouted out the cadence. His cleats were ugly. And so was his coach. And I hated their fans. When the final buzzer sounded, I wanted to march across the field and wipe that big smile off his face, with my fist, no less. And Turkey had better not show his face, either. Our season was over, for all intents and purposes, and Shane Hatfield's team was league champions. It shouldn't have happened; we should have won. And for a full thirty minutes after the game was over, our coach let us have it. We deserved it.

I don't think I've ever had such a headache. I think Donny Wilburn darned near died.

With Brutey standing next to him nodding at every statement, Coach O.J. lost it, which he had never done all season. He was generally a positive and supportive coach. But after we'd lost, 14-12, blowing a lead on the last play of the game, and ruining our chance for a championship in the process, he was anything but happy. He yelled like he's never done the whole season.

"You had this one. You had it!" he told us. "Then you let it get away."

He paced back and forth. He pointed at each of us individually. We all sat there with grass-stained uniforms and soaking-wet hair. Coach was so worked up he was sweating on an otherwise chilly day.

"Fellas, I can't play the game for you," he continued. "All I can do is teach you the way you're supposed to do it. And I thought we'd done that. We've worked on some basics all year long, practiced them over and over, and look at what happened today. We broke the number one rule on defense. The number one rule."

We knew what the number one rule was. No one had to ask. We all sat there like we'd just been to a funeral. As Coach Powers yelled, Donny sat quietly, his elbows on his knees, his head in his hands. Next to him was Lance. They both had played well, and neither was responsible for the last-second tragedy. But Coach always told us we won as a team and lost as a team.

"We lost this game because we weren't disciplined!" Coach yelled. "Come Tuesday, I'll show you discipline. Come Tuesday, I'll show you a lot of things."

The pounding in my head got even worse. I didn't bother to mention that we only had one more game in the season. Somehow, I didn't think Coach would care.

"Lance Penwell, how many times did we practice containment this week?" Coach asked.

"Every night, Coach." Lance's head was lowered now. It wasn't his fault, because he wasn't the left defensive end.

"Billy Hammock, what's the number one rule for a defensive end?"

"Turn the man inside." Billy Hammock had his head down; he practically whispered as he answered.

"Turn the man inside! Turn the man inside! Anyone here heard that before?!" Coach didn't really wait for an answer. He knew it. We all knew it. We'd heard it all week. It was the number one rule. It killed him that we lost because of a basic mistake. He probably would have had us do wind sprints right then if he thought he could get away with it.

He yelled about the mistake. He yelled because our lack of effort let them back into the game. "What happened down the stretch will not happen again! You got that?" We nodded in agreement, not sure we were telling the truth.

"We're better than this. We're capable of beating anybody in this league. We just have to quit beating ourselves."

Coach then calmed down a little and pointed out some positives. The offensive line blocked well, giving Donny plenty of running room and thus avoiding the butt whipping he had promised if they hadn't. He liked the way my brother John played at linebacker. And Lance caught some nice passes for some good gains. All in all, it had been a good game until the final minute.

Afterward, we all walked slowly to the K & W for something cold. It had been a tough game, with a bad result, and we had the physical and emotional wounds to show for it. I had a cut on my lip and a limp in my walk. My right shoulder had a tingle in it, too.

I loved every minute of it.

* * *

The houses along West Market Street were a study in contrast. In one house, there was death. In another, the specter of divorce.

There were still no solid clues on who was the mysterious driver of the reckless vehicle, something that added to the misery of Janet's family. John Spencer arrived in town a little past two o'clock in the afternoon, his eyes reddened, accompanied by his parents. He held his daughters for a full ten minutes in the front yard. Never had he experienced such a crushing loss. He wanted to hold his daughters tight for the rest of his life.

Charlie Reedy stopped by the house around three o'clock as he began his evening shift. It pained him that there was nothing more he could tell them about what happened. With no description of the vehicle, and no license number, and no real eyewitnesses, there was nothing to go on. John resisted the temptation to yell at Charlie and suggest he should spend every waking moment searching the entire universe for his wife's killer. After all, it wasn't Charlie's fault. Somewhere, a maniac was running loose, and he hoped God would strike him down and send him straight to hell.

"What kind of person could do such a thing? Run left of center, cause a beautiful woman to die, leave two girls without their mother for the rest of their lives, and then take off like a coward? Isn't that what those two people told you last night? The driver of that truck stopped, looked back, so he had to know what he'd done, and then take off. What is this world coming to? If I could find that guy, I'd tie him up, throw him in the street and then run over him."

Charlie just listened. He'd learned that grief expressed itself in many ways, primarily anger, something he had seen many times. He couldn't imagine his reaction if something had happened to either of his two boys. He adjusted his belt and looked for the right moment to excuse himself. Everyone knew the situation. There was no benefit in repeating it many times.

"Sounds like we just have to hope someone comes forward someday," John Spencer whispered. "And that never happens."

There was no disagreement.

As Charlie left, he saw Brutey and Norma getting out of his truck at the house next door. After a morning in which Brutey fixed the back door, cleaned out the garage and touched up the paint in the master bathroom, they had spent the afternoon at the peewee game. The sight of Charlie leaving the neighbor's house was sobering for the two of them. "I can't imagine what a mother goes through losing a child," Norma said. "I don't want to imagine it, either." They quickly walked inside. Brutey was in tears.

CHAPTER 18

Norma still hadn't told Brutey she had filed for divorce. The paperwork was getting processed and she would tell him just before Brutey just before being served, something she never dreamed would be so hard. It was especially hard after a day like today, when he was so attentive and so helpful around the house. She didn't know why he was acting like he was.

They spent the evening eating dinner and watching a movie until it was time to go to bed. Before turning out the lights, Brutey leaned over and kissed Norma on the cheek.

"Church starts in the morning at ten, right? I'll go with you, if that's okay." It was okay, of course, but Brutey hadn't been to church in years. Why now? Her mind was made up and she had already signed the divorce papers. There was only one answer.

He had to have found out what she was planning. But how?

Dr. Scott Swope, pictured with Mayor Jim Eyler, chief of police Carl Hirschbach and officer Charlie Reedy, came to Springboro in the early sixties and immediately made his presence known. He practiced medicine at the Springboro Clinic, plus started emergency medicine procedures and became the school's team physician.

CHAPTER 19

Hey, it's Batty-Hatty
From Cincinnati!
-- The Cool Ghoul
on WXIX, Ch. 19

TUESDAY, OCTOBER 31, 1972

When the final bell rang for the day, it was like a shotgun for an Olympic sprint. Kids bolted from their classrooms and quickly made their way to their lockers, where they dumped their books, grabbed their jackets and hustled outside. It was a beautiful fall afternoon, sunny and slightly chilly, and the end of the school day felt like a Friday. We were all in a good mood because it was Halloween, and for those of us in the seventh grade, it was probably our last chance to enjoy trick or treat.

I hooked up with Turkey and we walked from Mrs. Kuhn's Science class to our lockers. He was impressed that I'd gone almost two weeks without daydreaming in class.

"Worst thing that's ever happened to me," I said.

"It'll happen to me next," he said. "I couldn't keep my eyes open today."

"In Science class?" I asked, hoping for a partner in crime.

"Nah, English. It bores me to tears. Who would ever want read a whole book? As for me, I love Science class. I think Mrs. Kuhn is one of the best teachers I've ever had."

I wondered if I heard Turkey correctly. Was it possible that he was secretly delusional? Could it be that I was a friend with a guy who had deep-rooted mental problems? Next thing I knew he was going to tell me he wanted to move to Mason and play for the Comets. Then I would know he was really off his rocker.

"You still dreaming of playing lead guitar for Led Zeppelin?" I chuckled. Turkey was a master of the air guitar.

"Oh yeah. But today I was thinking about football, not music,. With Kings Mills coming to town Friday, I was dreaming about single-handedly stopping Testerman. Twenty carries for six yards. In his face all night. Afterward there was a parade in my honor."

"Good one."

"Might come true, too. Someday."

Fat chance of that and I decided that he was delusional, after all. He was lucky I liked him so much, or else I'd have been tempted to slam him all the time.

We reached our lockers and suddenly Turkey found fifteen other people to talk with. He was always in the middle of everything, and well liked as a result, by more than just me and Lance, despite his ornery nature. I put away my Science book and went to grab a notebook that I wanted to take home. But the notebook was stuck at the bottom of my locker and I had to tug to get it out. It took a lot of effort, and I tugged so hard that many of the things in my locker went sprawling all over the hall. At that same time Dodie Fetters, a blonde cheerleader in my class, walked by. She saw what had happened to me, and for reasons that were so obvious – I mean, really, how else was I supposed to interpret this? -- she picked up my pencil and handed it to me. "Here," she said. "I think this is yours."

It was incredible. Never before had I had such a flirtatious conversation with a girl. She held out her hand, and mine almost touched hers, and when I took the pencil back I could even see the hint of a smile. That's why I was in orbit the whole rest of that day. It gave me confidence.

I felt we were practically going steady.

I told Turkey about it later and he thought I was nuts. "So let me get this straight," he said. "Some girl cleans up your mess so the whole school doesn't trip over it, and break a leg in the process, and because of that one simple act you think she likes you? So what does that mean, if she actually waves hi to you in the hallway, is that like a marriage proposal? You're pretty desperate there, Kirb, aren't you?"

Hmmmmph. Little did he know. He was the one who was delusional, not me.

Of course, I didn't tell him that the very next day Dodie Fetters walked right by me and didn't even say hello. But she was really in a hurry and probably didn't see me. Yeah, that was it. That's what I figured.

As I walked past the locker room on my way out of school, I saw Dr. Swope tending to the sore knee of Steve Rottert, a senior defensive lineman. He'd twisted it late in the fourth quarter against Blanchester when he made a tackle that helped set up the last touchdown drive. Now Dr. Swope, who had volunteered as team doctor since coming to Springboro in the early sixties, was maneuvering the knee to see what was required to keep Steve in the lineup for the Kings game.

"Does that hurt?" Dr. Swope asked.

"Nope."

"How about that?"

"A little."

"Okay, stay off it tonight and keep it on ice. We'll see how it looks tomorrow."

"I'm playing Friday night, aren't I?" Steve wondered. He looked concerned, as was expected. As a senior, he had only two games left in his high school career.

"If I told you that you couldn't, would you still play?" Dr. Swope grinned.

"Unless someone chopped both legs off."

That was the answer Dr. Swope expected. He'd dealt with many a senior in his day, and he knew the intensity they had for their final season. Years earlier, he'd seen Bruce Smith's football career end because of an injury, and then it happened again in 1970 when Jerry Raffel was injured. In between, he had encountered seniors with some sore tendons and substantial bruises that were determined to play through the pain, even when those same injuries would have sidelined a lower classman.

"Okay, work in that ice and let's make sure you can play Friday."

Dr. Swope was from a family of doctors, seven in all, including his father. He grew up in Richmond, Indiana, but he spent a lot of time in Dayton because that's where his dad did most of his work. Dr. Swope spent some time in high school working as an orderly at Grandview Hospital in Dayton, an experience he found interesting, but not enough to encourage him to initially go into medicine.

After graduation, he studied engineering at Purdue because, as he says, he always has had an interest in everything mechanical. But after spending an internship in the desert in New Mexico one summer, he figured there had to be something better. So he changed majors to pre-med, graduating from Purdue in 1958.

He met his future wife Judy in high school in Richmond. Dr. Swope was a senior and she was only a sophomore. She had to ask her mother if it was okay to go out with a guy who was so much older, and she said yes, and they dated during Dr. Swope's senior year, and then whenever he came back to Richmond during his years at Purdue. When Judy graduated from Richmond she went to Ball State, which is also in Indiana, but – as was the practice in those days – she was not permitted to go visit him at Purdue, nor was he allowed to visit her at Ball State.

Soon, they married, and Dr. Swope went to medical school in Missouri. Then he took an internship back in Dayton at Grandview Hospital, and from there he fielded offers from both Eaton and Springboro to move there and establish a practice. In the end, Springboro won that bidding war, and the town benefited as a result.

In 1963 he went to work with Dr. Ted Garland, who had just established and built the Springboro Clinic, which was located on West Central Avenue, across from the Springboro Park, which in those early days was well outside the center of town. By now the Swopes had two sons, Brad and Todd, and they lived in a two-story house on the corner of Factory and Woods.

In addition to establishing his practice, he volunteered as the Panther team doctor. He who was on hand before all football and basketball games taping ankles, then checking on the bumps and bruises throughout the week – as he was doing that day I saw him with Steve Rottert. He also performed all the physicals for the student-athletes before each season, charging a nominal fee of $5, which he in turn donated to the athletic department.

He took on that role as team doctor after he joined the Lion's Club and met school superintendent Ray Perez and then-high school principal Jim Hough Sr. In the early years, they had ideas of a sports medicine program, but it wasn't until football started in 1965 that the idea really got off the ground. By the early seventies, Springboro had a full-fledged sports medicine program.

Dr. Swope helped start another valuable organization in those early years, too – Emergency Medical Services (EMS). He was on the scene when Bob Mockabee was killed in the summer of 1965, and that tragedy was a driving factor for Springboro – and municipalities everywhere – in obtaining their own ambulance and emergency medical staff. Before that, rescue officials had to contact local funeral homes to request a hearse to transport an injured person to the hospital. That, of course, required a late-night telephone call from a pay phone (since there were no cell phones back then) to a funeral director who could have been in any number of places throughout the day or night. That was only one of the problems. The other was the lack of training or equipment by any of the police officers or firefighters who arrived first on the scene.

He became a co-founder of the College of Emergency Physicians, an entity that trained emergency rescue personnel around the state.

By 1968, the Swopes had two daughters, Julie and Jenny, and it was then they moved from the two-story house on the corner of Factory to the big house on the hill down near Catalpa Drive. To those of us who lived in Royal Oaks, it was a mansion. In the years that followed, Brad and Todd became involved in peewee football, Little League baseball and Saturday morning basketball – just like the rest of us our age. So in addition to all of the varsity games, Dr. Swope and Judy had to go to all of those games, too.

They had become as synonymous with the Springboro athletic program as any player or coach whose name appeared in the sports pages.

"Hey, Doc, maybe you should take a look at Brutey. I haven't heard him say a word since he walked in, and it's been almost an hour," said Rottert as he limped toward the locker room.

Several of the other players and coaches turned towards Brutey, who was sitting in a chair reading a newspaper.

"Brutey, you okay?" Dr. Swope asked.

Brutey put the paper down and got up from the chair. "Yeah, I'm okay. I'm just worried that I did a good job of scouting Kings Mills," he said. "This is the biggest game of the year, and you guys are counting on me to get it right."

"You were close to Janet Spencer, too, weren't you?" Dr. Swope continued. "Someone said you were awfully shook up by her death the other night."

Brutey hesitated, for it was difficult to find the words. "She was like a daughter to me," he said finally. He then turned to walk out the door towards the practice field.

"Bet you'd like to kill the guy who ran her off the road, huh?"

Brutey was too far away to hear the question. Or so they thought.

* * *

A few hours later, I took a hit during football practice that sent my head spinning, and I could've used a few minutes with Dr. Swope myself. I tried to block a lineman so Donny Wilburn could break free, and evidently this lineman didn't like me much. Maybe he thought it was me who made threats to all the linemen, not Donny. Maybe he idolized Dick Butkus. Whatever it was, he saw me coming and he threw me to the ground and then body-slammed me. For a second, I couldn't breath. Then, when I got up, I couldn't see straight.

Oh, Dr. Swope? Got anything for a brain fracture? This gorilla just took my head off.

I sat out a few minutes and came back as good as new. Evidently, hurting my brain was the least worrisome injury I could've sustained. Break my legs or my right arm, well, and then we had a crisis. But my brain? Guess they figured I was already twisted in my thinking.

Afterward, when Coach O.J. was finished with us for the night, I walked home feeling a little dazed and confused, but mainly I was just dirty and sweaty. Oddly enough, it made me wish I could've run into any of the girls from school. This was my chance because I looked so cool! All I needed was a glance, because that would be enough for a wave. Then I could make my impression. I could show any of them just how strong and rugged I really was. After all, my hair was practically matted to my head, and I was injured. I'd never looked so good.

But I walked by the K & W and found no one. I walked down Factory, then across on Carey, then all the way up Market Street – past a dozen or so cute girls' houses. But still I found no one.

I finally made my way home, where I showered and changed into my Halloween costume, which was nothing more than a Joe Namath football jersey. As I showered, all that great dirt and mud and sweat disappeared down the drain.

I likened it to a Michelangelo masterpiece drawn in chalk being washed away by the rain. I would never look so good again. And I wasn't sure I'd ever have a moment as magical as the one at my locker that afternoon. Ahem.

That night, after Trick or Treat was over and the whole gang of us had our bag of candy, I walked towards an old farmhouse on the outskirts of town where a bunch of us would meet up for a Halloween "dare." We were dared by some sophomores that we wouldn't meet them out there at eight o'clock, the time they said the former owner of the house, a man who died sometime in the late sixties, would appear and try to scare anyone who was invading his property.

CHAPTER 19

"I'll do it," I announced bravely, intent on doing anything to challenge a sophomore.

"You're crazy," Lance responded, his eyes wide open. "Do you know how many kids have disappeared over at that house? I'm not going."

"I'll do it. I heard a couple of other guys say they'll do it, too." If I had a mission in life, it was to get the last laugh against sophomores.

The old abandoned farmhouse was way off of Central Avenue, over in the area across from the old Wright house and adjacent to that area of Renwood Place where it dead-ended (long before development changed all that). To get there, we either had to climb the fence at the end of Renwood, and crawl through the trees to get to the old house, or else we had to walk down the long driveway that was lined with creaky, overhanging trees and was about a million miles long.

I wasn't going to let a bunch of sophomores get to me. Not again. Not after what they did to me on the first day of school, which I hadn't forgotten. I didn't believe a word they said, so I set out to prove them wrong. The place wasn't haunted and there was no way some old man was going to appear and scare us off. I'd seen stuff just like this on The Twilight Zone and I knew it was fake the whole time. And I told everybody that all day.

Lance thought I was crazy, and Turkey began planning my funeral.

Four guys accepted the challenge, and we stood on Central at the beginning of the driveway right at eight o'clock – Tim, Todd, Brian and me. There was hardly any traffic that time of night, and on this night it was no exception. We were laughing and chomping on candy as we waited for anyone else to show up.

By five minutes after eight, it was clear that no one else was coming. So we took a few steps down the driveway. It was really dark there, and the wind howled through the trees. More than that, it was getting awfully cold, and I realized I was severely underdressed for this.

Then, one by one, my buddies dropped out. Tim remembered homework he had to do. Todd was told to be home by eight-fifteen, and Brian's mom wanted him home to help move a piece of furniture.

"You still going, Jeff?" Brian asked me.

"Yeah," I said. "No way are the sophomores getting me this time."

Brian shrugged his shoulders. "You're a braver man than me," he said, and turned and walked away.

I looked away for only a second, and when I looked back towards Brian it was like he had disappeared. The wind whirled through the barren trees, and it was as if the wind was saying something. I could see pieces of the full moon through the edges of the trees, and its light shone on the house in the distance. I did a double-take, but I was sure some old man was standing in the front yard. The shutters clanged in the distance, and with each step I took, the sound grew louder. I stayed exactly thirty-five seconds before I realized this was the stupidest thing I had ever done. Who was I kidding? Everyone knew this place was haunted, and that's why no one was ever out here.

When I was sure the coast was clear, I took a few steps backward to go back to the street. After a few steps I started to trot. Within seconds I was going full speed, doing what I had to do. Get. The. Heck. Out. Of. There.

I was never so scared in my whole life.

Then, out of the corner of my eye, I saw a gathering of people on the other side of the street. It was that same group of sophomores who had tricked me at the beginning of the school. They were laughing so hard they were practically falling over.

What was worse is that a few cute girls from my class were with them. Now I found them! Where were they a few hours ago when I was all beaten up and dirty?

At that moment, I didn't care, because there were two truths in my life. One had to do with staying away from freaky ghosts. And the other had to do with my opinion of sophomores.

Hated 'em. More than anything.

Except Mason, that is.

* * *

I got home and hibernated in my room while my brothers and sisters gathered downstairs with their candy thrown all over the living room floor. I finished up a little homework and then turned in for the night, listening to the sounds of WSAI as I fell asleep.

I wondered when the day would come that I wouldn't do anything stupid. Did that ever happen when I grew older? Would I ever be successful and be married? Were there many more lessons I had to learn the hard way?

Just then a Gilbert O'Sullivan song came on the radio, one that had been popular over the summer. As I listened I continued to think about my life and who I was. I was full of such hope and promise, but it seemed like I hit road blocks at every stop. It seemed that Lance and Mitch and Donny, even Turkey, had such confidence about who they were, and had reasons to back it up. The players on the varsity, the football players who were winding down their season and the basketball players who worked hard in open gym, they had everything. They were in great shape and talented, and on Friday nights they held center stage for the whole town to come cheer them on, and I really wanted that someday. Even the coaches, whose playing careers were gone, still did positive things to make a difference. Wouldn't that be something? I remembered again how appreciative I was when Brutey pulled me aside at football practice the other day. I wished I could have that kind of impact on somebody.

Yet I seemed to be such a goof-up. I had my moments when I seemed to get everything together, but then there were other moments – like this one – when I didn't think I did anything well. Was that ever going to change?

I thought about those questions as the song played on. The chorus seemed to have such truth for me:

To think that only yesterday
I was cheerful, bright and gay
Looking forward to well wouldn't do
The role I was about to play
But as if to knock me down
Reality came around
And without so much, as a mere touch
Cut me into little pieces
Leaving me to doubt
Talk about God and His mercy
Or if He really does exist
Why did He desert me
In my hour of need, I truly am indeed...
Alone again, naturally

The song had other meaning for the family of Janet Spencer. That awful Monday was the day that would forever live in infamy for them. In a small ceremony at a quiet cemetery just outside of Amherst, young Janet was buried.

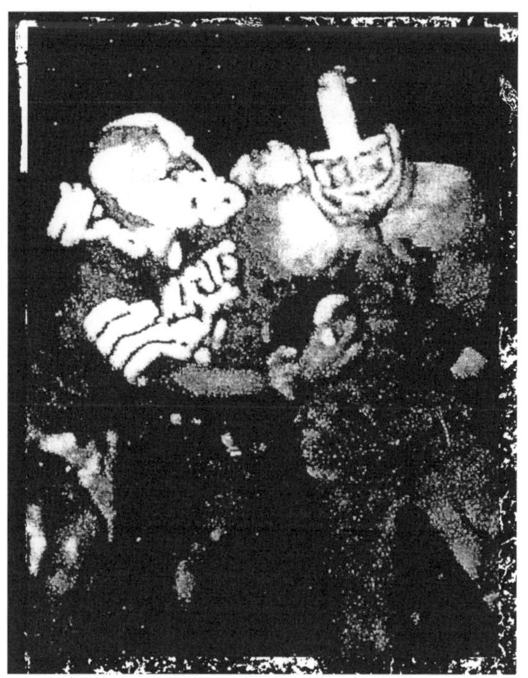

For an entire year, the return match-up against Kings Mills was THE game on the schedule. The defense would have to work hard to stop The Testerman Express, and Dave Dillon would have to earn a school rushing record the hard way. In the end, a leaping grab by Springboro's Dave Vicroy made the difference.

CHAPTER 20

Clint Eastwood, Steve McQueen
and James Bond were invincible,
but none were bigger than The Duke,
John Wayne, who was bigger than life
-- The movie heroes of '72

FRIDAY, NOVEMBER 3, 1972

The varsity players arrived, as required, two hours before kickoff. They met in the gymnasium, then stretched out on the floor or somewhere in the bleachers, and lay quietly for half an hour. This was a time to quiet down after a day of school. They were to be still and be focused, with no words spoken. Football is a game of emotion as much as anything else, and this was the time to get the emotion flowing in the right direction.

After that the players would dress, meet briefly for some initial instructions, and then go out and warm up before coming back in just before kickoff.

By the time they were dressed, the mood of the room was completely different.

The room was alive. Players were talkative, enthusiastic about the game at hand and occasionally laughing. Rod Dillon, the team's spiritual leader, was dressed first and went around the room, pounding lockers and challenging his teammates to get ready. "We only get one chance at this!" he said. "We've played and practiced for years for this one night! One chance! Who's with me on this? Who's ready to go make a statement? Right now, let's go!"

The room was predominantly full of seniors, all playing in their final conference game, with a conference championship still very much a possibility. This is what every peewee, junior high, junior varsity and varsity game they'd ever had prepared them for. And of course this was Kings Mills, the villain from a season ago. We owed them and wanted to show them. A loss this year virtually ended the season.

The seniors weren't going to let that happen. Rod spoke for all of them. If they'd been alive when they walked into the locker room, they were absolutely on fire moments before taking the field. They were ready to skip warm-ups, and skip the pre-game meeting, and start hitting right away.

The crowd was on edge, too. Though the rain continued to fall, no one stayed away. The stands were full well before kickoff. The older fans protected themselves with umbrellas and raincoats, but we kids ran around soaking wet, smiling. The wet field assured that the much bally-hooed running game would control the outcome of the game, as *The Western Star* said it would. After running for two hundred forty-one yards the week before against Blanchester, Dave Dillon was in a position to break the school rushing record. Kings Mills, meanwhile, had a bulldog of its own in Don Testerman, a junior who was being heavily recruited by the big colleges. Both defenses knew what they had to do. When the teams returned to the locker room for last-minute instructions, the men just below the press box analyzed every aspect of the game. Most predicted the Panthers would win, but only by three.

Coach Ross didn't need a fiery pre-game speech and he knew it. Instead, he put everything in perspective. "When you showed up in August, it was tonight that you were preparing for. Every game since then has been preparation for one thing, this game. So now let's go do it. This game will define this season. This game can be one that you'll remember for your whole life. Now, are you with me on this?"

"YES, SIR!"

Then they lined up and charged the field as the band played the school fight song. As was always the case, Rod Dillon trotted out last.

* * *

With no game to scout, Brutey was thrilled to be at the varsity game. He took the afternoon off work and spent it with Norma at the Dayton Mall, where they bought the boys some clothes and a new basketball. Brutey purposely stayed out of Mayor's Records, which was where the boys bought all their music, because he thought all rock stars looked like drug addicts. "Will you get a look at this Alice Cooper?" he'd say, picking up an album cover. "And which one of these guys is the real Lynyrd Skynrd?" Brutey preferred Pat Boone and Buddy Holly.

They had a quiet lunch and got home when the boys came home from school. Brutey fixed dinner before coming to the football field. Norma sat at the kitchen table and wondered who this man was. As she sent him off to the high school, she was glad to have an attentive husband again, but the mystery behind his sudden change was baffling.

Before the game, Brutey helped Rod Dillon tape his ankles. While doing so, he pumped confidence in the quarterback. He reassured Rod about his instincts and the game plan they had for Kings Mills. "Just trust your reads," Brutey said. "Wouldn't surprise me if the whole game came down to a play you were involved in."

Brutey loved the look on Rod's face as he prepared for one of the biggest games on his career.

"You know, I'd give anything to trade places with you for just one night," Brutey said softly. "We didn't have football back in the fifties, and I really wish we had. I'd give anything to have the chance you have tonight, to run out under those lights and be quarterback for this team. Cherish it. It's a memory you'll have for the rest of your life."

Rod appreciated the sentiment, but he kept his game face on. "It'll be a better memory if we win," Rod said.

As the game started, we had trouble moving the football. The wet field made it difficult for receivers to run their routes, and linemen had trouble digging in to make their blocks. Defensively, though, we dominated. Testerman had as hard a time running the football as Dave Dillon did.

The game was scoreless until very late in the second period when our rejuvenated passing game, not the running game, broke the ice. After starting a drive on our own 43-yard line, Rod found Dale Midkiff for 26 yards across the middle. With a first down on the Kings 31, Rod hit Dave Collins on a slant pattern for 15 yards, giving us a first down on the 16. Coach Ross called for a play-action pass and Rod -- again selling the fake like he had done the week before -- hit Dave Vicroy, taking us down to the two. From there everyone was sure the call would go to Dave Dillon through the middle. The Kings coaches were practically jumping up and down alerting its players to that, but that's where Rod – again playing the fake perfectly -- sent

Dave into the line empty-handed. Rod then rolled left to find Dale Midkiff wide-open in the end zone for the touchdown. The two-point conversion was good, giving us an 8-0 lead early in the second quarter.

But soon thereafter, disaster struck.

Kings Mills tricked us with a fake punt. Just like us, their quarterback was also their punter, and on a fourth down he faked a punt and threw a pass to a wide out for an unexpected first down. Seconds later, quarterback Mike Clutter threw a 45-yard bomb to Charlie Smith to tie the game, 8-8.

Then things got even worse. Rod threw a sideline pass to Dave, who was viciously tackled by Don Testerman, causing him to land directly on his shoulder.

"I could hear it pop when it happened," Rod said afterward. "And Dave never moaned in pain before. But when I heard him under the pile, I knew there was a problem."

Dr. Swope tended to Dave, who was eventually carted off the field in an ambulance as the game stopped for fifteen minutes. The whole field was silent; the Springboro fans were stunned. The score was tied in the biggest game of the season, and their best running back was on his way to the Springboro Clinic. Outwardly, the players expressed confidence that they could survive Dave's injury and still pull out a victory. Privately, though, many of them had their doubts. Coach Ross inserted sophomore Mark Jozwiak into the lineup, a tough runner. A good kid. But he wasn't Dave Dillon. No one was. The game moved on.

The teams exchanged punts. Jozwiak got a few carries and showed remarkable skill at finding the open field. But one drive ended on a fumble, the next on a punt. The momentum that Springboro had early in the game was clearly gone now.

"This is our moment, fellas!" Rod shouted on the sidelines. "Who's with me? C'mon!"

Meanwhile, Dr. Swope was with Dave and his dad at the clinic. X-rays were taken and the look on Dr. Swope's face said it all. The results were gloomy, and confirmed everything that Dr. Swope had suspected – the collarbone was separated, though fortunately it was not broken.

"You're done," he told Dave. Further injury was a certainty if he continued to play. Furthermore, he would play in a lot of pain. Being a junior, it was best for Dave to sit out and rest to avoid further complication to the shoulder.

Mr. Dillon was pained at the thought of Dave's potential record-setting season coming to an end. "Are you sure?" he finally asked.

CHAPTER 20

"Sure I'm sure," Dr. Swope replied.

Mr. Dillon asked Dave how he felt.

"I'm okay," he said. "I can play." No Dillon boy would ever tell his father he couldn't do something.

Mr. Dillon looked at Dr. Swope. Then he looked back at Dave, who was looking at Dr. Swope. Finally, a decision was made. "Bandage him up and get him back in there," Mr. Dillon said.

"I don't recommend this."

"I know. I'll sign whatever I have to. Patch him up."

Dave nodded in agreement. He suited back up and came back to the game sometime in the second half, his shoulder bandaged, with the score still tied. Mr. Dillon told Coach Ross that the shoulder was merely bruised and Dave could go back in, and the Coach obliged. Jozwiak came out, and Dave went back in.

The crowd was excited to see Dave return. So were his teammates, and results followed immediately.

Rod called Dave's number right away. Like a scene out of a movie, Dave immediately did something spectacular. He cut left, turned up field, cut again to his right, and pretty soon he was gone, racing twenty-eight yards untouched for a touchdown, putting us ahead, 16-8. It was incredible. As he came off the field there were handshakes and back slaps, but there was something else, too. Dave's pain was obvious. Mr. Dillon could see it in his son's eyes.

"Okay, you're done," he said, and Dave sat out the entire fourth quarter.

It was a dramatic fourth quarter too. The light rain at the start of the game had now turned into a downpour, making it hard just to hang on to the ball. The teams fought hard back and forth, and the game clock ticked away. A tie was very possible, which was as bad as a loss to us in our attempt to catch Clinton-Massie in the conference standings. For Springboro to win, something was going to have to happen in the air.

"Dave Collins has been open all night," I said. "Rod needs to keep looking for him."

"Or use him as a decoy," Wilburn said.

"I'll bet Rod is setting them up for something," Mitch said.

We were still standing in the end zone, soaking wet, hanging on every play.

We commented on every completed pass. We discussed every upcoming situation. If someone had offered us a pass to Disney World on the spot, we would have instead stayed at the game. This was awesome.

As it turned out, the coaches were indeed setting Rod up for something big. They ran Jozwiak to the left, to the right and up the middle. Soon Kings Mills began to think Jozwiak was the only offensive weapon Springboro had. The game clock kept ticking. With a minute thirty, we had a first down near midfield and Jozwiak ran for five yards. On second down Rod attempted a curl-in to Collins, but the pass was incomplete, stopping the clock with only seconds to go. Speculation ran wild about what play would come next – a quick-pitch to Jozwiak or a pass play to Collins. Coach Hefflin was talking to Coach Smith through the headsets, and then in turn to Coach Ross. After a moment's deliberation, the play was sent in. Rod broke the huddle and Collins flanked to the left while Dave Vicroy was spread out right. We were in the I-formation. Rod called the cadence and the ball was snapped in perhaps the most important play of his life.

He went for it all.

Rod faded back, looking left towards Collins. The Kings Mills rush came hard, and John Mockabee and Brian Smith fought to keep them away. The pads popped louder than ever. Rod stepped up in the pocket and cocked his mighty right arm. He turned and threw, higher and longer than any pass I'd ever seen before, to Vicroy who was streaking down the right side. It was a tight spiral, perfectly thrown, incredible since the rain was pelting everything. From our vantage point, we could see it as if it were happening in slow motion. The pass took forever to come down, the game clock ticking away in the distance. The ball sailed high and long, despite the rain.

It landed perfectly into the outstretched arms of Vicroy, who dove for it in the end zone.

"Touchdown! Touchdown!" shouted Wilburn.

"What did I tell you?" said Mitch.

"That's the most awesome pass I've ever seen," I said.

It was the greatest pass play I ever saw. We were jumping up and down, just like everyone else from Springboro. If I ever had moments where I wondered about the goodness of life, and whether I was somehow missing out on it, moments like this changed all of that. I was on cloud nine.

We won, 24-16, avenging the loss from the year before. At midfield there was a celebration one that looked like we had won the conference championship. Amid the mud and the rain and the sweat, there were smiles all around.

Everybody went home happy that night, even though Clinton-Massie also won and secured the conference title. The win was our fifth in a row, with the season's last game at home the following week. We were playing hard and winning. What's done was done. Under the circumstances, finishing second didn't feel so bad.

The season had been salvaged.

Springboro was founded by Quakers, and there are no less than seven churches in the small area in and around Olde Springboro. One is the Springboro Christian Church, which was led by Reverend Delbert Dawes for more than thirty years. That church is across from the old high school, near where Peg Leisz (L) and Evalyn Harris once were neighbors.

CHAPTER 21

"Come to me, all you who are weary and burdened, and I will give you rest."
-- The Bible

Sunday, November 5, 1972

When he was fifteen, Brutey got into a terrible fight with his dad over what he wanted to do when he grew older. The elder Mr. Baker had worked hard all his life at Armco, a steel mill in nearby Middletown, where he earned a nice living. Naturally, he wanted Brutey to do the same thing, and he talked to his son about it all the time. After nearly a year of Armco-this and Armco-that, Brutey finally told his dad that that's not what he wanted at all. He loved sports and wanted to coach. He didn't see any satisfaction in working around the drudgery and filth of the steel mill. His opinions did not set well with his dad. They yelled at one another for more than an hour, when Brutey left the house and took off running.

In the years since then, whether it was to blow off steam and just stay in shape, Brutey did a lot of running. When he lived on State Street, he would often run on Lower Springboro Road out to Ridgeville and back. But after he and Norma moved to Market Street, he went a different way. He took Catalpa Drive to Factory Road, where he turned right in the direction of the Wade family farm. A quarter-mile later, he would turn left onto Lower Springboro Road, which would take him past Weidner Road and the Springboro Cemetery, and then back into town by the United Church of Christ on the corner beside the high school. Then he took the streets of the Royal Oaks subdivision back to his house. It was a three-mile run in all, and by its end Brutey always felt energized and refreshed. For the thirty minutes he ran, Brutey was in his own personal sanctuary. He felt that each drop of sweat that left his body was also a worry that went away.

As usual, Brutey awoke at dawn on that cool November Sunday. He hadn't slept well now for over a week. He quietly fixed his coffee and walked down the driveway to retrieve his copy of *The Dayton Daily News*. Then he went inside to read it over coffee.

He liked his coffee with cream and sugar. He toasted two pieces of bread and peppered each of them with some grape jelly. He settled in at the kitchen table and took note of how quiet the house was at that time of the morning. Why couldn't life always be so peaceful? Wouldn't it be great to never have worries or regrets? Brutey felt good about all of his football teams, and he was excited about an even more success in basketball season. Things were clicking there. But in so many other areas of his life, he felt so conflicted. The thoughts kept rumbling through his head and he found it harder and harder to make sense of them. He needed to talk to someone, he figured, and the sooner the better.

He had to keep it together. He had to act natural.

He quickly sped through the paper, thinking that his run would clear his head a little. The sports page featured Ohio State's victory over Minnesota, putting the Buckeyes at 9-1 and setting up the showdown against Michigan in two weeks. After reading that, Brutey read Si Burick's column, because Si could make any part of the sports world relevant to a man sitting in his kitchen in little Springboro, Ohio. Then he read the piece about the 7-0 Miami Dolphins, who were playing in Buffalo that day, a game that was sure to be a challenge because the Dolphins had only beaten them by a point two weeks earlier in a game played in Miami.

All was still quiet as he set foot out of the door. No sooner than he turned right onto Factory Road, he saw Ralph Wade driving in his direction, slowing down to have a word with him. Mr. Wade mocked an attempt to run into Brutey, and they both shared a laugh.

"You headed for breakfast?" Brutey asked. "Some biscuits and gravy would go down pretty well on a cool morning like today."

"As a matter of fact, I am. I'm meeting a group of people at The Diner." Mr. Wade rubbed his tired eyes, but he flashed his trademark bright smile. "It feels normal to be up and at 'em through the week, but it feels awfully early on Sunday. I think I could have used a little more sleep."

"No rest for the weary," Brutey responded. "Who are you out helping this morning?"

"That family over on Market Street, the one right near your house as a matter of fact. They lost their daughter about a week ago and the guy who killed her just took off. It's just such a tragedy. Some guy ran left of center and ran her off the road – probably because he was drunk or something -- and then took off and left her to die. Two little girls in the car, too. The folks I'm meeting with this morning are going through an awful time. Just awful."

Brutey said he had heard people talk about the accident, and it was a terrible shame. The Richmonds had been his neighbors for years, and they were in shock. They hadn't been out of the house but a couple of times since the accident. He looked down at his running shoes. He kicked the rocks near his feet. "Any leads on the guy who did it?"

Mr. Wade shook his head. "I was talking to Charlie and Jimmy yesterday afternoon. Not a clue." He put his car in gear, indicating it was time to drive away. "If there was something I could do about that, I'd do it in a heartbeat. That fella' deserves to be taken out by the woodshed and beaten half to death."

No argument there. The driver was a scoundrel of the worst kind. Brutey took off running as Mr. Wade drove away.

* * *

Ralph Wade was Mr. Springboro, and was often regarded as its unofficial mayor. He loved being in the middle of everything around town, especially the sporting events, which he'd been involved with ever since settling in Springboro twenty years earlier. As a result, everyone knew him and had benefited from the things he'd done.

Mr. Wade actually graduated in 1944 from nearby Franklin High School, an arch-rival of Springboro's, where he played football with Jack and Lou Tracy, among others, and helped make the Wildcats a formidable team. He was a tenacious player who loved the aggressiveness of football, and the teamwork it required. Those were attributes that later carried over later into his business dealings. He came to Springboro and opened an insurance office in 1962 near the IGA, building his agency by working long hours and making connections. He sponsored teams and had a hand in running nearly every organization – namely Little League baseball and peewee football. He was also president of the school board, and was part of a group of men who funded and then built the football field. He had done all of this and was still only 45 years old. It seemed Mr. Wade never slept.

The Wade family farm was a twenty-acre tract west of town out on Factory Road, which was a working farm. His four children – Ed, Sandy, Dan and Ann – rose early and did chores before school each day, milking cows and feeding horses in the early morning chill. But life for them was not all work. They had free reign to ride horses all through the countryside, which for many years included all the land that later comprised Royal Oaks subdivision. Until 1959, when construction began on the homes in my neighborhood, virtually all of Springboro was countryside.

Mr. Wade was also fiercely protective of his home and family. For example, one day some vagrants showed up near his home. There were two of them, strangers to Springboro, and they had somehow drifted just outside of town near the farm. Mr. Wade, who was in the front yard tending to some of his bushes, knew something was up the moment he saw the car.

"What brings you out this way?" Mr. Wade asked them.

It was not a question designed to stimulate a friendly conversation. Don't mess with me, he was saying. I know you're not from these parts, and I want to know what brings you here.

No answer.

"I said, 'what brings you out this way?'"

The strangers looked at one another. Still no answer.

This was not an acceptable response. If they weren't going to answer the question voluntarily, then he'd have to find another way. He had a buckshot rifle that he kept handy. And he wasn't afraid to use it.

That's what he did on this occasion. As the two men scrambled for cover, Mr. Wade grabbed his shotgun. As the vagrants hurriedly put the car in gear, Mr. Wade took aim. Before they got very far down the road, Mr. Wade fired several rounds into the side of their car. Thanks for stopping by, fellas. Here's a little something to remember me by. Boom!

Not surprisingly, they never came back.

It was small town justice at its finest. When I first heard the story as a kid I never thought anything of it. It was a sign of the times. A man had a right to defend his home and his family. And no one protected his home and family better than Mr. Wade.

CHAPTER 21

The farm was a hangout for all the teenagers around town when his kids were in school. Sandy, the oldest, was a good student who went on to major in education. She has been principal of the Clearcreek Elementary, the Springboro Elementary and now the Dennis Elementary School over the past two decades. Oldest son Ed and younger son Danny were both talented athletes, with Ed serving as the second quarterback in school history, behind Tim Kirkpatrick, who was also a school board member's son. After varsity games and on warm summer night, guys went over to the two-story barn behind their house to talk and laugh and relive each play of the games. There were few other places to go in the mid-sixties, unless guys wanted to go to Middletown. The barn had an indoor basketball hoop that was the site of countless pick-up games. Plus it also had ten thousand bales of hay inside it, plenty to build an elaborate corn maze inside it.

"We used to have a blast there," Ed Wade remembered.

Ed spent many warm autumn nights as a teenager lying out in the middle of Factory Road, which was often desolate because it was way out in the country. With the warmth of the road on their backs, he and his friends would look up at the glory of the stars, wondering exactly where they eventually led. There was never a worry that a car would come by to disturb them. It was small town fun at its finest, the kind of stuff that couldn't be done in the big city.

When the children graduated and went off to college and then married, Mr. Wade stayed in Springboro, continuing to do all that public service he had always done. He went to all the games, partly because of his community activism but also partly because no dad who had ever followed his boy through a varsity season ever stayed away after his boy graduated. There was new talent to evaluate and old memories to rehash.

But, through it all, he always found someone in need. And he did something about it.

* * *

Mr. Wade's breakfast meeting ended with his promise to meet with as many police officers as he could to push the search for Janet's killer. Mr. Wade also contributed to a memorial fund in Janet's memory. And for all of that Bob and Hazel Richmond said all the usual things. Thanks so much. How can we ever repay you? You are such a valued member of the Springboro community. Mr. Wade humbly brushed all the comments aside and wished them well until they met again.

Then it was time for church. Janet's parents went to the Methodist Church, and Brutey and Norma – as they had done for several weeks now -- went to listen to Reverend Dawes at the Springboro Christian Church. Norma had temporarily put the divorce on hold.

As for my football teammates and me, we were the special guests of Pepper Dill and his father at the Springboro Baptist Church. His father said he wanted to recognize us in front of his congregation. Personally, I think he wanted to see if any of us knew how to shower and dress up.

We arrived promptly at ten, and the bunch of us gathered in a corner of the reception hall. Since my brother John and I were Catholic, I secretly worried that God would zap me if I walked into a Baptist church. But I was assured that the only zapping in a Baptist church was by the preacher, not God. And that kind of made me feel better, I think. It was stuff like that that made me stay away from church.

The service started on time, and we sat through four songs, all of them about fifteen minutes long with stanzas that all seemed to say the same thing. Then Pastor Dill delivered a passionate sermon about the decisions we make in life. He said we were confronted with them every day, from something as minor as what clothes to put on to something as major as how we choose to live our lives. Ultimately, we all have to make a decision about whether to live our lives by our own strength and understanding, or whether to allow God to lead us. He talked about times in his own life when life was particularly difficult, and many times it became even more so because he strayed from the principles found in the Bible. Then, when life was about to get really ugly, he swallowed his pride and humbly surrendered to its teachings, and soon life was better. We all faced similar decisions, he said, and God gives us the freedom to choose. Ever the renegade, I opted to choose Buffalo over the Miami Dolphins that afternoon.

Finally, after what seemed like hours, our football team was introduced. We stood up and turned around as our name was called. Then there was clapping. I felt as though I had done something really important, like score a touchdown or make a game-saving tackle. I only wished that Debbie Balyo had gone to that church. She'd have been so impressed seeing me in that big purple tie that practically swallowed my whole head.

Pepper's dad closed with a warm thought. "I've watched these boys practice and play for the past three months, and they really worked hard. More importantly, they're a great bunch of young men, the kind of men that will make this community proud." In unison every one of us stuck our chest out and grinned.

"May God bless each one of you boys."

We stayed afterward and had fried chicken, mashed potatoes and green beans, with some of the best lemonade I'd ever tasted. We topped it off with some chocolate cream pie. The entire Dill family thanked us for coming to their church, and welcomed us back any time we wanted.

Hmmm, football and great food. I decided I could go to that kind of church every week.

* * *

Around the corner at the Springboro Christian Church, Reverend Dawes preached about the integrity that every Christ-follower was called to demonstrate. "Jesus had chances to lie, but he never did. He had opportunities to look the other way, but he always stayed and helped. If we call ourselves disciples of Jesus Christ, then we are called to model the same behavior he did. So, I'm asking you this question this morning, are you modeling that same behavior? Or are you keeping secrets?"

His congregation hung on every word. Brutey and Norma sat in the back left side of the church, where they had sat for the second straight Sunday. Once again, Brutey felt like every word was directed at him. He wondered if Reverend Dawes followed him around all week and knew what he was doing. More importantly, he wondered if somehow the Reverend knew what he was thinking. Did he say "secrets?" Boy did that hit the mark. There were the usual secrets about a particular thought or action, something that presented no real problem, but at the moment there big secrets he was keeping. Was it enough just to confess it to God? Was he required to do something more? The thoughts weighed heavily on his mind.

Reverend Dawes saved his most poignant words for the end. "We all reach a time in our lives when we are at a crossroads," he said. "We face a choice: either we stay the way we have been and watch our lives slowly erode, little by little, and we lose the respect of the people in our lives. Or, we change direction. We embrace a new way of living, the way Jesus calls us to do, and we find a freedom we never felt before. We're more alive than ever. And in the process we make a larger impact on the people who are around us."

Now Brutey's mind was swimming. What should he do? Was there anyone who would understand? What would happen if someone were to know? Surely there were some secrets better kept.

The service closed with the traditional alter call, and several people went forward to dedicate their lives to the call Reverend Dawes talked about. In the previous week, Brutey looked around to see who else was at the church service. But on this morning, he had his head bowed and his eyes closed. Norma could see his lips moving. The words were not audible but it was clear what Brutey was doing. And the sight of it perplexed her all the more.

Brutey Baker, the man who never believed in church, was praying.

CHAPTER 22

A final time in uniform, a final hit and a final pass, and a final time in a huddle of teammates and friends...as a football career ends
--The feeling

FRIDAY, NOVEMBER 10, 1972

At six-thirty, our pilgrimage to the football field began. From our front doors, we could hear the band and see the lights in the distance. Regardless of where we lived in the subdivision, the music that filled the air served as a beacon to guide us to the game. My brothers and I started out on Redbud, where we soon caught up with the Wray kids – Bert, Sharon, Janet and Steve -- down the street. Once on Kesling we saw some of the Jozwiaks (Cindy, Matt and Greg, that is, no way we'd ever see ALL the Jozwiaks together at the same time), and on Factory we saw Otis Baty and the Swope boys. All of us were walking. There was no other option.

It was Senior Night, the last football game of the year. Players and cheerleaders took the field for the very last time, one after another, and they were introduced as they walked with one or both parents on each arm. Though it was regarded as a celebration, there was also sadness to it. All the years of practicing together, riding buses and celebrating victories was coming to an end.

There were six varsity cheerleaders – Captain Sandy Lawson, Robin Sharp, Vicki Ramey, Kathy Manning, Kathy England and Pam Hepp, the Homecoming queen who dated Rod. When they walked across the field and their names were called, I saw tears in their eyes. The same could be seen with their mothers.

Then the players were introduced: Steve Rottert ... Ed Sullivan ... Mike Colvin ... and many more. Then there was the guy known to everyone as Hog.

John "Hog" Mockabee, a senior tackle, number seventy-five, was a crowd favorite. He was not only a good football player, but he was also a good person, polite and sincere, a gentle giant that belied his nickname. He had lived his whole life in Springboro, having grown up in the small family house in Ridgeville east of town, as the fifth of Tom and Martha Mockabee's eight children. His walk across the field that night at Senior Night culminated a Springboro football career that began in the fifth grade.

"John Mockabee," announced Ray Perez, and the crowd cheered. In full pads, Big John was even bigger than usual. The parents beside him, the two people he always looked up to in life, suddenly didn't look very big by comparison. It was hard to believe he would never play football for Springboro again.

John's football career began in elementary school when E.B. Smith recruited a team to play in a traveling league. His size made him the perfect lineman, but ironically his size held him back in some of those games. "We went to Cincinnati one day to play a game and I was told that four of my guys were too big to play," Mr. Smith recalled. "John was one of them. He'd worked hard all week in practice, and it liked to kill me to go tell him he couldn't play." The maximum weight was one hundred thirty-five pounds; John weighed one sixty-five in the sixth grade.

The Mockabee house was the site of many pickup football and basketball games, beginning in the mid-sixties when older brother Bob frequently had all the starters on the state finalist basketball team over to the house. And John and younger brother Chuck and their Ridgeville friends occasionally rode into town and played against O.J. Powers and others, becoming known as the "Ridgeville Rugrats."

Starting in seventh grade, John played on the school football and basketball teams, starting in both. Then he quit playing basketball after ninth grade so he could focus on throwing the shot put. The track event became another of his passions, and he used the winter months to lift weights and run the steps at school in order to get his legs in better shape. By the time he was in high school, John started at right tackle on the football team and threw shot put and the discus for Coach Hefflin's track team.

He earned honors for his play in football, but he made it all the way to the state track meet for the shot put. It was at the state meet that John experienced one of the biggest highlights of his career. The highlight was a handshake, of all things. As John warmed up, an imposing figure walked across the field in his white shirt and black Ohio State hat. He smiled and spoke with everyone. "I always like to meet the big guys," he said, "because I'm always on the lookout for somebody who's agile and strong. If any of you are interested in coming to Ohio State, I'd be happy to talk with you." And the man extended his hand.

The man was Woody Hayes, the legendary football coach of the Buckeyes. When he told Brutey about that meeting later, Brutey practically wet his pants. Meeting Coach Hayes was always his dream.

John had grown up with an appreciation for good coaches and excellent players. Sports always meant a lot. When the backyard games were finished for the night, his family would often lounge under one of the old shady trees and listen to the Reds on WLW. Everyone knew the Reds players, and their opponent, plus the significance of the game in the league standings. Meanwhile, there may still be a game of horseshoes going on in the pits nearby.

Many summer nights he drove to the K & W to sit and talk and listen to the radio, and when it closed they all went to the high school parking lot, where they were often met by officers Charlie Reedy, Richard Wiseman and Jimmy Beavers, and they would talk and listen to music until late in the evening.

As he took the field against Madison to play his last football game ever in a Springboro uniform, John Mockabee knew he had given it everything he had. It had been enjoyable, and there had been success. More than anything, he knew he would miss it.

* * *

Madison didn't have a chance. Dick Mahan returned a punt for a touchdown. Mark Jozwiak ran 11 yards for one touchdown, and returned a punt 40 yards to set up another. Meanwhile, Madison was held to under 100 yards in total offense as we completed a season giving up only 92 points all year. A number of season school records were set – Rod had the most completions, Dave Collins had the most receiving yards and Dale Midkiff caught the most passes. We won hands down, 30-0.

Dave Dillon, broken collar bone and all, suited up for a valiant attempt to set the school rushing record, set years earlier by Jerry Raffel. Through three quarters, he had carried the ball nineteen times for 106 yards, giving him 1,126 for the season – just yards short of the record. But when he came back after every run, it was obvious to every guy in the huddle how much he was hurting.

He ran off Big John's right tackle for thirteen yards as the third quarter came to an end. He limped back to the huddle, teeth grinding, with his fist clenched. He was a gutsy, tough player, and he was determined to go as long as he could.

Finally, big brother Rod laid it out for him. "Dave, it's not worth it, bud," he said.

Dave didn't argue with him, so he left the game. Being a junior, he still had another year to set the record.

The horn finally sounded and the players shook hands with one another. Then they retired to the locker room as the fans, slowly but surely, made their way from their seats to their cars. Several of the clean-up crew began picking up the loose paper strewn around, and before long the lights were turned off for the last time that season.

As the players dressed, Coach Ross went around the room offering handshakes and words of encouragement. They didn't win the conference championship, but by season's end they proved to themselves and their community that they could play good, solid, excellent football. It had been a good season and it would always hold a special place in his thoughts. He would always regard these players as a special group of kids.

The players eventually dressed and poured out in the parking lot, with the celebration continuing. Many would get in their cars for the drive to Frisch's for the continuation of the post-game celebration. Somebody had a Rolling Stones song going full blast. Pam Hepp was waiting by Rod's car so they could go out on the town together.

Hog Mockabee got into his 1965 powder blue Grand Prix, wincing as he brought his injured left knee into the car. Tomorrow his body would be black and blue, as it was the day after every game, but he wouldn't mind. His body would heal and the pain would eventually go away. But the memories of playing football would stay with him forever, and they were good memories. He adjusted this rear-view mirror and then stopped for a second to look at the shadows that were cast in the direction of the empty football field. The sights and sounds of his high school career were now but a memory.

He drove away.

* * *

Brutey spent the evening watching from the sidelines. He had a few words for some of the players, but nothing more. The game was a blowout from the start, and besides, Brutey wasn't in a festive mood. The thoughts that had plagued him during Reverend Dawes' sermon continued to weigh on him, and he was to the point where something had to give.

He felt some temporary relief amid the post-game celebration. Though they were only second in the conference, they finished the season as one of the best teams in the area. Everybody wanted one more game. Maybe another after that. This team was in such high gear it believed it could whip anybody.

"Thanks, Coach," Rod Dillon told him, extending his right hand.

Brutey smiled and accepted the handshake. It was an act more satisfying than receiving any paycheck he could have been written.

He loved football. He loved these players.

He wanted more than anything to stay and savor the moment. He was in the Panther locker room, surrounded by some great guys, and celebrating a season-ending win. Aside from his wedding day and the birth of his two boys, this feeling was the greatest on earth. He didn't want it to end.

But life brings surprises sometimes. And that's not always a good thing.

* * *

They sat at the kitchen table just as Johnny Carson came on television. The boys were in bed and the only light was from the television in the next room. Surprisingly, Brutey found he was remarkably calm. It confirmed that he was doing the right thing.

But Norma didn't like the conversation at all. "You're kidding," she said. "You? I can't believe it." Then she started to sob.

Brutey shared with Norma the secret he had been carrying for weeks. It explained why he was suddenly focused on their relationship and time with the boys. It had nothing to do with her seeing a lawyer and filing for a divorce. Instead, it had everything to do with his own behavior.

"I have to come clean on this," Brutey said. "It's killing me inside. I've made all sorts of mistakes in my life, especially with you and the boys, and now I've gone and done this and it's pushed me over the edge."

Norma wasn't sure what to say. "So going to church, coming home early, paying attention to me and the boys – "

"All that started the day after all this happened."

Norma did the math. She had been curious for quite some time, and deep down she had known that the abrupt change had been caused by something wrong. She had had her suspicions. Now she knew it was true.

"So what do we do?" he asked, not sure where the plan took them beyond disclosure.

Norma wasn't so sure. She didn't know whether to walk out or reach out. Part of her wanted to strangle Brutey, the other wanted to hug him for telling the truth. Brutey's disclosure ran deep, and she didn't know what to do. She decided privately that she would call her lawyer on Monday morning.

Then they'd go from there.

* * *

For being such a young franchise, it was amazing that the Cincinnati Bengals were already in a Super Bowl. But they were, and coach Paul Brown had told the media all week long that his team wasn't just there for show. They came to win. Across the way were Bud Grant and the Minnesota Vikings, the best team in football.

Late in the fourth quarter, the Vikings were leading, 38-33, in what had proven to be the most exciting Super Bowl ever. That was a fact that the TV announcers, Curt Gowdy and Al DeRogatis, mentioned time and time again. Nationwide, millions of people were watching.

"The Bengals have three minutes to go and they have the ball on their own 32-yard line."

"Curt, the Bengals have plenty of time. They still have two timeouts. So they can afford to run the ball a few times with Archie Griffin. That way they can set up the pass…Anderson is under center. Their go-to guy, Jeff Kirby, is flanked to the bottom of your screen. He's caught nineteen passes today for over two hundred yards and all five Cincinnati touchdowns. It's been an amazing effort. He's been triple covered all day long."

CHAPTER 22

The ball was snapped and Anderson handed off to Griffin around left end. The crowd cheered as he rounded the corner and gained thirteen yards before he was run out of bounds, stopping the clock. The announcers were impressed. "Did you see that block Kirby threw? I'm telling you, if Cincinnati goes on to win this ball game, there's no question about who their MVP is."

With two minutes, thirty-one seconds left, the Bengals have a first down on their own forty. "Kirby is lined up as a wide-out at the top of your screen. It looks like the Vikings are showing blitz –"

"—Watch for Anderson to look for Kirby going long then."

"Anderson takes the snap, steps up to avoid Alan Page and Carl Eller, he's looking long! There it is! Kirby's beat his man! Touchdown! Touchdown! The Cincinnati Bengals have …"

The Cincinnati Bengals have…Bengals have….

And soon I was fast asleep. Football season may have been over, but the dreams continued. This time Mrs. Kuhn couldn't disturb it, either.

Kneeling — From Left to Right — Gene Anspach, Barry Glass, Steve Hoefler, Doug Gephart. Standing — From Left to Right — Bruce Smith, Daryl Jackson, Dale Kearns, Glenn Jackson, Coach Gerald Saunders, Bob Mockabee, Mike Blevins, George Burkhart, Denny Kearns.

Long-time Springboro residents remember Jimmy Hough, who was like a coach on the basketball court, shown here finding the open man from an unlikely position. Or they remember even further back, when the '65 team electrified the town by going to the state tournament.

HOT DOG

PART 2

CHAPTER 23

Thirty-five years later, the memories of Coach Hall and that '72-73 team are as fresh as if the action just occurred – does anyone else remember them, too?
-- A personal reflection

A BASKETBALL FRIDAY NIGHT

JANUARY 6, 2006

From his customary spot at the top of the gymnasium, way behind the home bench, he still coached the game.

"Inside to the big man! Inside to Ballard! Come on, fellas, this time next year he'll be playing at Ohio State. Give him his due." Time was winding down in a classic battle between two schools that were fast becoming big rivals, whose coaches were the best of friends. For the past three years Mike Holweger and Troy Holtrey coached together at Springboro. Now Holweger was head coach at Lebanon. And the Warriors were giving the Panthers fits in a very close game.

"Pick up your man! Watch him going left!" Brutey roared at Springboro guard Andy Ungerman like he'd known him his whole life.

"All right, way to go! Now you're doing it right!" Holweger called timeout as Springboro clung to a slim lead with only two minutes remaining.

Once a coach, always a coach. There was a time when Brutey Baker's seat was down on the bench. He wore a shirt and tie, as all coaches used to do back then. He'd have his clipboard in hand, his arm wrapped around a player discussing a particular situation, and his face glowing with a smile. He would point and clap and mark down statistics that would come in handy during halftime. He would do all of this and pay no attention to the cheerleaders, the talkative parents and the line toward the concession stand. And then, two hours later, he would sit in the locker room, hoarse from all the yelling. His scratchy voice would congratulate names like Charlton and Leisz and Hough and Howard. And he would go home a happy man.

"I can still see that old gym that was such a magic place," he said during the timeout. "Boy, we had some good games there. Remember the home win against Waynesville in '65? George Burkhart had such a touch. Then, years later, Russ Spicer was such a great ball handler. And there were nights I swear I thought Jeff Howard was going to jump through the roof." He would say these things and look off in the distance, oblivious to the world around him.

"Those were some awesome days, all right. When there was a basketball game on a Friday night, nothing else happened in this town. Walk down Main Street and you could hear a pin drop. Then go anywhere around town and people were talking basketball. Kids played ball in the park all through the winter, no matter how cold it got."

He was interrupted. "Things change, man. We've talked about that."

"Oh, you ain't a kidding. You know what's a rare sight around here anymore? Some vacant land. Everywhere you look they're building a house or a restaurant anymore. Remember years ago that you didn't know you were in Springboro until you got to the corner of Central and Main? Remember that? Nothing north until you got to the Mall, and nothing west until you got to Franklin. And Waynesville seemed like a million miles away.

"Now, shoot, they've developed all the land. Interest rates went through the floor and the builders came along and ate up all the fields and green grass. Pretty soon the whole town will be a pile of concrete. I miss my small little town."

The timeout ended and Lebanon in bounded from underneath the Springboro basket. This game was going to be decided in the final seconds, and the capacity crowd was on its feet. The teams traded baskets, keeping the score within one point, and then with forty seconds left, Troy Holtrey called his final timeout. The tension in the air was as thick as Smokey Mountain fog. Brutey continued talking.

"You were born for the sidelines, weren't you?" I responded. "Years ago, I'd see you down there next to Coach Hall, shouting instructions and analyzing the game. That was always in your blood, so it has to be tough sitting up here far away from the action."

CHAPTER 23

He grimaced. "That's not what makes sitting up here so difficult. What's hard is I have to hear all these parents yap about what's wrong with everything. Crimany, you'd think this team hadn't won a game all season. This set of parents complain because we set up in a zone, then a few minutes later this other set of parents complain because we're in man-to-man. We're up fifteen against an undefeated team and to hear some of these folks you'd think we were losing to a team that hadn't won all year."

"It's been that way forever, Brutey. It was the same back when you were coaching."

"Yeah, but it's gotten worse since then. Everybody's a critic anymore and no one hesitates to just spit out what they are feeling, no matter how destructive their comments may be. You know what I mean? I blame all those dang talk shows and TV shows where anybody with a microphone is suddenly an expert and they generate all their ratings by questioning the talents of everybody who's actually doing something. Ever listen on those programs? 'This coach should have done this and that player should have done that.' As if it's not the easiest thing in the world and sit back after something's happened and second-guess the decision that was made. Everything's backwards anymore. Sometimes I'd like to have my own show where all I do is poke fun at the talking heads and let them get a taste of their own medicine."

The Panthers broke the huddle and took the floor. Just then, Mike Holweger called a timeout. The plot thickened.

"When I played back in the 'fifties, I don't remember any parents giving my coach a hard time," Brutey said. "It just wasn't done. Mom and Dad knew that the coach had training and experience, and so they let him do his job. Sure, they had opinions, but I don't ever remember a time when my parents, or anyone else's, would come up to him to complain about the way he was doing everything.

"Coach Hough was a good man. One day I looked at a scrapbook that had all of his records and game highlights. It's easy to play for a man who knows what he's talking about. I tried to be just like him years later when I coached his son."

Then he added, "Of course, Jimmy was so good he didn't need anyone to take care of him."

Jim Hough, Jr., who was also known to some as Jimmy, was a three-year starter in the early seventies. He was a captain and starting guard on the '72-'73 team. When Brutey coached kids my age back in those days, he always told us to watch Jimmy's technique. He always shot jump shots with his shoulders square to the basket. He always dribbled with his head up. He knew where everyone was on the floor, and where they should be. "No sooner would I jump up to tell him something, and then I would see him already doing it," Brutey said. "He was amazing that way."

Brutey saw all the guards come through since then, but he wasn't sure any of them fully compared with Jimmy. "Some of them were great ball handlers, some of them passed well, and others were excellent shooters. I can't say any of them had the whole package like he did. That's why Jimmy was so much fun to watch."

Play resumed as Ungerman dribbled around the perimeter, looking to take as much time off the clock as possible. Holtrey was on his feet, shouting instructions, making it clear that he did not want a shot taken too soon.

That triggered a new line of conversation with Brutey, one that always brought a smile to his face. He loved Springboro's newest basketball coach. He thought Troy Holtrey was amazing. He was involved with the whole program, from seventh grade on up, so that all the kids knew his style of play. The younger kids saw the varsity winning and it made them work harder to get to that level one day. Holtrey's teams kept on winning.

"Twenty years ago, you'd have never dreamed we'd be the powerhouse we are. When Harry stepped down, we had a lot of good coaches – Coach Hefflin, Kevin Kirkpatrick, and Harry Krohn – but no one really took us to the next level. Then they brought that Collins fella' in, and it just wasn't the right fit. He was too intense for this level. I mean, kids need to be pushed – God knows they do, especially now – but he went a little far, don't you think? This town wasn't ready for anyone like him. I'm not sure anyone was."

Don Ross, who was in his final years of teaching, was brought in to help repair the program's image. And he did the excellent job everyone expected. But then Holtrey took over and the basketball program took off. Cain Daliboa's team made it to the Regionals in '95-'96. Later, a team with Seth Daliboa and Chip James, among others, made a mockery of the Mid-Miami League, the much bigger and supposedly better league than the FAVC. And after that, the '02-'03 team made it to the Regionals once again. And along the way there were MML championships and accolades galore.

"You can say what you want to about talent, how a coach can't win without talent. And that's true. But let me tell you something: talent don't grow on trees. The best thing Troy does is take some kids in eighth and ninth grade and work with them and make them something better than anyone ever thought. Troy knows the value of junior high and freshmen basketball. He knows the value of those coaches, and so he gets good ones and keeps them. That, my friend, is how you build a program."

CHAPTER 23

Springboro missed its final shot. But Jake Ballard, the dominating presence inside at six-foot-seven, was there for the tip-in. The play down the stretch was a frenzied panic, with Lebanon desperate for a good final shot. But it never came, and Springboro won the game, 44-43. The two coaches embraced at midcourt, knowing they had just endured the best of what high school basketball had to offer. Lebanon vowed to beat Springboro in the rematch at their place a month later.

"Brutey, why don't you coach now?" I asked. "There's nothing stopping you. You still know the game, you still have a passion for it, and now with your boys grown and out of the house – they are out of the house, right?"

"Yeah."

"Good. With the boys gone, you have all the time in the world. I'll bet Norma would be glad to see you out a little more."

He chuckled. We both knew that was true.

"Troy's got a good crew. There wouldn't be any place for me. I'd be getting in the middle of a situation that already works; all I would do is mess it up."

I held my ground, though. "Who says you have to coach high school or junior high? I'm just saying coaching is in your blood. I've seen you do it. You love the kids and you love the game. I just feel part of you is never really alive until you get back to doing what you do best."

He turned and looked at me. He scowled a little, but I could tell he seriously considered what I said. He was just looking for the right words. "There's more to it than that. I mean, there was a reason I quit coaching in the first place. I did a terrible thing, and I paid a big price for it. I just don't think this town is ready to forgive me for that."

I said I understood his reservations. "But it seems to me that a very wise man I know spends an awful lot of time grumbling about how times have changed. And if that's true, then maybe this town has long since forgotten what you did. Just like it seems to have forgotten what a nice quiet walk down Main Street seems like."

That felt like check mate. Brutey had no place to go.

He thought about that as he told me the rest of the story.

CHAPTER 24

Be more concerned with your character than your reputation because your character is what you really are, while your reputation is merely what others think you are.
-- The Wizard of Westwood
John Wooden
UCLA basketball coach

WEDNESDAY, NOVEMBER 15, 1972

The football gear was tucked away to the back of the closet, where it could gather dust for another year. The jersey had more grass stains on the sleeves than before, plus a new rip around the collar. The cleats were grass-stained and muddy, kept for safekeeping even though I would surely outgrow them in a year. Don't ask me why I hadn't thrown away the mouthpiece, which was all mangled and dirty. It's a good thing Mom never looked in my closet.

In its place, the basketball gear came out of the closet, all brand-new and ready for the season ahead. Shorts and T-shirts and wristbands, all in matching Panther colors, were ready for sweat stains. My socks were the long tube socks, one pair all white and another with blue stripes at the top. I couldn't be cool without them. But the crown jewel was the hallmark of all Springboro basketball players – Converse Chuck Taylor high-top tennis shoes, white in color. Among the many rules head coach Harry Hall had implemented for the entire program, which included us seventh-graders, wearing these babies was among the top. At the steep price of $17 a pair, it took me a while to save up enough money to buy them.

CHAPTER 24

The freshness of fall was giving way to the brutal cold of winter. Leaves were falling and frost was accumulating. That meant one thing – basketball was in the air.

A kid growing up in Springboro comes to know that early on. That's because basketball was *the* sport in town.

The final school bell of the day rang at 3:05 and it was the sweetest sound in the whole wide world. With no varsity game to look forward to, it had been a long week – and it was only Wednesday. It was made more difficult knowing that basketball try-outs started on Saturday. Even Mitch and Donny, the best players in the whole seventh grade, were nervous. The rest of us were beyond nervous. The experience made sitting in Mrs. Kuhn's class seem like a piece of cake.

Some of us thought an after-school shooting session would ease the jitters. Brutey had opened the gym for us the night before, and that had been a great workout, but with all this nervous energy inside us, we needed more. So we locked our books away in our lockers for the evening and made our way to the gym. Mitch was there, and Lance and Turkey, Roger and Donny. Others would follow. As we got to the bottom of the steps of the junior high wing (I never got near the senior high wing again, thanks to the crappy sophomores), Shane Hatfield was shouting for us to wait up, and almost immediately he and Donny started jawing at one another. Then Kruer entered the fray and the scene was almost a certifiable riot. As usual, I just listened.

"Kruer, you could build a house with the way you shoot free throws," Mitch kidded. "Brick city, man."

"Ha! That takes a lot of guts for you to say," Danny shot back. "Is that your hair on top of your head or did a crazy clown throw up on your head?"

Donny doubled over laughing. "I was just thinking that Hatfield here dribbles about the same way he runs a football. How many steps are you allowed anyway, Shane? Three or four?"

"Yeah, this from the guy who'd kick his mom's butt if she didn't block for him."

The other kids who weren't playing basketball walked and talked their way out the doors for the walk home. The Clearcreek Elementary School across the street was emptying out, too. The K & W would be packed in a matter of minutes. From there, kids would separate and go off in all the directions around the subdivision. Only a few kids we knew took the bus.

"Hey, Mitch, do you know this difference between a Hatfield and a puppy?"

Donny asked, with Shane in obvious earshot.

"Now don't be starting that crap again," Shane fired back.

"The puppy is cute and lovable," Donny laughed.

"Yeah, and it can kick the butt of anyone named Wilburn."

"Ooh, must be a bulldog puppy," Donny retorted, and laughed again.

We walked past the cafeteria and around the corner towards the gym. The band room was on our right and the girls' locker room on the left. When we opened the gym doors, we abruptly realized that we wouldn't be playing any basketball that afternoon. At least not in that gym anyway.

That was okay, though because what we got to watch instead was much, much better.

* * *

One night over the summer, Brutey saw a bunch of us playing basketball at the park near his house. Being a coach, not to mention a former basketball player for Springboro, he came out for a while and showed us the proper form for a jump shot. This went on for about an hour, until we were all thirsty, so Brutey took us up to Lawson's Market for something to drink and then we sat around the park listening to all of his basketball stories. He played for the Panthers in the mid fifties and had been a coach ever since, so he had seen all the good players. He told us about Jim Hough Sr.'s two big free throws to win a game in the late forties. He saw every one of the tournament games when the '65 team went to state. And he was excited about what the current varsity team could accomplish in the coming winter.

We soaked in all the information. We couldn't wait for basketball. There was no greater thrill in our town than starting for the basketball team. The reason for that was simple. While Springboro had an interest and enthusiasm about football, especially in recent years, that enthusiasm did not reach the same level that the town had for its basketball teams. The town went absolutely crazy over basketball. There was always standing room only for the home games, with late-comers turned away. A caravan of trucks and cars followed the team to the away games, and basketball was the hot topic at The Diner, at the K & W, at the grocery and in lunchrooms all over. Nearby Franklin was generally considered a football town, but Springboro was obviously a basketball town.

CHAPTER 24

There were a couple of reasons for this. For starters, football was still relatively new in Springboro, having only been started seven years earlier, in 1965. But the other reason had to do with flat-out wins and losses. While football had its share of wins, the basketball program had been far more successful over a much longer period of time. We were coming off a championship season from the '71-'72 season, the second conference championship since Coach Harry Hall took over the program in 1967. And the town was still talking about the '65 team that went to the state finals, which was far and away the most successful Panther basketball team ever.

I had neighbors who went to every game that season, and teachers who could still remember the scores. Though I was not yet five when that team was making town history, I still remember the decorations around town and the parade that sent them off to Columbus. Brutey talked about that team all the time, saying it embodied both the talent and the work ethic that every team should aspire to possess. Of course, he was an integral part in the development of some of the team's major players, or so he told us.

That team had a starting five that had no weaknesses. Mike Blevins, a junior, was a six-five, two hundred-twenty-pound center, who was as big as anyone had ever seen. He combined the physical strength of Wilt Chamberlain and the delicate touch of Jerry West. He was joined up front by Glenn Jackson, a senior six-three forward, who was strong and aggressive, and Bob Mockabee, another senior, who played much taller than he was because of his leaping ability. The guards were George Burkhart, an excellent outside shooter, and Dale Kearns, a hard-working point guard who was like the team's spark plug. Both of them were seniors, too.

They played well throughout the regular season, winning the Warren County championship, but they really caught fire in the Class A post-season tournament, winning five games before losing their final game in Columbus. The success made celebrities out of the players. Their future plans were the topic of much discussion. The task of living up to their standards became the challenge of every Springboro team ever since.

Blevins went on to play guard for the University of Jacksonville, which ultimately advanced to the Final Four, largely because of a center named Artis Gilmore. Kearns went to college and was back in Springboro as the jayvee basketball coach. And Bob Mockabee had plans to go to Ohio Northern on a basketball scholarship.

Like all the Springboro teams, their picture was hung in the corridor outside the south entrance to the gymnasium. None of the teams had been looked at and talked about more than that one. It would forever stand out as one of Springboro's best.

But the '72-'73 was a contender for that distinction. They were experienced, solid, and competitive. Almost every newspaper had predicted that we would win the conference championship, a prediction Coach Hall publicly downplayed because he feared the consequences. No coach ever downplayed the future success of his team any better than Harry Hall. We often joked that he could take over the UCLA Bruins, winners of ten national championships, and somehow predict they would be lucky to win more than half of their games.

"You sure it's okay that we sit here?" I asked, looking around. "Coach isn't going to like a bunch of kids in here."

Mitch put my mind at ease. "We're not just a bunch of kids anymore, Jeff. We're part of this program."

I practically laughed out loud. They were the varsity, the guys who were the talk of the town. We were a bunch of kids in sweatshirts, jeans and tennis shoes, with a dollar in our pocket for a milkshake at the K & W. There wasn't anyone around town paying money to come watch me play.

"Okay, if you say so," I told Mitch. But for good measure I squatted down instead of sitting. That way I could fly out of there if Coach Hall buzzed us out of there.

Jim Hough and Gary Patton were the guards. Jim had been the team's leading scorer as a junior and was named all-conference. He was a point guard who was like a quarterback on the basketball floor. Gary, meanwhile, was tall for a guard at six-three, but he was a good ball handler and excellent outside shot. First man off the bench was guard Dave Collins, who was only a week removed from catching footballs from Rod Dillon. All of them were seniors.

Across the front were Jeff Howard, a six-three forward who played six inches taller because of how high he could jump and Gordy Gregg, who, though he was only six-two, was a bulldog. "I'm here to set picks and rebound," he would joke. "That's all I'm good for." They were seniors, too.

At center was six-four Chuck Mockabee, Bob and John's younger brother, who was the only junior who saw any regular playing time. Chuck was a solid force in the middle, a good rebounder, but he also befuddled opponents with an ability to shoot fifteen-footers with incredible accuracy. He was a natural at basketball, much like Bob had been, and he enjoyed success at each step up the ranks, even getting some varsity playing time as a sophomore. He had earned the respect of his senior teammates, and he was as optimistic about the coming season as everyone else.

CHAPTER 24

Chuck brought to this season his incredible talent, plus his experience, and a confidence that was contagious. But he also brought with him a memory that he would never, ever forget.

Actually, no one would. A plaque was placed on the wall in the gymnasium to serve as a memory to what the town of Springboro experienced generally, but what the Mockabee family experienced intimately. It all happened one awful night in July 1965, only four months after the Panther varsity made it to the state finals.

* * *

Tom and Martha Mockabee moved to Springboro in 1954 to get away from the city life. Mr. Mockabee delivered gasoline and home-heating oil for a living, and after years of living near Miami Valley Hospital in Dayton they purchased a small house on two acres on Lower Springboro Road near Ridgeville, which was a community of homes around a church east of town. One acre of the property was fully devoted to a garden, and while in season the Mockabee children were required to work so many rows before they were free to break out and have fun.

There were eight children in all. David, the oldest, was a 1961 graduate of Springboro. Then came Tom, who was two years younger, then Mary – the 1963 Homecoming queen – a year after that. After Bob there was Barney, John, Chuck, a 1974 grad, and Carol, who graduated a year later.

They were a close-knit, hard-working family who attended church regularly. That influence was largely presented to them by their mother, whose father was a minister.

All of the children had their unique characteristics and special talents. Bob's was basketball, and he was a forward on that memorable '65 team. For every game, the family was in the stands cheering. The Panthers breezed through the regular season, going 17-1 and easily winning the Warren County tournament. The frenzy really grew intense during the post-season tournament, when they won a District title, then the Regional, and went all the way to the state Class A finals. Bob scored in double digits many of those games. His family was proud of how he handled himself along the way, but they were even more proud that he was a good student with a great personality, someone who was loved by everybody.

Because of his playing ability, he earned a scholarship to play basketball at Ohio Northern University. Teammates Dale Kearns and Glenn Jackson were going there, too. So after graduation he had to keep his game in shape. Amid the chores each day, he played basketball all over the county to stay sharp. He hoped to make a good impression on his new coach and team.

On Saturday, July 17, 1965, not two months after graduation, the chores around the Mockabee house had been delegated and each of the children was drenched with sweat by one o'clock. After that, they made their plans to scatter and do what they wanted to do. John and Chuck and older brother Barney, pre-teenagers at the time, went to a social at the Ridgeville Christian Church that evening. Tom and Mary were going out with friends. Bob, meanwhile, was going to Mason with some former teammates to play basketball.

"I'll be home later, Mom," he said as he was leaving.

"Okay. Be careful," she replied. Bob piled into a car with several others to make the trip.

Bob never made it home. Around 11:30 that night, as the heat of the hot summer day gave way to the coolness of the night, Bob was in the passenger seat in a vehicle fast approaching Red Lion, another small collection of homes around a church south of town. Red Lion sits squarely in the middle of the intersection of St. Rt. 741 and St. Rt. 122, with an artery of St. Rt. 123 also there. A Buddy Holly song was on the radio and the guys were laughing about a joke they'd heard earlier in the day. It had been a great Saturday night.

The intersection there is one of the most confusing intersections in the whole area. St. Rt. 122 is a straightaway east and west. St. Rt. 741 is a straightaway north and south, connecting Springboro to a western part of Lebanon and then, at its final point, Mason. What makes it confusing is there is a fifth road to that intersection, an artery of St. Rt. 123 that turns south out of Red Lion as it twists and turns all the way to Lebanon. Traffic going east and west on 122 had the right-of-way, with no stop sign, while the other three roads were required to stop. That meant the drivers from one of those three had to look left and right, but also across the way in at least two other directions. There was no traffic light in those days.

The vehicle stopped at the stop sign on 123 right at the 122 intersection. To get to Springboro, they needed to cross 122 and hit 741 going north. With the radio blaring and the guys laughing, the driver looked left and right and straight ahead. The problem was that he didn't look into the east very carefully.

He pulled out without seeing the tractor-trailer that was coming from the right.

The truck was traveling at full speed and its driver didn't have an opportunity to apply the brakes. The rig hit the vehicle Bob was in at full impact, directly at the point that Bob was sitting. The car was carried down the road before it finally stopped, wedged underneath the tractor-trailer. Immediately, it was clear that Bob suffered the worst injury. He had broken bones and contusions, and a loss of consciousness. But, amazingly, he was still alive. He was transported by the emergency squad to Middletown Hospital, where he was listed in critical condition.

Chuck, John and the other members of his family were at the church that Saturday night when they learned what had happened to Bob. They rushed to the hospital, where they waited throughout the night for word about Bob's condition. Meanwhile, the news spread all over town and people dropped to their knees and cried. Bob was like a son to so many. He was loved and appreciated. They were devastated.

The next morning, at church services all over town, news of the crash spread. Special prayers were said for the recovery of Bob Mockabee.

Later that day, as John and Chuck Mockabee worshipped at the Ridgeville Christian Church, they learned that Bob had died. He was only seventeen years old.

Don Ross was serving as director of Camp Hook near Carlisle when he got the phone call from Gerald Saunders, Bob's coach, about the accident. The town mourned in the same way the country mourned when John F. Kennedy had been assassinated two years earlier. The funeral procession was miles long.

Brutey told me that he had never been so depressed than the day he heard Bob Mockabee had been killed. He took off work for several days, and huddled with all the other townspeople who were grieving the same way he was. Bob had so much talent, and was such a likeable kid, Brutey told me, and it was such a tragedy for him to lose his life so young.

"I can remember like it was yesterday watching that boy work up a sweat by working so hard in practice," Brutey would say. "I really admired that about him. He had such a talent that he could have just relied on that, but he didn't. He worked even harder. When you're out there playing basketball, you ought to remember that.

"He was a special kid. It was one of the worst tragedies this town had ever seen."

* * *

"Hustle, fellas," Coach Hall barked. "We've got less than a week and I guarantee you Carlisle's going to be gunning for you. Now, let's go!"

There was no wasted movement. The players moved quickly to different stations, allowing for no standing around or goofing off. Coach Hall, who himself had been an all-American at Fairmont State (W. Va.) College, barked orders while the players kept moving. At 6'5" he was taller than anyone on the team, with a deep voice, horn-rimmed glasses, and a clipboard at his side at all times to tell him of what was next on the rigid agenda. Though he downplayed his expectations about this team, he privately knew the predictions were correct. To combat a letdown, they were at least going to work hard and be prepared, trusting that the results would follow.

"Big men on the boards. Ball handlers on the line. Let's go! Let's go!"

The season started in seven days at Carlisle, a small community in the western most portion of Warren County. It was opening a new gym, and Springboro was an arch-rival. The place was sure to be packed, and loud. But we were still favored, as we were in the four games after that one. But then we would play at Franklin, the bigger town right next to us, and at Madison – which had killed us a year ago en route to the state finals in its own dream season. Then we would start the meat of the conference schedule, at Mason, no less. That would be a tough stretch, for sure.

"Fellas, let's work, because you play a game like you practice," Coach Hall told them. "If you mess around and get sloppy in practice, you'll mess around and get sloppy in games." Coach was always full of these witty sayings.

Their passes were crisp. Their shots were calculated. If the bank board could be used, it was. No one had hair down over their ears, and everyone wore the same socks and tennis shoes. The whistle blew and instructions were given, and each player fell into place automatically. It was no wonder this team was so good.

"Watch this," Mitch whispered. "Jimmy will slide off that pick and shoot the jumper. Perfect form. Boom! He could do that all day if he wanted to."

At another basket, Chuck Mockabee hooked up with Gordy Gregg in a rebounding drill. Chuck was taller but Gordy was stronger; it wasn't clear who had more of the advantage. And off to one side, Dave Collins, Gary Patton and Jeff Howard were in a ball-handling drill.

We watched for nearly an hour. We would see the team plenty more times, sometimes in practice but all the time during games. It would not be the last time that we would be in awe of what they could do.

Watching them made me so ready to go play basketball somewhere. I would shoot jumpers from the corner and the wing, pretending that I was leading a major comeback for my school. The crowd would be on edge, and time after time I would do something so astounding that people would shake their heads in disbelief. The game announcer would say my name a hundred times, and I would be the game's leading scorer. The next morning, there would be a big news story with my name in the headlines and my picture underneath.

I was so ready for basketball.

Try-outs couldn't come quickly enough.

The varsity cheerleaders in 1972-73, shown at top, were captain Sandy Lawson, Robyn Sharp, Vicki Ramey, Kathy Manning, Cathi England and Pam Hepp. The junior high cheeleaders were (L-R) Lana Beavers, Sonya Antrobus, Rhonda Riley, Debbie Balyo, Sherry Burnett, Starr Koogler and Dorene Fetters.

CHAPTER 25

In the span of one week, I'd laugh at Hawkeye, Jethro, Gomer and Flip. And then on Thursday I waited for THE line – "Book him Dano. Murder one."
-- The Prime Time Lineup

THURSDAY, NOVEMBER 16, 1972

Brutey's appointment with my dad was set for one-thirty. Brutey picked up Norma at the house at one, having gone to the office for half a day, though once he got there he wondered what he was thinking. His thoughts were such a mess he couldn't concentrate on anything. He left without telling anyone where he was going, which was common practice anyway since he was a salesman. In many ways, he felt like he had an appointment with the executioner.

He and Norma drove the four miles into Franklin in total silence. Since the time Brutey made his confession to Norma, they had talked several times about the situation. There would be a lot of talk around town, with some finger-pointing and turning of heads, all of which would affect the boys. In small-town, squeaky-clean Springboro, even the slightest blemish in a family's reputation was magnified a thousand fold.

"Honey, I'm sorry," Brutey kept saying.

"I know, I know," Norma responded. She couldn't land on just one emotion. Instead, she alternated between three primary feelings – hurt, anger and disappointment – and she did her best to honor her husband's honesty.

The road between Franklin and Springboro was a two-lane highway that was virtually barren. The only buildings along that stretch west of town were Dr. Guenther's veterinary office and Edwards Furniture, which competed fiercely with Eyler's Furniture, the town's newest furniture store that was owned by Mayor Jim Eyler. As they passed Edwards' they took note that six cars were out front – which seemed like a lot for that time of day. Must be having a sale, Brutey thought. Eyler would fire back with a sale of his own by morning.

My dad's office was in downtown Franklin in a renovated house next to Kinney's Restaurant, which was located next to Cookie's grocery. It was a nice old place, but small. The upstairs was a renovated apartment that was rented out. Downstairs, the living room, dining room and a large family room were all converted into offices, three in all. Dad partnered with James D. Ruppert and Dallas Powers in a firm that proudly displayed the letterhead of Ruppert, Kirby & Powers.

Brutey and Norma arrived fifteen minutes before their scheduled appointment, and learned from the secretary that Dad was on the telephone. They both felt surprisingly calm as sat in the make-shift waiting room and read magazines. The calmness told them they were doing the right thing.

"Hey, Brutey. Hello, Norma. Come on back and let's talk."

Once inside Dad's office, there was no discussion about Norma's prior visit to file for a divorce. For all Dad knew, they were there to update their wills or make out a new deed to their house in order to avoid probate. He had seen lots of situations where someone wanted a divorce one day, then they were renewing their wedding vows the next. So he didn't ask questions until he knew for sure what they wanted to talk about. They chatted for a few minutes about kids and the problems that always occur in owning a home, and how winter was fast approaching.

"So what brings you two in today?" Time to get down to business.

There was a long pause. Brutey looked over at Norma, and she reached over to hold his hand. Tears welled up in her eyes. Then she nodded for Brutey to say what he came to say.

"Tom, I've done a terrible thing," he began. "There was this woman, a younger woman who grew up in Springboro and is a few years younger than Norma and me. Anyway, about a month ago, on a Friday night after the Blanchester game, I –"

"-- You knew this woman?"

"Yes."

"That's what this is all about?"

CHAPTER 25

"Yes. I mean, no." He was flustered, and angry. "Tom let me finish."

Brutey took a deep breath. "There was a crash a few weeks ago where a woman was killed. The driver of the vehicle that ran her off the road had been drinking, so he took off and everyone's been looking for him ever since."

Dad nodded as if to say he'd heard about the crash. "Charlie Reedy was talking about it at the courthouse the other day. Sad situation. The woman had two young daughters, didn't she?"

Brutey agreed.

"But Charlie specifically told me they didn't know anything about the other driver, so they don't know the driver had been drinking. How did you know that?"

Brutey didn't blink. He'd rehearsed this moment ever since they made the appointment. He sat up in his chair and leaned his arms across the edge of my dad's desk. Norma, meanwhile, put her hand on Brutey's arm.

"Tom, you're looking at the other driver. I'm the one they're looking for."

Norma broke down crying and Brutey hugged her. For several minutes, no one said anything, since there was nothing to say. The clock ticked away and a typewriter clicked away in the next room. Brutey looked at Dad in a way that said only one thing, "Look what I've done."

Brutey told Dad the entire story. He had some beer in the car, as he always did, and he started drinking the minute he got into the car for the drive home back to Springboro. He listened to the radio and sipped his beer as he negotiated the twists and turns on State Route 73. He passed by a state highway patrolman at the intersection of 73 and State Route 48, but because he wasn't speeding or weaving, there was no reason for the officer to pay attention to him.

"I went past Bunnell Hill when I finished my second beer. I held the steering wheel with my left hand, and I reached back behind the seat for the beer with my right. There was no one on the road that time of night. There never is. Then I came up over a little hill just as you get to Bob Lovely's place on the right, and she was in that curve. When I saw her it was too late. I pulled –"

Brutey began crying like he hadn't since he was in the second grade. The memory of what he did to Janet Spencer was so fresh it was as if it had happened only moments earlier.

Dad broke the silence. "Charlie Reedy told me she swerved right to miss you, then overcompensated when she went off the side of the road. Her tires hit pavement and it slung the car into the telephone pole."

"I wasn't drunk," Brutey said.

"Two beers in an hour, probably not. The legal limit is .15%. You probably would have tested about half that. But that leads to the most challenging question, Brutey."

"I know."

"Why did you take off?" Dad asked.

Brutey put his hands together. He had anticipated the question and he struggled to find a sensible answer. "I wanted to stick around. I knew it was the right thing to do. But I had beer on my breath and beer in the car. I just knew I'd get arrested for DWI or worse, and I didn't want to go to jail. I panicked. It don't matter who I am, Charlie Reedy and Jimmy Beavers would've had me behind bars in no time for killing a woman while I was drinking beer."

Dad couldn't argue with that.

"So what's going to happen to me, Tom? What am I looking at?" It was the second thing he had rehearsed over and over. The possible answers scared Brutey more than anything ever had.

As he listened to the answer, part of him wished he'd kept quiet.

* * *

My dad personally knew the destructive effects of alcohol. What he heard from Brutey Baker only reinforced his own experiences. It brought back a lot of bad memories from his childhood.

A day that my dad will always remember was a day when he was around fourteen years old, a kid growing up in Franklin during a time when the country was experiencing an unprecedented time of peace and patriotism. World War II was finally over and life was getting back to normal, and the mood around the country was generally a positive one.

He and my grandparents lived in a rented home on River Street, just a few blocks from downtown and just around the corner from the St. Mary's Catholic Church. Grandpa Burt was a mill worker and Grandma Violet, who was the first child to ever play piano on the radio station WLW on Sunday afternoons, was a homemaker. Dad had a younger brother Jack and a younger sister, Bernie. From the street their home may have looked like something out of a postcard – simple, relaxed and enjoyable.

But it was anything but that. And on that June afternoon in 1949, the reality of that hit my dad full throttle.

It was a Friday. Though generally Friday is a happy day because it signifies the end of the work week and the beginning of the weekend, Friday instead was the worst day in his home. That's because it was payday, the day Grandpa Kirby was given money to put in his pocket and spend on what he wanted.

And what he wanted, invariably, was something to drink. So he would stop at one of the taverns along the way, order drinks until the pain and disappointments of life were washed away, and then stumble home. That's the way it was this particular day. He walked in the front door, slamming it behind him, expecting that he would be greeted warmly and promptly served his supper. Instead, he found that supper that he failed to show up for hours earlier was cold and the family was upstairs a little too relaxed sitting around listening to the radio.

"Violet, where's dinner?" he shouted. "I work hard all day and all you do is loaf around all day." He punched the wall next to him. "WHERE'S DINNER? And don't tell me to heat it up myself!"

What followed was another of the nasty episodes that generally happened when Grandpa had been drinking. Grandpa and Grandma would fight and Dad would intervene on Grandma's behalf, and usually he was told it was none of his business. The verbal assault on Grandma would continue, and more punches would be thrown, and stuff would be broken, and Grandma and the kids would retreat to their rooms in despair. The entire evening was ruined. Meanwhile, Grandpa passed out. It was not an *Ozzie and Harriett* way of living, and Dad began to see how different his home life was than some of the other kids in town.

By thirteen, Dad had to work to help support the family. Everyone in the family sacrificed, either financially or in the things they couldn't have. They'd scrimp and save and make leftovers stretch out for several days. As a result, Dad grew up believing that he did not measure up with everyone else, and that he had to try harder – and work more – in order to achieve.

He would lay awake at night and wonder why God didn't make a world without any suffering. It pained him to feel the frustration in his own life, and it tortured him to see it in other people. He didn't understand it because, in his mind, there was nothing to understand. If God were as powerful as the Bible taught, then He had the power to make this life as wonderful as heaven, should he so choose. But because this life did involve pain and suffering, the inescapable conclusion was that God was either not as powerful as we may hope, or he wasn't as loving as we may hope.

His mom was a devoted Catholic who prayed or went to church every day, and she encouraged her oldest son to follow her there. But Dad was reluctant; it was hard to praise a God who left him in such a mess, he thought, and apparently was ignoring the cries of so many other people whose situation was worse than his.

"Tommy, God'll get you if you don't go to church," Grandma would say.

"I'd say God's got me pretty good already," he would mumble in return.

The patriotism of the post-World War II era affected Dad, and so after he graduated from Franklin in 1953 he entered the Air Force. It was his hope to serve his country, see the world and get away from his troubled surroundings at home. And it was there that he hoped to fulfill a lifelong dream – to fly fighter jets. He served his country proudly, but Grandpa thought he was wasting his time. Come home, get a job at Frigidaire or NCR or Armco, and live your life. There was nothing more to it than that, Grandpa believed.

Two things kept my dad from flying, though. The first was a college education, something that would elevate him to officer's training. The second was the damage to his hearing by working around jet engines. None of the mechanics wore protection over their ears in those days. It was another blow to him, and when he left the service after his four years, he went through a phase when he wasn't sure of what he wanted to do. He took a few jobs but didn't like them. He moved around a few places, but nothing felt like the place to settle.

Using the GI Bill, he decided to do what no one else in his family had done, he went to college. He started at Ohio State, and then transferred to the University of Dayton, a Catholic school, where he took classes – oddly enough – in philosophy and the Bible. He was still searching for God's ultimate plan for this world that involved human pain and suffering. Grandpa, meanwhile, still thought he should settle into a job and get on with his life.

In 1959 he met my mom, Patricia Buckley, at a nightclub in Dayton. They married in November of that year and rented a home on Legion Court in Franklin. Less than a year later, I was born. Then, in successive years, Mom gave birth to John, Jenny, Julie and Joey. He continued to go to college and work at Frigidaire and somehow find time to be Santa Claus and the Easter Bunny and, simply put, Dad. It was a hard time, with both money and energy running short. And though the family was healthy and progress was being made, life still didn't seem to be fair.

CHAPTER 25

Grandpa died in 1963 when I was three; I only knew him through the stories I've been told. At the cemetery after the funeral, Dad slid off to himself and reflected on the life of his father. He remembered all the drunken episodes that ended up with punches thrown and lamps broken, and came to some sobering realizations.

First, he found it incredibly odd that in spite of every terrible thing his father had ever done, he still loved him, and maybe pitied him. And secondly, perhaps more importantly, Dad realized who actually the strong one was.

He would have never characterized himself as strong until then. But he was, and to assure himself of it all he had to do was consider everything that he had accomplished – military service, a college degree, a home and a family -- all in the wake of no parental support and incredible odds.

He was 28 years old. He realized his loneliness in this world was not a sudden development.

He had been alone for a long time.

* * *

"So you think I'm going to prison, huh?"

Brutey wasn't sure what he thought he would hear, but he still didn't like to hear the word prison. That meant losing his job, and maybe losing Norma and the boys. He surely wouldn't coach anymore, in Springboro or anywhere for that matter. That thought hurt him as much as the other two.

"I didn't say that," Dad said. "I said involuntary manslaughter carries the potential of prison. A judge has several options, if you're found guilty. You can be put on probation, or you can spend time in the county jail, on a work release, or worst case scenario, you could go to prison."

"You know what her family's going to want."

"Yeah, well, that's where you driving away and leaving them hanging for the last month could really work against you. So all of this may affect whether you want me to disclose this." Brutey later learned that a lawyer must keep all communication with a client confidential, unless the client was planning on breaking the law, in which case he had a responsibility to turn him in. Like many things with the legal system, he couldn't understand this fully.

"No, I have to do this. I may hate every step of the way, and it might kill me –"

"And me," Norma interjected.

"But I'm going through with this. I just need your help getting through this."

"Tom, how can we possibly keep Brutey from going to prison? I know he did wrong, and I feel so awful for that family. But prison? Why prison? And as mad as they're going to be when we come forward, how can we possibly get him through this without a prison sentence?"

They expected Dad to say it would be difficult, and he did. He didn't sugar coat a thing. A meeting would be scheduled with the county prosecutor, then the judge, and Dad would do his best. But, in the end, it would be a crapshoot, and we have to be prepared for the worst.

Instead, Dad asked a question: "Brutey, how far back was that other car that was behind you that night?"

"You mean the Wrenns? Shoot, I could barely see their lights. I took off because I knew they'd be there in a minute. Why?"

Dad had a quizzical look on his face, like something was clicking but he wasn't sure it would get there. "Brutey, I have an idea."

CHAPTER 26

"Bite your tongue, Margaret.
Or better yet, let me do it."
-- Hawkeye Pierce
*M*A*S*H*

FRIDAY, NOVEMBER 17, 1972

There was no regular group of kids to walk to school with, because it never happened that we could get up, get ready, eat breakfast and be out the door at the exact same time. Sometimes I walked with Alan Little, who lived across the street. Other times I found Roger or Donny. Occasionally I made the fifteen-minute walk all by myself.

I ran into Ricky Baker as he rounded the corner from Walnut Place onto Redbud Drive, just down the street from my house. We both wore bell-bottom jeans and football jerseys. With basketball try-outs starting the next day, we both followed the rule Coach Harry Hall had for the entire program and had our hair cut short. As we walked, some of the high-schoolers drove by in their souped up Camaros and Firebirds.

Since I didn't know anything about Brutey's legal problems (my dad kept all that stuff at the office), I had no reason to bring the subject up. I blabbered on about watching the varsity practice a couple of nights earlier, and how cool that had been. I also talked about being a little nervous about try-outs. Ricky didn't interrupt me; he just let me talk. If he was aware of the problems Brutey had, he never talked about it, ever.

From all I could see, Ricky's life went on just like before. He spoke up in class, he laughed when someone said something funny. And when we got to school and encountered a bunch of older kids by the front door, Ricky walked right on by like it was no big deal. This amazed me because some of the older kids were jerks. And I didn't like them. So I did everything I could to avoid them.

* * *

I learned very quickly to hate sophomores. They were scum -- too young to be the rulers of the high school, but old enough to have power over some of the younger guys, like us seventh graders. They got a thrill out of kicking us every chance they could, which was kind of ridiculous actually. After all, they were guys with car keys, beards and mustaches. Meanwhile, we were boys with bicycles and peach fuzz. It was about the same as us going back to the Jonathan Wright to pick on some kindergarteners. Oh, the joy.

It started on the very first day of school, which was a tough day for us seventh graders. We'd never before changed classes every hour throughout the school day, and that was intimidating. Where were we supposed to go? How could we be so sure we were in the right class? What's more, we were in the same building as the high school kids, which included the scum-sucking sophomores. So how was I supposed to know that the building was divided into two parts, one for the junior high and another for the high school? There were no signs, no student handbook and no announcement to that effect. So I guess we were just expected to know. Or else find out the hard way.

On the first day of school, everyone showed up wearing the newest clothes they had in the closet so they could make a really good first impression. Well, I blew it. I made my mistake of wandering over into the senior high. I kept looking at room numbers, not the students who were surrounding me, so I never noticed that I gradually entered a world of mustaches and big burley guys. Before long, I was trapped in the worst situation any kid had ever seen. I was lost, confused and stupid, and I wondered how in the world I was ever going to survive in my new world. The sophomores smelled the blood, too.

As I neared Mr. Vince Ross' principal's office, there was a bunch of them standing there – looking greasy and grimy and goofy as all get out. I almost didn't say anything, but for some reason I did. "Uh, where's the science room?" I felt like the lion in *The Wizard of Oz*, a coward in search of his courage.

The sophomores smirked at the sound of my squeaky voice. They pointed at my new matching shirt and pants, then laughed as they huddled. Looking back, I should have known I had just been fed to the wolves.

"Oh, you'll love Mrs. Kuhn," one of them said. I would say he was the stupid one, but in that crowd it was hard to tell. "We all loved her. Just be careful and make sure you don't pay too much attention in her class or else you'll look really dumb. If you hang on her every word she'll think you don't know anything."

"Okay." I tucked my books under my arm to better support them. I'd been walking for quite a while and they were getting heavy. "But where's her room?"

They pointed up a flight of stairs. "Up this way and down the hall. Turn left to another flight of stairs. Go up them. It's on the third floor, near the pool. You better hurry, though. It'll take a while to get there." The fat head said this with a straight face, too.

I looked around and decided I didn't have a choice. I took off up the steps. When I got halfway up, the slimy sophomores started laughing out loud and pointing in my direction. Finally, senior Dave Collins came to my rescue. I had known him for several years, and his younger brother Brian and I played baseball together. "What are you doing up here, Jeff?" he said. "All your classes are down in the junior high wing. Don't listen to those guys."

I was late for science class and Mrs. Kuhn wasn't happy about it one bit. After that, I think she really had it in for me, too.

* * *

For the first hundred and thirty years Springboro existed, all the kids went to various one-room schools scattered in and around Clearcreek Township, in which Springboro is located. One was in the center of town, another south of town, and another to the east in Ridgeville. One teacher tended to all of the students in each building, and with no competitive sports there was rarely any interaction among the different schools.

In the early 1900s the town built its first official school for the entire community. Known as The Little Red School, it was located one block west of Main Street on the cusp of all the farm country that Ralph Wade's children later rode their horses. For nearly a half-century it was the only school in town. All the one-room schools funneled their children into this school.

But by 1928, school enrollment for the entire district reached four hundred and it was difficult to house all the children in one school. So they built Clearcreek Township High School, which later became known as Springboro High School, just south of town, leaving the Little Red School to house the kindergarten through ninth grades. A decade later, the new gym was constructed in the rear of the new high school. Around that same time, the Little Red School was torn down so they could build the Jonathan Wright Elementary, so named for the founder of Springboro, which initially held classes for kindergarten through the sixth grades. In 1970, Clearcreek Elementary School was built for grades four through six, with Mr. Bill Gordon named as principal, leaving the younger grades still at the Jonathan Wright, where Mr. James Dalton was the principal.

I wanted a new school that put all the sophomores in the bathroom.

Was that too much to ask?

* * *

I ran into Ricky at lunchtime that day, and again he plowed through a smelly batch of sophomores and walked right into the cafeteria, which was as crowded as I had ever seen. Our school had open lunch, so we were free to leave the building at 11:30 so long as we were back by 12:45. Sometimes we walked over to Mitch's house. Other times we walked to the K & W. Since it was raining outside, we had no choice but to stay in.

I sat at a table with Ricky and the rest of the guys. I was at the end of our table, near Mitch. Just to my left was another group, mostly eighth graders, one of whom was Mark Dillon, younger brother to Rod and Dave. All of us had Sloppy Joes, which was about our favorite thing in the world to eat. The messier, the better, too.

Some of the guys were still discussing the Reds' loss to the Oakland A's in the World Series. Others talked about the news from the NFL, which was halfway through its season. Some of the guys were still Browns fans, while others – like me – embraced the Bengals. Conversation went a mile a minute.

"The Dolphins are going to go undefeated, man," I said. "They're the baddest bunch of guys the league has ever seen."

"No one's ever gone undefeated the whole year," Wilburn said. "Watch the Vikings." I scoffed. No way was I rooting for something called a "Purple People Eater."

CHAPTER 26

Lance offered his opinion. "I like the Redskins," he said.

"No way, man," Kruer said. "Billy Kilmer hasn't thrown a spiral in ten years. My grandma throws better than him."

We all followed football. We could watch the varsity play in person on Friday nights, but there were college and pro games on TV on the weekends. NFL games featured tough guys and real athletes, and you could always tell what quarter a game was in by how dirty the uniforms were. Games in Cleveland were played in the mud, while games in Minnesota were in the driving snow. I loved the image of a running back walking off the field, the scoreboard showing victory in the background, with him covered in mud.

"I still say Miami will go all the way. Look at them, they don't have a weakness."

"Yeah, but Griese got hurt yesterday."

"I know. But Earl Morrell can do a good job." I was holding my ground.

"Earl Morrell?!" Kruer responded. "My grandma looks younger than that guy. Ever see him? He looks like George Gobel in football cleats. He couldn't outrun my kitchen table."

The whole table laughed, but I held my ground. I predicted that the Dolphins would keep winning, even with a quarterback who seemed better suited for *The Hollywood Squares*. From there the conversation turned to the Ohio State-Michigan game and then to the beginning of the upcoming basketball season.

Just before lunch was over, the coolest thing happened. It was the one thing that made me like being in a school with the high school kids.

* * *

I came face-to-face with guys I never dreamed I would be around. I was in the presence of athletic giants. As I opened my carton of milk, I looked up and saw Rod Dillon, Jim Hough, Jeff Howard and Gary Patton sit down right across from me. This could not have been more exciting than if Pete Rose and Johnny Bench had invited me into the Reds' dugout to sit next to them.

Rod found a seat next to Mark, his brother. And like all the seniors, Rod knew Mitch. And so, right in front of me, taking special care to wipe away any of the germs on his fork and his knife, sat the Springboro varsity quarterback. And the three stars of the upcoming basketball team. My idols. I practically peed my pants.

"Hey, Kirby," Rod said.

He knew my name! Now I really had to go.

A moment later Dale Midkiff and John Mockabee sat down. They were having Sloppy Joes, too, just like me, with pears and potato chips and white milk, just like me. Dale sat next to Rod, while John sat next to Jimmy, Gary and Jeff. I sat there with my eyes wide open, trying to act like I was in my element but no doubt failing miserably. Mitch, meanwhile, carried on with all of them like it was no big thing, which was hardly surprising because Mitch knew everybody, no matter how old they were. Pretty soon all of the guys were talking about old football games and future basketball games, and in between they told some risqué stories about stuff that was going on with other players. I laughed right along with them, even though I didn't have a clue what half the stories were about.

Though I finished my lunch long before they did, I didn't dare leave that table. It was so cool. I felt like I knew a lot of the players personally. I'd tell my brothers later on that I was now practically a member of the varsity, and I'd watch them freak out.

Turkey told me later that none of those seniors would ever remember me or that particular lunch for the rest of their lives.

I thought about that for a second, and a one-word answer popped to mind.

So?

CHAPTER 27

Hough, Hefflin, Blevins,
Wight, Kemper, Shoemaker,
Patton, Howard ...Kirby (?)
-- The Panther basketball fraternity

SATURDAY, NOVEMBER 18, 1972

The maple trees in front of the high school were virtually bare. As winter snaked its way into town on a brisk, blustery morning, there were no kids riding bikes or walking barefoot to the K & W for an ice cream cone. Those hot summer days during which we played basketball at the park seemed like such a long time ago. Now it was time to show off our talents for basketball try-outs.

This was scary. Nobody was ever cut from a baseball or football team, and the Saturday morning basketball program was for everybody, too. Sixty guys would try out for the seventh grade team; less than twenty would make the team. Our first game was three weeks away, and by then the chill of late fall would give way to the brutal cold of winter.

Our coach was Mike Wilson, a tall lefthander with a Kentucky accent, who was our Ohio History teacher. Brutey was our unofficial assistant coach, just as he had been with the junior high football program. He was the official scout for the varsity, reporting to Coach Hall, and then he spent his extra time at our practices and games, helping out in whatever way was needed. He was good that way. When Coach Hall came to town as a rookie, Brutey never tried to throw his weight around, and was also supportive of our head coach. He would do the same for Coach Wilson.

Guys poured into the gym and spread out among the six baskets. Everyone wanted a basketball to dribble and shoot around, but there weren't enough to go around. I gathered in a group that included Mitch Leisz, who would clearly be our starting guard because he handled the ball better than a lot of sophomores, though I'm not sure that was saying anything. Mitch had had a bunch of us at his house the night before for some pick-up games. When practice was over, he'd asked us to come back over to watch the Ohio State-Michigan football game.

"Look at him, he can dribble circles around the rest of us," Lance said. Mitch was already in mid-season form.

Those of us who had a good chance of making the team took short jumpers and made nice passes to one another. Then there were the yahoos who took half-court shots and tried dribbling between their legs. Some of them would be scratched from the list before we got through calisthenics.

Suddenly, the whistle blew, and Coach Wilson entered the gym. "Fellas, before we get started, I want you to all take a seat here at midcourt," Coach told us. He stood tall in the center of the gym, wearing a white shirt and grey sweat pants, with a whistle around his neck. Brutey, meanwhile, stood off in the distance holding a basketball.

"Today marks the first day of what can be an awesome journey for every single one of you," he said. He stepped back and looked at all the championship banners behind him, and it gave me chills down my back. "One day, your name can be on a starting lineup for the varsity, and you can join the ranks of some pretty big names – Belvins, Jackson, Hough, Charlton, and Hefflin…even Mr. Baker over there. Every one of those guys started in the spot where you are right now."

He looked around at us guys on the floor. It occurred to me that I was sitting in the very spot that a big varsity game would take place that winter. The stands would be full and excitement would be in the air, and on the very spot I sat a major play in a big game would occur. I couldn't believe I was there.

"One day I hope to see each of you wearing a varsity uniform and proudly representing this town. The journey to that level begins today. So let's hustle."

With that, we started practice. We loosened up and then did some running. We heard Brutey talk about the importance of defense. Then the coaches lined us up for lay-ups, with right-hand lay-ups first and then left-handed ones. Most of us did well on the right-hand lay-ups, except for the goof-offs, of course, and some of them missed the entire backboard. The left-handed lay-ups were more difficult for everyone, which is the case everywhere because most of us were right-handed. I had practiced and practiced this for weeks.

CHAPTER 27

When it was my turn, I just followed my routine. I dribbled left-handed and then counted my steps properly to the basket. Once there I put up the shot left-handed, then watched it bounce off the backboard and into the net. I swelled with pride and did a fist-pump to congratulate myself. Then I looked over at Coach Wilson, who was making a mark on his clipboard. Brutey told me later I made the seventh grade basketball team right then and there.

Meanwhile, I could see that all my other friends were playing well, too. Lance hit five straight free throws, and Donny and Shane teamed up in a two-man drill where they annihilated everyone. And then of course there was Mitch, everybody's all-American.

From the time I was eight or nine, Mitch and I had played every sport imaginable at his house. His backyard made for a perfect baseball field, and his free-standing garage held a hoop for one of the best basketball courts anywhere. Just beyond his fence were the high school and its enormous yard. The football field was only thirty yards from Mitch's house. We went to Mitch's a lot after varsity games.

Mitch was naturally gifted, but he also had lots of help. Because of where his house was, and because he had older relatives, Mitch's house was a social hub for just about every athlete since the mid-sixties. Everybody knew about Mitch's house. And I mean *everybody.*

The Leisz family had given a lot back to Springboro over the years, starting way back almost fifty years earlier.

In 1927, Ed and Lucy Leisz scoured the area outside of town, just past where Springboro Road winds through the trees and cornfields, looking for farmland. They found just what they were looking for when they purchased an old farmhouse and surrounding acreage so that Ed could pursue a lifelong dream of farming. Until then Ed hauled coal with a team of horses, and while it earned him a decent wage, it wasn't the work he wanted to do. In Springboro Ed raised crops and tended to livestock, and he and Lucy had their children.

I always had a hard time keeping track of Mitch's family tree. Ed and Lucy Leisz had five children. Charles was the oldest, then there was Jane, and Bob was the youngest of them all, with Ruth being the one older than him. Mitch's dad, Ward, was the middle child. Like the others, he worked before and after school and learned the ropes of farming. He also played basketball and baseball during his days at Springboro High School, from which he graduated in 1948.

Ward met Peggy Dunaway while in high school; she lived right across the street from the school. She was a good athlete, too, but the school didn't offer any team competition for her best sport, which was archery. She a national champion, a distinction that would later get her enshrined in the Springboro High sports Hall of Fame. Like Ward, she was a 1948 graduate of Springboro, and after two years of dating she and Ward were married.

The Leisz family grew. In just about every class and part of town, there was a member of the Leisz family.

Jane Leisz married Don Charlton, and their first son was Scott, a member of the '65 state runner-up team. Then came Rod, who played basketball until his graduation in 1970, and Mike, Robyn and Chris, all of whom played in the mid-seventies and beyond. Ward Leisz and Peggy had their daughter Kim first, in 1957, and then Mitch three years later. Oldest son Charles married, and his oldest son was Russ, who played basketball with Rod Charlton in the same class of 1970.

Mitch initially learned to play basketball with his mother on their driveway court on the house they owned on Cherry Street, where they lived before Mitch started school. Then, in 1965, they purchased the home on Lookout Street, right behind the high school and across the street from E.B. Smith, for $9,600. It was a nice home with three bedrooms, a living room and a utility room, but it also had a flat driveway and a free-standing garage that made for a natural basketball court. A nine-foot goal was erected above the garage door, and Mitch and his mom continued their games there.

By this time Russ Leisz and Rod Charlton, Mitch's cousins, were in junior high school. As they grew older, they were old enough to watch Mitch when his parents were away. They all played a lot of basketball with young Mitch. "I only had one rule for them," Mrs. Leisz says, "They could block Mitch's shots, but they couldn't jump to do it."

Soon Russ and Rod invited their friends over to Mitch's house, and the friends invited their friends. Corky Jackson, Tom Henderson and Larry Henderson were classmates who came over, then it was guys like Jeff Kees and Jerry Raffel, and before long it was Jimmy Hough, Jeff Howard, Gordy Gregg and everyone else from the class of 1973.

Many times the school called Mrs. Leisz when several students were missing in class. "You got Russ over there?" the school would ask. "How about Charlton or Jackson?"

Mrs. Leisz would often have coffee at the Diner and the conversation would turn to all the big athletes Springboro's had over the years. She'd take a sip and listen to all the famous names. The men would tell stories about the plays each of the athletes had made over the years. It would be a highlight reel of touchdowns, big plays and outside jump shots. "Yes, sir, I've seen them all," Mr. Leisz would say.

But Mrs. Leisz had a different perspective. "I've *fed* them all."

There were a thousand people, it seemed, at Mitch's house that afternoon, and all eyes were on the television. The Ohio State-Michigan game was like a national holiday to us. Archie Griffin was a freshmen sensation. And Bo Schembechler was a nuisance to us. We couldn't wait for the kickoff.

Brutey was there as a guest of Mitch's dad. Mitch's dad had been a senior when Brutey was still in elementary school, and there had been a time he looked up to Mitch's dad. They often got together to talk about the old days, and the games they played in. I overheard part of their conversation when I walked by them to use the bathroom. Brutey was rubbing his eyes and mumbling words in a hushed voice. Mitch's dad was leaned over, elbows on his knees, whispering support to his very good friend.

"Brutey, bud, it could have happened to anybody. Accidents happen, you know. You come over a hill and it doesn't take much to throw you on the other side of the road. Certainly the law has to take all that into consideration."

There was a pause. "Tom says I could be charged with a felony, involuntary manslaughter, not to mention leaving the scene of the accident. He said it carries prison time. I just can't believe I put myself in a position to do this to Norma and the boys. It would be awful to be carted away like some animal. But then that's better than being carted away in a box like that woman was. I can't believe I could've been so stupid."

I snuck back through to go back to where everyone else was sitting. Mr. Leisz kept talking, "You leave everything to Tom, Brutey. You go out and be the best husband, father and coach you know to be. Trust Tom to work through the legal stuff."

"I suppose you're right," Brutey said. "That's the only choice I got."

Pretty soon Ohio State kicked off to Michigan, and the whole bunch of us huddled around Mitch's television. There was a lot of laughing and carrying on, and Ohio State went on to win the game, 14-11, to give Michigan its first loss of the season. Brutey stayed until midway through the third quarter, when he abruptly announced that he needed to get home and help Norma cook dinner.

He didn't say much the whole time he was there.

And he didn't have a single beer, and that was the most unusual thing of all.

Starting at forward, number fifty-two, Gordy Gregg!....The Panthers opened their season with an easy victory at Carlisle, providing the kind of start that was expected by athletic director Neil Clingman and by all the kids like Mitch Leisz who packed the stands on Friday nights.

CHAPTER 28

There's life itself, and friends and family, and there are sunsets and warm summer afternoons, with good music and laughter.
-- The Thanksgiving

WEDNESDAY, NOVEMBER 22, 1972

The meeting was set for three o'clock in the afternoon at The Diner. At such an hour, the lunch crowd was long gone and the dinner crowd was still two hours away. Dad had called the Springboro Police Department and arranged a meeting with two of its best officers, Charlie Reedy and Jimmy Beavers. Though they both pressed him for details over the phone, Dad wouldn't give them any. All he assured them of was that it would be well worth their time.

Charlie and Jimmy were in a booth drinking coffee when Dad walked in. Sure enough, there wasn't a soul in sight. The lone waitress was sitting in the back reading *The Western Star* and its preview article about Springboro's high school basketball opener that night at Carlisle. Shrugging off coffee, Dad sat down next to Jimmy. There was no room next to big ol' Charlie.

"What do you got, Tom?" Charlie asked. So much for small talk.

Dad took the bait and jumped right in.

"Let me ask you something. If last Friday night I drove all the way from Middletown to Springboro, and I was drunk, and I come tell you about it but you never saw it happen, can you arrest me for DWI?" Dad knew the answer. He was just building up to his point.

"You know I can't. I have to see you personally. What's that got to do with anything? You want to confess to something?" Charlie was busy.

"I have information about that accident about a month ago."

"The one where that woman was killed? Who was it?"

"Not so fast."

"We've been looking for that guy ever since it happened. What a coward. C'mon, Tom, who is it?"

The department got phone calls on this case every day. The prosecutor's office was getting pressure. The family wanted constant updates. It put all the officers on edge, but Charlie and Jimmy especially since they had been first ones on the scene.

"It's someone you know," Dad continued, stirring his coffee. "He lives here and knows everybody. He made a mistake and he panicked, and then everything just got a whole lot more complicated for him. As the days and weeks moved along, he became more and more remorseful and so he wants to come clean."

Charlie and Jimmy weren't convinced. "Yeah, well then why would he come to you? Why not just come to us? Guess he only wants to come clean if it works for him?" Jimmy was also anxious.

Charlie, meanwhile, was out of patience. "Tom, if a man wants to come clean all he has to do is pick up the telephone. We answer our phone twenty-four hours a day. Sounds like he wants to come clean as long as he don't get in too much trouble. Now who is it?"

Dad poured cream and sugar in his cup of coffee. "He's only human, so there's a little of that. You're talking about a woman who was killed. Most people don't know the difference between murder and manslaughter. All they know is somebody's dead and they think you want them to go to the electric chair."

"We do! Just look what the man has done. So who is it?"

Dad stayed composed. He was in no hurry to do this under any other terms. "I want to turn him in and I want an O.R. bond. We'll plea to vehicular homicide, a misdemeanor, and I want him to get probation," he said. "He's not going anywhere. There's no need to arrest him and make him post bond before he's released. And under the circumstances, he shouldn't get any jail time."

The reaction was as expected. "You're out of your mind, Tom. We don't make those decisions. You know that. You gotta' talk to one of the county prosecutors or one of the judges for that. Just gimme the name and I'll go from there."

"But they listen to you two. If you two are okay with a reduced charge and an O.R. bond, so will they."

"Yeah, but that depends on who we're talking about. There are some scumbags in this town that I wouldn't trust as far as I could throw 'em."

"My client is not a scumbag."

"You mean except for the fact that he was apparently drunk and went left and center and killed an innocent woman, then took off." Charlie could stand his ground, too.

"He made a mistake."

"Who are we talking about, Tom? You're playing games with us."

"You know me better than that." By this time no one was sipping coffee. The meeting had turned into a full-blown confrontation. The officers were desperate to solve their case and the attorney was focused on protecting his client's best interest. "I'll tell you what, let me follow you down to the station. Let's get the prosecutor and the judge on the phone. If I hear that he gets a reduced charge and an O.R. bond, I'll have him in your office in a half-hour."

Charlie grimaced and Jimmy shook his head. "Nobody's going to give him a reduced charge. He was probably drunk and took off and left a woman to die. Prosecutors don't make deals with scumbags like that, you know that. And he is a scumbag, no matter what you say. What circumstances are you talking about?"

"Charlie, remember the first question I asked you about, drinking and driving and later admitting it to you?"

"Yeah. So?"

"So this is the very same thing. I can give you a name, but that doesn't give you a case."

"The hell it don't."

"And even if he tells you what happened, you still may not have a case."

"Well then there's no sense you holding out on us, is there?"

Dad had considered that point, but he wanted to make the phone calls anyway. Let's see if a deal can be struck first. Then go from there.

* * *

An hour later, Brutey was with the rest of the Springboro basketball team as it traveled by bus to nearby Carlisle for the opening game of the season. He hadn't heard anything from Dad before he left, so he spent the night pretending like it was any other night. He tried to be upbeat and also tried to laugh, but he found both of them difficult to do. He kept expecting the nearest police officer to arrest him and take him to jail.

After a while, though, he settled down. Basketball season was about to begin and nothing trumped Springboro basketball. While Brutey milled around the scorer's table waiting for the game to begin, I sat in the top row with Roger Woolery and his dad and we were awestruck by everything we saw. This was the opening night for Carlisle's new gymnasium and it was spectacular, a gem for all of Carlisle to cherish. It was only fitting that its first game would feature a rivalry such as the one between our two towns.

As the band played and the cheerleaders led chants, I saw Brutey standing one row behind our varsity bench talking with Mr. Hough and Mr. Howard, fathers of two of our starters. Coach Hall stood near mid-court, giving Gary Patton some last-minute pointers on how to stop Carlisle's Kenny Crowe, their leading scorer. Brutey had given Coach Hall a three-page spread sheet on what he saw during Carlisle's preseason scrimmage games, and Kenny Crowe was at the top of the list of players to worry about.

"Love those blue uniforms," I said to Roger, which obviously indicated where my head was. "I don't go to many away games, so I never see these uniforms."

"Why do we have different numbers than when we're home?" Roger asked.

"I don't know," I said. "Jimmy's number twenty-four at home, but then he's twenty-five for away games. They don't do that in football. I'm not sure why they do it."

"Probably has something to do with superstition," Roger said. "Like, I'm number twelve in baseball but then I wear twenty in football. I like both numbers. Jimmy must like both twenty-four and twenty-five."

That sounded pretty good to me, but Roger's dad couldn't stand it any longer. "Guys, it's to help out the officials. When they signal to the scorer's table for a foul, no one can get confused because there's only one guy wearing a particular number." Then he chuckled at how silly we were.

But I still liked the superstition thing.

We jumped out on Carlisle very early, and Kenny Crowe never really got in a rhythm. Jimmy Hough scored at will and Jeff Howard jumped over guys who were several inches taller. Dave Collins came off the bench and played great, and Gordy Gregg was a bulldog inside. With us way out in front as the third quarter began, Roger's dad suggested that we leave in order to avoid the traffic jam. We went home that night knowing we were in for a special season – with great players who were fun to watch.

"I'm ready to go play basketball right now," Roger said in the car.

"Me, too. Too bad it's dark."

"And cold," Roger added.

But we had a plan anyway. "So let's play tomorrow, at the park," I said. "I'll call Donny and Shane. You call Mitch and Lance and Turkey. Be there at two."

"But it's Thanksgiving," Mr. Woolery interrupted.

"Oh, right," Roger said, with hesitation. "Better make it three then."

"Afterward, we'll play football."

The varsity lived up to its billing that night, and Ron's Pizza was abuzz when the crowd poured in after the game. Roger and I sat in a booth reliving every play. I knew I would dream of making corner jump shots all night long.

At the bar, Paul Sowers talked politics with some other older men. Every so often, we heard a roar of laughter coming from their area.

Brutey was no where to be found, though.

Brutey sat quietly in the front of a very noisy team bus on the way home from Carlisle. Once back at the school, he slipped past the girls who were waiting for their boyfriends and quickly made his way to his car. He sat there for a full ten minutes before starting the engine, questioning again how he could have went left of center and caused the death of a young mother. Did he do the right thing in turning himself in? Was everything going to turn out okay? He reflected on the events of the evening, and thought about Norma and his boys and his parents, and how everything in his life meant so much to him. It would be awful to have to leave it.

For the second time since the night of the crash, Brutey cried. He sat there with the engine running, and the radio playing softly, until the parking lot was empty. After what seemed like an eternity, he finally found some composure.

He arrived home at about a quarter to eleven, thinking everyone would be asleep. The boys were in bed but Norma was in the family room, with the Reverend Delbert Dawes and his wife Omalee. They were sipping tea and making small talk. Brutey wasn't sure what to make of it.

"Honey, I told Reverend Dawes at church tonight what happened. I hope you don't mind," she said. She rose from her chair to offer Brutey a kiss on the cheek. Brutey said nothing. Norma needed as much support as he did, he realized. And Reverend Dawes could be trusted.

"We won the game tonight. We whipped Carlisle pretty good at their place," he said finally, not sure what was appropriate to say.

Reverend Dawes stood up. His towering presence practically smothered Brutey. He then gave Brutey the first male hug he received since he was probably ten years old, and Brutey appreciated the gesture. "We're going to get you through this thing," Reverend Dawes said, his eyes fixing squarely on Brutey's. "With God's help, we're going to do it."

Brutey closed his eyes, and then chuckled. "I'm glad to hear you say that, 'cause it's kind of your fault. If you weren't so dang convincing, I might have just kept this to myself."

Reverend Dawes grabbed Brutey's arm. "I'm terribly sorry about the crash. But son, I am so proud of you. And God is too, so much so that he's going to take care of you."

Brutey cried again. This time his cry was one of reassurance. Things were going to be okay, somehow, even though he didn't feel he deserved it. He so believed in what Reverend Dawes told him. He so trusted that it all would be true.

Just then they heard a siren out front of the house. The lights of a police cruiser were flashing through the curtains.

For a moment, Brutey lost his breath. He was sure that Charlie Reedy or Jimmy Beavers, men he had forever known and respected, were there to take him to jail. Norma looked through the window. Reverend Dawes put his hand on Brutey's shoulder.

"They've stopped a carload of kids out there," she said finally. "Brutey, they're not here for you."

Brutey let out a sigh of relief. *At least not yet.*

Harry Hall took over the Springboro basketball program at an almost impossible time, just a year after the school advanced all the way to the state finals. But Coach Hall saw the talent he had, and he molded it so that Springboro continued its winning ways. Wayne Kemper (24) and Al Wight helped the Panthers to FAVC championships, and then some post-season success, almost beating the mighty Middletown Middies. After going 11-1 to win the conference in '71-'72, hopes were high for the Panthers the next year.

CHAPTER 29

A rooster crows only when it sees the light.
Put him in the dark and he'll never crow.
I have seen the light and I'm crowing.
-- The champ
Muhammad Ali

Saturday, December 2, 1972

In the ten days since approaching Charlie Reedy and Jimmy Beavers, Dad had serious negotiations with the Warren County prosecutor and his staff. Morris Turkelson had just assumed the office of prosecutor, and already his administration was hit with an explosive case. An innocent young mother of two was dead, and her killer had taken off. The family was livid. The public outcry was strong. But secretly, the prosecution wondered how it was going to get a conviction. As crazy as it sounded to people outside the legal system, a confession alone wasn't enough.

The politically correct thing to do was prosecute to the full. That's what people like out of their prosecutor – aggressive, tough on crime, and willing to stand up for victims. But the pragmatic thing to do was consider a plea bargain. Evidentiary issues would be eliminated. Plus the defendant still would be held accountable in some way. The problem was it looked to outsiders like a killer would literally get away with murder.

"Hey, I didn't write the law. But it's my job to use it to my client's advantage. To do otherwise would get me sued for malpractice," Dad had said.

"I can't deal with you until you give me a name," the prosecution responded.

CHAPTER 29

"And I can't give you a name until you make a deal. C'mon, Turk, you know you've got nothing without a statement. Your guys have been searching for over a month. You've got nothing. You have nothing to lose by working with me."

Finally, the prosecutor agreed to mull it over and get back with him. By late Friday afternoon Dad still had not received a phone call. Brutey checked in with Dad's office around four o'clock that Friday afternoon, just before getting on the bus for the varsity game at Waynesville. He was frustrated that nothing had come of Dad's offer. Brutey appreciated Dad's efforts, but he was tired of the waiting.

He wanted to come clean, deal or no deal. Whatever happened, happened. He had to trust that what was best was what would happen. He enjoyed the game at Waynesville, which was another convincing win by the Panthers, because he was at peace with that decision. Maybe he would regret it, but something inside him told him it was time to come clean.

He called my dad at home first thing Saturday morning. Dad, of course, recommended Brutey not do anything drastic until he knew something more. Brutey said he understood, but at least he wanted to tell some people close to him. He felt he owed it to them.

"Like who?" Dad asked.

"Mainly our coaches, Coach Hall for one. We're in the middle of a season and I think he should know before anything happens."

"Anyone else?"

"My parents. My brothers. Tom, this is all coming to a head soon. I feel I owe it to them to be prepared for it."

The phone call ended with that understanding. Come Monday, Dad would give the prosecution the name of Brutey Baker, deal or no deal. And then they would brace for the onslaught of attention and the legal troubles that went with it. In that respect, Brutey was going to face the biggest contest of his life.

Coach Hall agreed to meet Brutey at 4 o'clock at the high school on Saturday afternoon. The Panthers played Edgewood at home that night. They had won their first three games against Carlisle, Kings Mills and Waynesville in convincing fashion. Edgewood, though, a school in the bigger Mid-Miami League, was supposed to be a tougher challenge. Coach Hall, in a surprise to no one, told reporters he expected Edgewood to win by ten points. The reporters smiled as they wrote the quote in their notebooks. "Yeah, and Nixon is as clueless as he tries to say," one of them grumbled.

"Brutey, my boy. I was looking to have a talk with you, so it's just as well you wanted to meet with me. What's this all about?" Coach Hall did everything confidently. He was self-assured in the way he walked, and talked, and in the way he coached.

Brutey shifted gears for a second. "You were going to meet with me? Have I done something wrong?"

Coach Hall waved him off. "No, not at all. I've always loved having you as a part of this program. You work hard and you're loyal to what we're trying to do. I could never ask for anything more than that."

Brutey settled down and smiled. Coach Hall offered him a seat across from him. "It's just you seem preoccupied anymore. More distant. I crack jokes and you don't laugh. I look to you for a witty comment and all of a sudden you're quiet. What's up?"

"That's what I wanted to talk to you about," Brutey said, rubbing his chin.

"All right then. Out with it. There's nothing you can say that will ever change my opinion of you."

Brutey started talking because he trusted Coach Hall. He only hoped that the Coach meant what he said, because his story was a doozy.

* * *

Harry Hall came to Springboro in the spring of 1966 when, after coaching for a year at Hillsboro High School in Highland County, he learned that Gerald Saunders had resigned a very successful tenure as Panther head coach. It was just one season removed from the state finals season, so community interest in the program was as intense as ever. Coach Hall brought with him coaching experience but also huge success as a player. He starred on his own high school team before graduating in 1958, and then averaged more than twenty-eight points a game at Fairmont State College in West Virginia, where he was an All-American. He learned early on as a player that discipline and preparation were the two key ingredients to winning. And Coach Hall never compromised either one.

From the time he arrived, Coach Hall made his players wear shirts and ties on game days, and purchased blue sport jackets with a team patch on the left front that they were to wear, too. At all times they were uniform in spirit and in dress.

CHAPTER 28

Haircuts were above the ear, and no facial hair, a tough rule in light of the hippie fashion that was so prevalent at the time. Every practice was outlined in detail so that every minute was productive, and he kept the practice outlines on file so he could remember from one year to the next what was practiced before particular opponents. Players were required to wear kneepads to encourage scrambling for loose balls.

He also made his basketball players run cross country in the fall. None of them particularly liked it, but they knew it was good for them. With several months of running miles on end, they started basketball season in excellent shape. There was also another reason to run cross country – he wouldn't let anyone into open gym unless they were active in a fall sport.

Coach Hall also took the fifth and sixth grade basketball program away from the parents, and gave each team one varsity player as a head coach, and a jayvee player as an assistant. That's how Jeff Howard ended up as my coach for two years.

Maybe some of the parents didn't like that. But the kids loved it.

His first team in '66-'67 returned only one letterman and went 4-15, but they lost seven games by a total of fifteen points, three in overtime. In a small town, it was common for talent to vary drastically from year-to-year, and the handwriting had been on the wall for several years that the program would go through a down period.

The record improved to 8-13 the next year, which was better, but Coach Hall was particularly encouraged that the young team won many games late in the year. That gave them momentum and a confidence going into the next season. That momentum carried over to the '68-'69 season, as a team with players like Al Wight, Wayne Kemper, Dale Bost, Charlie Johnson and Rod Charlton went undefeated in the conference, giving Springboro its first-ever FAVC title, and a 17-3 record. They made a strong showing in the post-season tournament before losing a one-point heartbreaker to Middletown in the sectional finals.

With Wight and Kemper graduated, Springboro wasn't expected to do as well in the '69-'70 season, but Coach Hall did a masterful job of coordinating a good team. That year they surprised people, going 15-4 and finishing second in the conference. The stars that year were Cork Jackson, Tom Shoemaker and Jeff Kees. By now, Coach Hall had established himself as a winner. He was in total control of the program. As a result, the town embraced the methods of its new young coach, and looked forward to the years to come.

The '70-'71 basketball season was another rebuilding year. Sophomore Jimmy Hough was point guard and leading scorer that year, and Doug Patton, Gary's older brother, and Scott Bradstreet were other team leaders. That team went 5-14 and finished fifth in the conference, which may not have been much to brag about, but something else happened. It marked the beginning of something bigger.

A group of excellent players was banding together.

When the 1971-72 season rolled around, Hough, Howard, Patton and company were juniors and little was known and expected from them, at least outside of Springboro. A pre-season newspaper poll ranked them fifth in the FAVC, a news item that Coach Hall cut out and put on the locker room bulletin board so the players would look at it every day before practice in order to fire them up. He'd have made a banner of it if he could have. It didn't take long for them to prove the prediction wrong. That team, playing with only one senior – Bradstreet – went 11-1 in the conference, and went 13-5 overall. It lost to Mason in the first round of the tournament, which was a shocker. But overall it was considered a successful season.

Coach Hall turned the tournament setback into a positive, however. He reminded his team that upsets were the rule in tournament play, and they had simply fallen victim to that reality. Over the summer, they had a choice, to either fall apart because of such a loss, or go the other way. Use it as a motivator. Use it to make themselves better for the next season.

By the end of that year, everybody knew about Springboro's star players. Beyond their talent, they were mentally tough. They were competitors, with a killer instinct, and all of them worked hard in the off-season. When the players gathered nightly to play basketball either at the high school or at the Miami University-Middletown campus or any place where good competition could be found, the memory of the Mason loss remained fresh. They were eager to atone for it, too.

The pre-season pundits were all but handing Springboro the conference championship before the beginning of the 1972-73 season. A seed in the post-season tournament was expected and a repeat of what the magical team of '64-'65 had accomplished remained in the hopes and dreams of everyone in town. Coach Hall cringed every time he heard that, though he secretly expected it, too.

The constant through all of this was Coach Hall. His confidence was sometimes seen as arrogance, and his rules were not always popular. But the town could see the proof in the numbers.

* * *

The Panthers were 3-0 going into the Edgewood game, playing well and working hard to get better. That's all Coach could ask of them.

CHAPTER 28

A real test of what the team was made of would come in the next few weeks, when the team had three difficult opponents, all on the road. First they would go to Franklin, the backyard rival that was bigger in many ways. Then they would go to Madison, a team that walloped Springboro 100-61 the year before on its way to the state finals. Last, but certainly not least, they would go to Mason. Say no more.

The games would be tough, but no one doubted that Coach Hall would have his team prepared for them.

Brutey told the whole story and it was worse than Coach Hall anticipated. The fallout would no doubt be devastating, and Coach Hall worried about the distraction to his team and damage to the program. Brutey said he understood. He apologized over and over and also told Coach Hall how proud he was of him and the way he runs his basketball team. He volunteered to step aside as coach of the junior high and perhaps he could still be a scout on Friday nights. Coach Hall said that sounded like a good plan, but he needed to think it over.

"I hate to lose you. These kids really look up to you," Coach told him. "Keep me posted what's going on. Once you're in the clear, I'll take you back in a heartbeat. I do what's right for the kids, no matter what the public might think. Everybody knows that."

So Brutey watched the Panthers clobber Edgewood from the stands that Saturday night. He felt like such an outsider, like a runaway father who returned to watch his boy play ball from a distance. The more he couldn't be part of the team, the more he wanted to be in the middle of it. He suffered silently.

Gary Patton caught fire in the second quarter to break the game open. Dave Collins made some outstanding defensive plays. Later, outside the locker room after the game, Coach Hall praised Edgewood and its coaches. "They're a good team, but we managed to get some lucky breaks. We'll need to be lucky next week at Franklin. And then at Madison after that. Remember last year. They came here and whipped us like a drum."

This time, the reporters believed Harry Hall.

Brutey hung around for a little while after the game. He shook hands and chatted with Ray Perez, the school superintendent, and Vince Ross, the high school principal, for fifteen minutes. Even though he didn't possess a high position like the both of them, he could tell he held their respect. They talked and joked with him like they were all part of a big fraternity. They sought Brutey's opinion on the basketball team just as if they were talking to Coach Hall himself.

He was sad as he walked home that night. He wondered what their opinion would be of him come Monday.

Bloody Monday.

Judge P. Daniel Fedders, circa 1972

Prosecutor Morris Turkelson

Defense Counsel Fred Jones

Judge William Young Circa 1972

Eddie Lawson

Thomas B. Kirby Jr. My Dad

There was a time when a $100 fee was a big retainer to pay a lawyer. In Warren County, there were two common pleas court judges, William Young (bottom left) and P. Daniel Fedders (top left). Morris Turkelson (middle to) was the county prosecutor, and Fred Jones (top right) was one of the more highly-regarded lawyers in the county. Eddie Lawson (middle bottom) and Tom Kirby were lawyers who lived in Springboro.

CHAPTER 30

My dad fought to get people out of jail, and I thought he must have been enormously successful at it, because he never came home with a single scratch on him.

-- The Misconception

Thursday, December 7, 1972

On Monday, the phone call was made first thing in the morning, and Brutey gave his statement to the authorities later that afternoon. He told the entire story to Charlie Reedy, Jimmy Beavers, Springboro chief of police Carl Hirshbach and an Ohio State trooper, and didn't leave out a single detail, either. When he left, he felt relieved that his secret was finally out in the open.

By Tuesday, the prosecution assembled a grand jury. By Thursday, Brutey appeared in court for his first court appearance. Before all of this, he had thought that the court system moved slowly. But not anymore. For him, it moved at warp speed, which hardly seemed fair, and he was convinced the public assassination of his character would move faster than that.

The old Warren County courthouse was a grand but aging structure built in the mid-1800s on Silver Street in Lebanon, the county seat. It was four blocks from historic downtown and housed three entire courts in the three-story building, as well as the county administration offices. The whole building was alive as Brutey marched through the front doors that morning. Norma was beside him and my dad was already there waiting on him. But so was the family of Janet Spencer. The arraignment in State of Ohio vs. Harold Benjamin Baker was scheduled for eight-thirty in front of Judge P. Daniel Fedders.

CHAPTER 30

Seeing the family of Janet Spencer worried Norma. "What are they doing here?" Norma whispered to Dad. "Are they going to ask that Brutey go to jail today?"

Dad shook his head. "It's common for the family of a homicide victim to be present at all court hearings. It's part of the healing process. It shows that they loved their daughter and they don't want her to be left out in any of the discussions.

"Is Brutey going to go to prison?"

"It's too early for me to know the answer to that. I'm sure going to do everything I can to make sure it doesn't happen."

Brutey entered the conversation. "What do I say today? Is the judge going to ask me anything?"

Dad told him to relax and that he would do all the talking. An arraignment consisted of nothing more than answering the charges, and for today – since the defense had the right to require the prosecution to prove its case – the plea would be not guilty and a request would be made to schedule a pre-trial conference, something that would likely be scheduled in late January. Until then, Dad would request that the prosecutor provide him all the witnesses and evidence that he had against Brutey.

"How can I plead not guilty when I did it? I was driving the car."

"I know. I know. But what you did may not be involuntary manslaughter. That's what we have to look into. We will probably have a motion hearing well in advance of trial on that very issue."

"Gawd, I'm a nervous wreck." It made a tie game going into overtime look like a walk in the park.

Dad sat with Brutey and Norma at the back of the big courtroom. Up at the counsel table, county prosecutor Morris Turkelson flipped through some files and made notes. P.B. Stockman, the judge's bailiff who was known throughout Springboro for his announcements of the band and because he served on the Springboro school board, poured water into a glass on the judge's bench. Meanwhile, other defendants and their lawyers filtered into the courtroom. There was the occasional whisper; otherwise, there was silence. Dad used to say that the moments just before a judge entering a courtroom were a lot like being in church. Only scarier.

"Kirby, it's good seeing you, my boy." Dad looked up to see Fred Jones, a Lebanon lawyer who was a few years older and many years more experienced than he. Mr. Jones was there that day representing a Maineville man for murder, having charged him $25,000, reported to be the highest fee ever charged in a Warren

County case. But money was no object since Mr. Jones was generally thought to be *the* man in the county. He didn't just persuade juries, he virtually threatened them. He dared them to find against his client, and they rarely did. As a result, Mr. Jones walked through the courthouse the way Moses walked through the Red Sea.

Mr. Jones was dressed as he normally was, in a three-piece charcoal suit and burgundy tie, with a black topcoat and burgundy briefcase at his side. People did a double take when they saw him, because he was instantly recognizable in and around the courthouse, and his presence indicated that a big case was taking place.

"Hey, Fred. Nice job on the Witt case last week. I caught the last part of your closing argument."

"Got lucky. The prosecutor never saw where I was coming from, and by the time I tied it all up in closing, it was too late for him. He couldn't catch up."

"You get lucky like that a lot."

Mr. Jones then turned to Brutey Baker. "Fred Jones, nice to meet you."

"You, too." They shook hands.

"You've got a good lawyer here. The best. If he can't help you, nobody can." Then he turned and walked to the counsel table where almost immediately he and the prosecutor began to argue. A half-minute later, Judge Fedders entered the courtroom and P.B. Stockman told everyone to rise. Court was now in session.

"Mr. Turkelson, are we handling Mr. Jones' case first?"

"Yes, your honor."

The common pleas court, on the top floor, handled all the felony charges and civil lawsuits involving more than five thousand dollars. It was also where all the divorces were handled. There were two common pleas court judges, Judge William Young and Judge Fedders. Elsewhere in the building, the county municipal court, with Judge Herdman, occupied the basement. Misdemeanor criminal citations and traffic tickets were handled there, plus civil lawsuits under five thousand dollars. The probate and juvenile court, with Judge Bowers, occupied the first floor, and he handled delinquent juveniles as well as all matters that settled estates.

Brutey's case was called second, right after Fred Jones' murder case, and Brutey stood nervously at the podium. With his mind going in a million directions and his lips tightened, he was glad he wouldn't have to say anything.

"Your honor, the defense acknowledges receipt of the indictment and waives any defects in service, including the twenty-four hour rule. We ask that the case be set for a hearing on our motion to dismiss."

The prosecutor interrupted. "Dismiss? How do you figure?"

"It'll all be in my brief."

"But he admitted to everything. You were there when he did it. There was no coercion. His statement was made freely and voluntarily, you know that."

"That's not the basis for my motion."

"Well, what –"

"Gentlemen, gentlemen!" Judge Fedders interrupted. "When you speak in court, you address the court, not each other."

"Yes, sir."

"Yes, your honor."

Judge Fedders lowered his head, something he often did when he chose his words carefully. "The hearing on the motion will be heard January 23. Until then, Mr. Baker will remain free on his own recognizance. Mr. Baker, stay in touch with Mr. Kirby. That's all for today. Call the next case."

The two attorneys jawed with one another for a few seconds more and then Brutey and Dad walked out the back of the courtroom. The first court appearance was over and Brutey hadn't ended up in jail. That by itself felt like a victory for him. He and Norma promised to schedule an appointment in the next week, and all three took off away from the courthouse. It was only nine o'clock and Brutey felt like he had already put in a full day. If he hadn't been so determined to quit drinking, it would have been the perfect time to stop off some place for a belt.

The next thing he had to brace for was the public reaction to the news. No doubt he would be blasted at every turn. There was nothing that lit up a town like a good ball game or a scandal.

Brutey would be the focus of the scandal. He was just thrilled that the basketball team had the promise of taking everyone's mind off of him and onto it instead.

* * *

By four-fifteen, the bleachers on our side of the gym were still fairly empty.

Our junior high teams played host to Lebanon that night, and in typical fashion, the seventh grade game was the warm-up for the eighth grade game two hours later. It was hard for parents to get to the start of our game, so it wasn't unusual for the stands to be empty when the game started and then almost full by the time it ended.

We were in our usual pre-game routine, with ten guys in two lines taking turns doing lay-ups. It didn't have near the fan-fare of the varsity warm-up, because we didn't do The Star and there was no band playing the school fight song, but I was pumped up nonetheless. We were wearing Springboro uniforms and I was on the same floor that Jim Hough made twenty-footers; my imagination took it from there. I was a Panther just the same.

"Okay, guys, now we go," Coach Wilson told us in the huddle. "Mitch, I want you to look for Shane and Donny on the wings."

"I'll be open," Donny announced.

"Me, too," Shane shot back.

"Of course. I have no doubt," Coach said. "You guys, look inside to Jerry. If he's open, get the ball inside. Otherwise, look for the short jumper. Mitch, make your way to the corner. You're deadly from there."

"And what about me?" Donny asked, half-joking.

"Or me?" Shane jumped in.

Coach Wilson chuckled. "Shane, Donny, if I can just make sure you are as competitive with other teams as you are with each other, we're winning everything."

The rest of us took our place on the bench. Our cheerleaders were to our left, in front of where our parents would eventually be. I glanced over quickly and saw that Debbie Balyo was on the far end, in between Dodie Fetters and Lana Beavers. Oooh man, I couldn't wait to get into the game and do something to impress the three of them. Maybe I would make a long jump shot. Maybe I could block a shot from the other team. Better yet, maybe I would go crashing into the bleachers diving for a loose ball and get a concussion or something. Yeah, that would really impress them.

Jerry Monnin won the jump and tipped it to Donny. He quickly passed to Mitch, who dribbled and then fired to Shane in the corner. Donny cut to the basket and Shane made a perfect bounce pass that hit Donny in stride, leading to an easy lay-up. We were ahead, 2-0, and it had been the teamwork of Donny and Shane that had produced the early lead.

"Nice pass, Shane."

"Hey, thanks. Nice cut."

Brutey found it difficult to sit in the stands. Since his son Ricky played, he came to all of our games. But out of respect for Coach Hall and the legal troubles he was in, he honored the request to not coach. He sat about five rows behind the bench, next to Norma, and we never saw anything out of him except for clapping for a nice play. He respected all the other parents, but listening to their selfish and irresponsible comments often drove him crazy, and that's when we would see him standing at the door to the coaches' room. From there the cheerleaders stood between him and the parents, which allowed him to enjoy the game more, though he still ached to be sitting on the bench.

So he picked his moments. When Mitch grew tired late in the first half, I entered the game with us ahead by only four, 14-10. Lebanon's Randy Callahan missed a short jump shot, and Jerry Monnin ripped down the rebound. He hit Donny on an outlet pass, and Donny quickly threw the ball to me. I dribbled down into the corner, when Callahan then knocked the ball out of bounds. I then stood right next to Brutey as the referee threw me the ball for the inbounds play.

"Watch for Shane off the pick," Brutey whispered. "Give the play a chance to develop. Be patient. There it is!"

I made a perfect pass and Shane made the shot. For ten minutes all everyone could do was congratulate me on such a great play, but the truth was I had nothing to do with it. Brutey deserved the credit. We went on to win our third straight game, and afterward we sat in the stands watching the eighth graders (and the cheerleaders). Brutey, meanwhile, stood in the corner and continued to dish out helpful hints when he could.

More than once he told himself that he was simply making the best of a bad situation.

But more than that he told himself that life was full of major disappointments. Why couldn't he have just stayed in his proper lane of travel? It was a question he could never answer. Where was the peace he had before he decided to come forward? And how was he ever going to act normal until January 23?

No judge could punish him any more than he already punished himself.

Gordy Gregg took over the role of inside bulldog once Scott Bradstreet (50) graduated. Though only six-two, Gordy muscled his way inside, grabbing rebounds and setting picks and also scoring. Though the seventh-grades like Lance Penwell, Jeff Kirby, Roger Woolery, Shane Hatfield and Todd Thompson noticed only the leading scorers, the coaches knew what value Gordy Gregg was to the varsity.

CHAPTER 31

Every tree needs roots and every boat needs a rudder. Sometimes the players who don't get headlines are just as important as the stars.
-- The truth coaches told me

FRIDAY, DECEMBER 15, 1972

The first few flakes of snow began to fall just before lunch. We could see them from the window in Mr. Terry Lawson's room, and fifteen minutes later the ground was a solid blanket of white. Danny Kruer predicted eighteen inches of snow, which sounded like great news to all of us, but then we had to remember how much Danny tended to exaggerate things. He was also the guy who, over the summer, had told us that he made like Evel Knievel and jumped his bicycle over Clear Creek, in the big section of water right next door to the Chmeil house. That was quite an accomplishment, if it were true, but no one had been able to confirm his report.

By the time we finished lunch, the snow was falling heavily and it was clear they had to send us home early. Sure enough, a little after lunch, we were told to report to fifth period, get our assignments, and then we could leave for the day. The home basketball game that night against Blanchester was cancelled. Our seventh grade practice set for Saturday morning was also cancelled.

We had the afternoon free. And we had the weekend to ourselves. For a second, it seemed like summertime again.

I sat between Michele Brown and Linda Fish in fourth period English class. I had known both of them since kindergarten and as we watched the snow come down in a hurry, we couldn't remember the last time we'd been sent home from school early on account of the weather. Back in second grade, when we all had Mrs. Tillie Simpson as a teacher, it seemed like we'd been out a school for a whole week one time. A few years later, when we had Mr. C. Gordon in the fifth grade, we had a huge snow that kept us home for three straight days.

This was only for an afternoon, but it didn't matter. Missing school for ten minutes was always a pleasure.

Some of the kids gleefully walked home; others stopped at the K & W, proving that there was never a day too cold for ice cream. I was among twenty or so kids who walked to Mitch's house, where we found some of the high schoolers already there playing ping-pong. Gordy Gregg was up ten to five on Gary Patton as a dozen others watched. We walked into the backdoor and saw Mrs. Leisz standing at the stove. Kim was nearby pouring her world-famous chili into a bowl for somebody. From our vantage point we could see inside the living room, and it was full. The music coming from inside it was loud.

"C'mon, look at what I've got," Mitch said.

We followed him as if he had just discovered a national treasure. We walked through the living room, past John Mockabee on the couch and over Dave Dillon who was lying in the middle of the living room, and on to Mitch's room which was at the far end of the house, next to Kim's.

"I got this the other day," he said, pulling out a baseball card and handling it like it was a forty-karat diamond.

It was a Pete Rose rookie card, mint condition. None of us had ever seen something so magnificent. Pete Rose was a player we idolized. We went to Reds games just to watch him run to first base after a walk, or slide into third base head first. We imitated his play while on the playground, and modeled our own style of play during our Little League games. And yet there it was, right in front of us, the most-prized baseball card any of us could dare to get a hold of.

"Man, how did you get that?" I asked, envious.

"I had an extra Johnny Bench and Willie Mays and I traded for it with my cousin Russ," Mitch said.

"Oh, man. You're kidding," I said. "I've got an extra Tony Perez, and I'd have given up my Hank Aaron and my Jim Brown for that one."

"Does he have any more?" Lance asked. We could sit and talk about baseball and football cards for hours.

CHAPTER 31

But throughout all this, a kid named Sam clearly wasn't impressed.

"I wouldn't want it if you did," Sam murmured. "About the only thing it's good for is to put in the spokes on your bicycle. Pete Rose, who needs him? I'll take Roberto Clemente every day. He could run circles around Charlie Hustle."

The whole place stopped. It's like there was this total deafening silence that lasted for hours, maybe days. Everyone was stunned at what they just heard. We were in the heart of Reds country, and they'd just been in the World Series for the second time in three years. People were beginning to refer to them as 'The Big Red Machine' and Pete Rose was perhaps the most important player they had. And here Sam dared to offer criticism.

"You can't be serious." Donny Wilburn said.

"Does a bear go in the woods? Of course I'm serious. The Reds are my team but Pete's just not my guy."

This led to a rousing discussion about big league baseball, its players and its teams, and the games we had seen through the years first at Old Crosley Field and then later at Riverfront. We were twelve years old, with no responsibility and – thanks to the snow – no school, so if we wanted to spend a few hours talking about baseball and cards and games we had seen, there was nothing stopping us.

"Hey Mitch," Ricky Baker said finally. "What would it take for you to trade Pete?"

Mitch chuckled. The price would be steep. "Nothing short of Babe Ruth, Joe DiMaggio and Mickey Mantle," he said jokingly.

"Is that all?" Ricky asked.

"Yeah, okay. Throw in Ted Kluszewski."

"Okay."

"Okay what?" Mitch fired back. His eyes were wide and his voice pitched higher. This negotiation session was really getting good.

"I can do that."

Mitch's jaw dropped to the floor. The rest of us looked at him like he was some sort of god, like he had done something superhuman, like kissing a girl on the lips. "You've got all those guys?" Mitch asked. "You can't be serious."

"My grandpa died a couple of years ago and he left all of his cards to me and Larry. I've got a whole box. You should see them."

"Does Brutey know you want to trade?"

"I can't trade. I just wanted to know if you wanted to see them."

"Let's go."

And with that twenty kids halfway zipped up their coats and walked the five blocks to Market Street, throwing snowballs and cracking jokes the whole way. Yeah, go ahead and say it. Sometimes it was soooooo difficult being a kid.

* * *

The only bad part about the snow was that there wouldn't be a varsity game that night, which everyone in town was looking forward to. The varsity had been beaten for the first time of the season the week before at Franklin, a game where three of our starters fouled out, which infuriated everyone because it seemed a pattern of being treated unfairly there was developing. The memory of Dave Dillon's eighty-yard touchdown being called back in the football game at Franklin was still fresh in everyone's mind. Now Blanchester was scheduled to come to town, and the goal was to take out our frustration on them. Light it up, we'd say! Hough, Howard and Patton teaming up for eighty. Boom!

But the snow changed everything. Coach Hall wanted the team in the gym at five-thirty for practice. Snow or no snow, the team needed practice. A return match-up with Madison was on the horizon, and then the conference schedule swung into full gear after Christmas and New Year's. Before they got there, Coach Hall said the zone press needed refined and the motion offense needed work. We were shooting well from outside, but our guards weren't coming off picks the way they should, leaving a huge part of the offense unused. A pick-and-roll drill would be practiced all night until they got it right.

The big man who was a large part of that aspect of the offense was Gordy Gregg. He was a senior and a starter, but rarely did Gordy get a headline or a large write-up in the paper. "My job is to set picks and rebound," he would joke. He was also pretty good at taking a charge now and then. But though he wasn't generally known for shooting or handling the ball, he did average seven points a game. Only six-two, he was a power forward, often assigned to an opponent's inside strong man. He did his job well because he was smart enough to put himself in the correct position, and because he was as strong as an ox.

While Jimmy Hough, Jeff Howard and Gary Patton got the headlines, everyone close to the team knew Gordy's quiet contributions were as important as all the points scored.

Such an auspicious senior year was not envisioned when young Gordy began his schooling in Springboro. His parents James and Esther moved to Springboro from Lebanon to be closer to their extended family. Rick Black, another senior and basketball teammate from town, was his cousin. And James Eyler, the mayor of Springboro, was his uncle. After renting the home at the corner of South and Gilpin in 1962, they purchased the home at 410 Factory brand new a year later.

Gordy owed a lot to Mr. Carl Gordon, who he had as a teacher in the fifth grade, which was the year the basketball team went all the way to state. Gordy went to some of the games, but wasn't particularly interested because sports just didn't appeal to him that much. He remembers reading a book while some of the game action went on right in front of him.

That changed in the spring of his fifth grade year when, during lunch and recess, "Mr. C" as Carl Gordon was known, would go out back of the school and play football and basketball with the boys. He learned the way games were played and saw the enjoyment that could be had while playing them. From then on, he spent a lot of time at the park or at the school, playing and practicing and working to improve, and enjoying himself in the process.

A setback came in seventh grade when he failed to make the seventh grade basketball team. "Just wasn't good enough," he said later. Despite the disappointment, though, he continued to play and practice, and when the season was over, coach Ted Hall – who was also the eighth grade coach – noticed how he much had improved, and commented to some of the other players that they were about to get caught by him unless they continued to work hard, too. By this time Gordy was walking to most of the home varsity football and basketball games all the time, and enjoying himself.

He made the eighth grade team, playing behind Big John Mockabee, and then a year later benefited from Big John's decision to work on his shot-put skills in the winter rather than play basketball. Gordy became a starter that year and then, a year later, became one of four members of the class of 1973 to make the varsity as a sophomore – Jim Hough, Gary Patton and Rod Dillon being the others.

He had two memories of his sophomore year, both away from the actual game action. The first happened on the very first night of the season. Coach Hall required haircuts above the ears, and Gordy's mom generally cut his hair. As Gordy got ready to leave for that first game, he walked in to have his mom trim his hair. But she had a migraine that day and was unable to do it. And, like many things, money for a haircut was not in the family budget. When he walked into the gym with his hair too long, Coach Hall wouldn't let him dress. "Never happened again," Gordy said.

The second memory had to do with being on the varsity. It was an honor and a privilege to be there, but he never got to play. So he decided to do something about it. "One day I marched down to Coach's office and told him that I'd only been playing for two years; what I needed was game experience. I wanted to play jayvee," he remembered. "I thought I made a pretty good case too."

But Coach kept him on the varsity. "Showed me what I knew."

He played a lot his junior year, coming off the bench to give starting center Scott Bradstreet a breather. By the time his senior season came around, his goal was to be a starter, thus becoming a poster child to all kids who get cut in junior high and want to believe that their playing career is over. He traveled the circuit with all the other guys that summer, playing in schools all over, driving his green '67 Chevy pick-up everywhere they went.

When the first starting line-up was announced at Carlisle when the season began, Gordy was in it.

That didn't change the rest of the season.

He averaged thirty picks and fifteen rebounds a game, though none of that could be found anywhere in the box scores.

But Gordy knew what he had done. And so did his teammates.

* * *

With the snow continuing to fall, the Springboro Police Department had little to do. No one was leaving their homes. Traffic, which was already light in the one stoplight town, was even lighter. When Charlie and Jimmy, the only two officers on duty, met for supper at The Diner, they discussed how the only calls they were getting were from the local merchants wanting to know if they should close early.

Charlie had meatloaf and mashed potatoes. Jimmy, ever the southern boy at heart, ordered biscuits and gravy. They talked about their kids and some of the politics within the department. They also talked about Christmas presents they still had to buy, and how they were glad they still had more than a week in order to buy them and have them wrapped. But they also talked about their cases, one in particular.

CHAPTER 31

"I was in county court the other day on that DWI we got down by the taxidermy," Charlie mentioned.

"You mean that fella' who crashed into the bridge? What did he try to claim, that the bridge moved and so it wasn't his fault that he hit it?" They both laughed.

"He pled out. Anyway, the prosecutor pulled me aside to talk about the Baker case. Wanted to know how I felt about Brutey."

"What did you tell him?" Jimmy took a sip of coffee.

"I told him what anybody in this town would tell him. Brutey's a great guy. He's coached just about every kid who's ever put on a jock strap in this town, and most of them realize how much better off they are because of his influence. I said it looks like he made a terrible mistake and he's owned up to it, and he seems to be awfully sorry for what he done."

"You ain't a kiddin'. I saw him at the ball game the other night and he was barely talking to people. That ain't like him. So what did the prosecutor say?"

Charlie set his dish to the side. "He said they had a meeting with the family the other day. They discussed the case and Brutey. They were trying to figure out what they might offer to settle the case. They wanted to determine what should happen to Brutey."

"How'd they sound?"

"No deals, they said. The family is hurt beyond belief and they want Brutey held accountable. They want to punish him and send a message to the community." He took one last sip of coffee.

"So they won't go along with probation?" Jimmy asked.

"Nope. They want Brutey in prison."

For nearly two decades, the Mockabee name dominated the Springboro class lists. Bob was a starter on the '65 state basketball team, while John was a tackle and shot-putter for the Class of '73. And Chuck, behind Kim Zech, was the lone junior starter on the star-studded team that won its final ten regular season games.

CHAPTER 32

Bing Crosby dreamt for it to be white
and Charlie Brown wondered what
it was really all about. All I knew was
that Christmas meant I got something good.
-- The simple observation

Sunday, December 24, 1972

The scenes all over town made it clear that it was Christmas. The Church of Christ on Main Street had a nativity scene with a tiny light under a blanket to signify the baby Jesus. Almost all of the homes on Willow Street had lights hanging from gutters and around windows and front doors. Then there was the granddaddy of them all, a two-story house at the corner of Woods and Duncan Court that had lights around the perimeter of the roof and house, plus around all windows and in the trees in the yard. People came from miles around to see that one.

It was not a white Christmas. The snow that had closed school and cancelled the varsity basketball game a couple of weeks earlier had melted. The air was chilly and the leaves on the trees were long gone, but the most we could expect come Christmas morning was a few snow flurries that covered over the frosty brown grass. That was okay, because all the hype about a white Christmas was overrated anyway.

My sisters wanted Santa to bring an Easy-Bake oven, and my brothers were hoping for a Hot Wheels track and matching car set.

"I want a RED car," Joey would say. "I want it to race my RED fire truck. Get it?"

"Shut up," responded my brother John, who had red hair, and was sensitive about it.

"Red."

"I said shut up!"

"Red. Red." Joey had fun teasing John all day long.

Me? I wanted a new baseball glove and a new basketball. I also wanted a Tim McCarver book that explained what it meant to be a catcher. And a Jim Croce record. But more than anything I wanted an electric football game which pitted the Chiefs against the Jets. I could plug it in and play with it for hours, and it would be much better than the football card game that Mitch and I had made up.

"Hey, if you get that we can play it, too," my brother Joey offered. "I'll be the Jets. John can be the Chiefs. What color are they again, John?"

"Red," John said, not thinking.

"Man, now you're doing it for me."

John chased Joey out the door and down the street, barefooted, but never caught up with him. But he'd get him later.

The Sunday paper was extra thick, with ads from Sears and J.C. Penney's and Rike's that promised good prices for last-minute shoppers, plus the ever-ridiculous after-Christmas sales. As I made the short ride from my house to the place where I was to pick up all the papers I was to deliver, I knew I would be in for a long morning. The cold wind in my face felt like knives cutting me, and before long my fingers and toes were frozen. On cold winter mornings such as this it was a blessing to have the Gilpin Apartments on my route. There I could sit inside and read the paper while my tingling toes and fingers warmed up.

"Merry Christmas" was the banner headline at the top of the front page of the *The Dayton Daily News*. Below it was a story about Watergate, and down below it was a story about the war in Vietnam. Those stories were always on the front page, and at the top of the evening news, so I knew everything I needed to know about both of them. I quickly passed to the sports section, which focused primarily on the national sports scene and only casually mentioned local games. Not much had happened locally the day before. The varsity had followed up its loss at Madison on Wednesday with a win at Clinton-Massie on Friday, but that was not reported in the Sunday paper. All the other local schools were on break, too, as was the University of Dayton basketball team, which was our favorite local college team.

The big story that morning was about a play that had been shown and re-shown a hundred times the day before on television. On the last play of the Oakland Raiders' playoff game at Pittsburgh, Terry Bradshaw's last-second pass had deflected off the helmet of a Raider. The Steelers' Franco Harris caught the pass just before it hit the ground, and then ran forty yards past a stunned Raider defense for a touchdown. Already they were calling it "The Immaculate Reception." Already Curt Gowdy was predicting that it would likely be the most re-played play in the history of football. I tended to agree with that prediction because I personally had seen it more than any other play in sports history – except maybe Pete Rose's headfirst slide in the 1970 All-Star game.

The sports page showed Bradshaw in shock, grasping the top of his helmet and leaning back as if he couldn't believe what had just happened. The victory earned them the right to play the AFC championship game against the undefeated Miami Dolphins, who beat the Cleveland Browns. The winner of that game would go on to play in the Super Bowl in a few weeks.

Like all of my friends, I knew the stars and statistics of every team. I knew which teams were leading which divisions, and I knew what players led the leagues in various categories. Mom only wished that I could rattle off math quotients with the same ease.

We would re-enact the play on the playground that afternoon and make predictions about who would be in the Super Bowl. It didn't matter if it was Christmas Eve. After all, it was still a Sunday afternoon.

While everyone else in town was busy wrapping and cooking, a bunch of us met at Mitch's to play football. Practically everyone was there, wearing our jeans and tennis shoes but with an extra hooded sweatshirt overtop of our normal sweatshirt. Donny and Shane were named captains, and they took turns choosing teams. I ended up on a team with Roger, Lance and Shane Hatfield, who was still my nemesis even though football season had ended two months earlier. What made matters worse was that he insisted on being quarterback, not me. So I secretly devised a plan to sabotage Shane and somehow make him look bad.

"Okay, everybody go long," Shane said in the huddle. "But let Wilburn blitz through. He's about to buy a bulls eye in the jewels. Ready, let's break."

Roger hiked the ball and Shane instantly knew he was in trouble. Donny sent everyone into rush, with no steamboats at that, and Shane was slammed to the ground. It was pretty funny really, but Shane didn't see it that way. He tossed the ball away and jumped up, cussing as we huddled back up.

"Man, get over it. It was a joke," Donny smiled.

"A joke? Yeah, funny. Ha."

It hadn't been but a week ago, in our seventh-grade game against Madison, that Donny and Shane combined to lead us to victory. They were magic together, each playing off the other, passing as if each had a sixth sense and trapping as if they had practiced it their whole life. As a result, Madison didn't have a chance. We won easily, 30-14, as Donny had eight points and Shane seven.

"Hey, Shane. You know what ten football players call one wimp?" Donny asked.

Shane ignored him for a moment while he repositioned his sweatshirt. Finally, he decided to answer: "What?"

"Quarterback!"

His team laughed like there was no tomorrow. And then, amid their fun, they looked at me and realized what had been said was not funny to everybody, especially me. I was a quarterback, too, they realized. And while the smiles didn't disappear, the mood changed drastically. Now, not only did they have Shane to deal with it, but they also had a ticked-off me. So Shane and I huddled to do something about it. When play resumed, I went long as fast as I possibly could, catching a perfect spiral from Shane down the left sideline. We were up 1-0 in a heartbeat. And we weren't finished.

Shane intercepted a pass, giving us the ball back. This time I ran a post-pattern, faking to the outside and turning in, wide-open. Shane's pass was once again right on target. Now it was 2-0. A few minutes later it was 3-0 and we were still going strong.

By the time it was over, and all of us scattered to get home for our Christmas get-togethers, Shane and I combined for seven touchdowns and we won easily, 10-4.

Game Over. I loved Shane Hatfield.

Anyone who told you otherwise was a dang liar.

* * *

When he awoke, his eyes were quickly filled with the same tears he'd had the night before, and he was consumed with sadness. Brutey was reminded that Janet Spencer's family, her two little girls in particular, were finding little reason to celebrate

CHAPTER 32

Christmas. There would be one less stocking over the fireplace, a few less presents under the tree. Brutey was as down as he had ever been. He was tempted to pull into the garage and leave the truck running. Or maybe take a drive over Clear Creek and take a right into the water. Or maybe find another use for that silver-handled pistol his uncle gave him years ago. Why did he have to go left of center? Why did she have to be coming the opposite way at just that very moment? How could he have been so stupid? How could he live with such pain and remorse for the rest of his life?

Nothing seemed to ease the pain, even the knowledge that by turning himself in he had done the right thing.

He had his coffee with the morning paper, but he found it difficult to focus on any of the news. While Norma and the kids slept, he sat in his chair in the living room, with no lights on and no television running, and buried his head in his hands and cried. Far and away, this was the worst day of his life. There would be no jog through the country today. His goal, if he had any, was to make it until nine o'clock. If he did that, his goal was to make it to ten. He couldn't see his life having any existence beyond that.

"Please, God, help me," he cried. "Bring her back if you can. Kill me instead of her. I'd rather be the one who's dead than to have to live with this regret the rest of my life."

He repeated one word for several minutes: Please.

Before all of this, he would have never thought to pray for anything. He didn't like any church he'd ever been in, and wasn't sure he could accept the idea of some higher being that created the universe. Church was something that weaker and less intelligent people did on a Sunday to try and make themselves feel better, nothing more.

Just then he was startled by the ringing of the telephone. He didn't know who could be calling at such an early hour. It was Sunday, Christmas Eve day. Surely most people knew that it was a day to sleep in.

It rang a second time and then a third. Brutey stared at the phone and considered not picking it up, believing it was Janet Spencer's family, calling to remind him of what he had done and of the devastation he had caused. That was the last thing he needed. Or maybe it was Coach Hall or Coach Ross telling him that he was no longer needed as any part of the Springboro athletic program. Or maybe it was my dad, calling to say that the police were on their way to make sure he spent Christmas in jail.

He picked it up after the fourth ring. His voice gave out as he said hello.

It was Reverend Dawes, already wide awake and sounding as chipper as if it were a Saturday afternoon. Church would begin in a couple of hours, but he was already in his office, reviewing his sermon notes and praying, when he suddenly felt the compulsion to give Brutey a call. He would never know just how strategic this particular call was.

"Brutey Baker, I just wanted you to know this fine morning that God loves you," Reverend Dawes began. "He knows what you've done and he knows your heart, and there's nothing you could ever do that would make him stop loving you." He let the words hang for a moment so Brutey could absorb them.

"Reverend Dawes, I appreciate the gesture," he said. "But I did such a horrible thing. I can't expect God to forgive me."

The response came quickly. "Brutey, let me ask you something. Suppose one of those fine boys you have sleeping away in your house were to one day do something that hurt somebody."

"Okay. Let's hope not. I wouldn't wish that on anybody."

"Fair enough. But if that were to happen, do you suppose they would feel miserable?"

"Sure."

"And would there be times they felt so miserable that they wouldn't want to go on living?"

Brutey hesitated. Was Reverend Dawes in the next room? How did he know all this? "I suppose they would have moments feeling like that, yes," Brutey said.

"So they would do something awful and they would feel miserable and they would feel like they have no reason to keep on living. Would you still love them, though? Would you still see the beauty inside their hearts and know the goodness they possess, and love them even when other people – or themselves – seem to see it?"

Brutey felt like he'd been nailed by a classic cross-examination. He instantly recognized Reverend Dawes' point, and appreciated it.

"My boss is an amazing man, Brutey," Reverend Dawes responded.

Maybe he was, Brutey thought. This was a side of spirituality he had never been exposed to before, that maybe God does care about his people here on Earth. "Thanks," he said, rubbing his eyes. "See you in a couple of hours."

CHAPTER 32

Brutey spent the rest of the day in a much better mood. Reverend Dawes preached on how giving of oneself was as necessary as giving of one's presents and money. So he invited the congregation to do little acts of service – helping out around the house, smiling at strangers, listening to friends and family when they talk – as a gift for Christmas.

Brutey's prayer that night was one of thanksgiving, for his life, and for his children. He prayed for the emotional comfort of Janet Spencer's family, and hoped that one day they could finally come to forgive him. But especially he was thankful for Norma, who he regarded as the world's most remarkable woman. He drifted off to sleep with his arm over her right shoulder.

How quickly life changes.

CHAPTER 33

There was the walk to the game, and the electricity in the air. And then there was t he smell of the gym, and the sight of our players warming up to the music. Oh, what I night!
-- The greatest moment

FRIDAY, JANUARY 19, 1973

The bell rang and the shuffle towards the last period of the day began. Books were removed and lockers were slammed and Donny Wilburn made eyes with a pretty girl who just moved into town. Not surprisingly, she looked back and smiled, and I wondered how a guy could be so lucky. I grabbed my science book and trudged to the end of the hall, eyes half-shut and totally bored, counting the minutes to the end of the school day. But there was no way to know what fun I had in store.

Sometimes when a teacher had a doctor's appointment or some other reason to leave the school, a high school student was asked to monitor our class. Most of the times this happened for a study hall, or maybe gym class, but on this afternoon we had a substitute in Science class. I couldn't have been more thrilled. That alone was a reason for me to enjoy the time. But it was memorable for other reasons as well.

For starters, it was a Friday, which had a freedom all its own anyway. Add to that the fact that midway through the period we were adjourning to the gymnasium for a pep rally, which was always a blast; the town was on fire for the basketball team which, after an auspicious 5-3 start, had won three games in a row. It was hosting Waynesville that night in a conference rematch. Seats would be hard to come by and the enthusiasm was bound to blow the ceiling off.

The final part of the mix was the student teacher who was our substitute. Dave Dillon, the junior class clown / running back we watched on football Friday nights, walked in carrying a book and a pencil. When he wasn't pulling pranks himself, Dave had a secret aspiration of being a teacher someday.

Fireworks were assured the minute he walked in. He walked around the room, made his way to the front of the room, sat at Mrs. Kuhn's desk, looked up and saw Danny Kruer, our class clown / basketball player, sitting in front of him with pencils stuck up his nose.

Dave stared at him, deadpan. Two could play at this game, he thought.

"That's the best look you've got," Dave quipped, barely breaking stride. "It's better than your fingers up there, which is what I normally see out of you."

The class roared.

Dave was the master at this. He was as fun-loving and daring as older brother Rod was responsible and conservative. There was no joke, no prank, and no situation that Danny could ever throw at him that Dave himself hadn't already done.

"All right, listen up," Dave continued. "You have a test on Monday. You are to use this time to study for that test. Got that? You smart kids over here – Lance McKinney, Laura, Linda – I know you know what that means. But I'm not so sure about these guys." He was looking in our direction – me, Ricky, Lance, Mitch and Kruer, of course.

"Look at these guys," he said looking right at me. "There's dust on the top of Kirby's book. Kruer, I'll bet if open your book the pages will crackle."

"I don't need it," Danny spoke up. "I'll be on scholarship someday, and then I'll make a lot of money playing pro basketball."

"Scholarship? Yeah. The only scholarship you're gonna' get is to the Lebanon Correctional Institute."

More laughter. Dave smiled wide, because he was having fun. He knew how impossible it was to settle us down for just half a period, with a pep rally on the way. But he had a job to do. And most of us knew he could pound us, unofficially, if we didn't listen.

"Now study," he said. "I'm going to take a nap."

Five minutes later, Jeff Linton walked to the front of the room and stood silently by the teacher's desk, waiting to be acknowledged. Finally, Jeff cleared his throat, an obvious attempt to get Dave's attention.

"No," Dave said, not looking up.

"But..."

"No, go away."

"But I need to go to the rest room."

Dave looked up from his magazine, rubbed his eyes, and looked straight at Jeff. "What for?" he asked.

Jeff was astounded. He started wiggling in a way that it was obvious why he needed to go to the rest room. "What do you mean, 'What for?' I have to use the rest room." Jeff was beginning to sweat.

"How do I know that?"

"How do ...I can't believe this. If you don't let me go, it's going to come out."

"Okay. I want to see it come out."

Laughter.

"If I see it coming out, then you can go to the rest room."

We were now laughing hysterically. Jeff was buckling at the knees, looking confused. He didn't know what to do, literally.

Finally, Dave waved him on and Jeff fled from the room, holding his crotch. He never asked to go to the rest room during class the rest of the year.

And I think Dave's ambition of being a teacher ended right there on the spot. Kids are animals.

* * *

We arrived a half-hour before the reserve game and we still had to wait in line. Snow drifted and the cold wind blew as we waited patiently for our chance to get in the door. Lowell Hayes, a warm, funny man who was on the school board, sold tickets to the high school basketball games, and he could see how cold we were standing in front of him. So he got us through quickly. As always, he took our seventy-five cents and gave us a ticket, but he also often gave us more than that. He remembered our names and knew our ambitions. Knowing how much we worshipped the varsity players, he encouraged us to work hard so that, one day, we could be on the varsity, too.

"One day a kid's going to stand in line and watch you play," he'd say. I'd hear that and practically float into the gym. Was such a dream possible?

Tickets to the Waynesville game sold out by the middle of the reserve game. With Waynesville being only five miles to the west, another farm community like ours, it had a huge fan base that was willing to make the short trip. Plus it had Mike Hartsock, a senior guard who was the pick by many as the pre-season MVP, a guy who later went into broadcasting and is now the sports anchor for Channel 7.

It was like a championship game atmosphere. Applause was more intense and the cheers were louder. At halftime of the reserve game, the varsity players went to the locker room to get ready. Meanwhile, other people milled in and out of the cramped gymnasium. "I really need to go the bathroom," I heard a guy behind me say, "but I'm afraid I'll never get back in."

It may have been Jeff Linton, but I doubted it.

Our gym was typical in the sense that it had twelve rows of bleachers on each side, allowing a maximum capacity of five or six hundred. But it was unique in the sense that its wooden floor was especially hard and unforgiving; it was as if the ends of two-by-fours were lined up one after another to make it up, giving our gym a look and a feel that was much different than anyone else's.

The Springboro parents sat directly behind the scorer's table. The student and band section was to their left, behind the Panther players. All the other Springboro people sat behind the visiting team or across the way next to where the visitors and their parents sat. Myrtle Reedy, Charlie's mother, was a fixture right behind the scorer's table, sitting with Eleanor Cushman and keeping score. Incredibly, when the official scorers had a question about a statistic, they turned to Myrtle for correction. No one ever argued with her.

We always sat in the first row or two near the visiting team. On this night I sat next to Lance and in front of Donny and Mitch. Roger was down front, as were my brothers, John and Joey. We were surrounded by other kids of all ages, from fourth grade up through the eighth. All of the older kids were down in the high school student section.

Springboro had a huge home court advantage because of this atmosphere. The crowd inspired the Panthers to play at another level. I enjoyed just being in the room, feeling the intensity that infected every square inch.

Brutey stood near the doorway to the coaches' office, having finally given up ever trying to sit in the stands to begin with. The varsity had turned the town on its head, yet there were still some parents and men from town who shouted out the stupidest things. Often Brutey didn't know whether to be embarrassed or angry. He ultimately settled for both.

Our reserves scored five points in the final twenty-five seconds to break away and win their game, 50-43. Denny Hall led the way with fourteen points, and Mike Flynn and Mike Charlton both had twelve apiece, allowing the reserves to gain a rare victory. The teams shook hands and quickly made their way to the locker room. Just as Mike Charlton, the last of the reserve players, had walked out the door, I could see Coach Hall standing tall ready to lead the varsity into the gym.

This was it.

The pep band, under the direction of Robert McNutt, who was a visionary in the sense that he allowed popular rock music to infiltrate the band's repertoire, was in fine form, blaring out a rock tune loudly and proudly. The opening strum of Chicago's *25 or 6 to 4* was as distinct as any song on the radio, and it was an exact replica. It was a great song, with a kick-butt beat. I just couldn't figure out what the heck the words meant.

Then out came the Panthers, each wearing a white cotton warm-up jacket with 'Panthers' written on the back in gold lettering. Jim Hough was first, then Gary Patton and Jeff Howard. They circled the south half of the floor once, and then broke into several groups for their warm-up exercise known as 'The Star.' The band was so loud I couldn't hear a word by anyone sitting close to me.

After completing their pre-game warm-up, the players circled the foul lane and shot free throws; Jim and Gary broke outside to shoot eighteen footers from the wing. The two had been sick all week and there was much speculation at The Diner about whether or not they would even play. But they had shown up at school that morning, ready to try, and if they were truly sick they didn't show it, because both pounded their outside jumpers with ease. The real question probably would be how long could they play.

Starting lineups were announced. Then the national anthem was played. As I listened and watched, I could feel my heart pounding. And I was only a spectator.

I loved it.

Jeff Howard won the jump and quickly scored when Gordy Gregg posted up and fed him a pass on the baseline, proving once more that Gordy did many things that didn't show up in the box scores. Jim Goode, taking over as team leader with Hartsock out with illness, took Waynesville's first shot, but it was off the mark and, Jeff, who always played much bigger than his 6'3" frame, leaped high to snag the rebound. From there Jimmy set up the offense, hit Gary on the wing, and from there Chuck Mockabee got the ball in the corner. His twenty-footer was nothing but net, giving us a 4-0 lead and the beginning stages of what felt like a nuclear explosion.

When Goode called timeout, our fans gave the team a standing ovation. It looked like there was going to be a rout.

But Waynesville came charging back. Goode made excellent passes, plus rebounded and scored baskets, and slowly but surely the Spartans fought their way back, so much so that by the end of the first quarter, it didn't look like we were even going to beat Waynesville, let alone do it running away. We led only by a point, 12-11, when the second quarter got its start.

Jeff hit a turnaround jumper to start the second quarter. Later, he tipped in an errant shot to give us a five-point lead. Midway through the quarter he rolled off a pick set by Gordy and knocked down a nine-foot fade away jumper that gave us the nine point lead that we held at halftime, 31-22.

Coach Hall had good things to say at halftime. He praised the efforts of his sick starting guards, and Gordy Gregg was having a fine game. But he was especially impressed with Jeff Howard who, though he was only the third-leading scorer on the team, many thought he was the most talented.

* * *

He was a guy with dreams and the talent to get him there. He was fiercely competitive and yet one of the nicest kids around town. Jeff Howard was one of the most valuable members of our team, if not our community.

I followed Jeff's varsity career because he was the one player I knew the best. In the two years before this season, back when I was in the fifth and sixth grade program, Jeff had been my coach both seasons. He taught me fundamentals that I had never heard of before. What's more, he taught me the game. As I sat there that evening as a member of the seventh grade basketball team, I owed every bit of basketball knowledge and training I had to him.

He moved to Springboro in the seventh grade, in 1967, when his parents Bryan and Glee Howard moved from nearby Xenia to Bunnell Hill Road. Mr. Howard's sister, Janice Patton, already lived on Lower Springboro Road, and her two sons, Doug and Gary, were already involved in the basketball program and demonstrating an ability to start on the varsity one day.

Gary Patton and Jeff had known one another all their lives, but when Jeff moved to town they became teammates. They did everything together. They were both cut-ups who enjoyed one another's humor. They rode their bikes to one another's houses before they were able to drive, which was no small task given that they lived three miles from one another. One day, they rode their bikes all the way to Middletown, taking St. Rt. 122 the whole way.

While they had other interests, clearly basketball was their primary interest. They played at school and in town. Eventually, Jeff had the chance to play at his own house, too.

Mr. Howard erected a ten-foot basketball hoop in the grass at their new home, and through the years Jeff played and practiced and dreamed of where a life of basketball could lead him. In seventh and eighth grade, Jeff and Gary started on teams that lost a total of one game. Their future looked bright.

Like everyone else who grew up playing ball in Springboro, he appreciated the positive feedback of all his coaches. After every game, he could count on Brutey coming up to him and commenting on something he did well. Sometimes it was his shooting, other times his rebounding or defense. Jeff always knew he had a fan in Brutey. "Too bad I can't interest you in the scarlet and gray, though," Brutey would say. "You'd make a helluva Buckeye, Jeff."

But there was only one college on Jeff's radar screen. On winter evenings, the Howard family listened to University of Kentucky basketball games on the radio, and lived and died on the outcome of those games. Jeff became a fan of Pistol Pete Maravich, even though he didn't play for Kentucky, and Dr. J, Julius Erving, because both were flashy with their awesome talent. Perhaps to the dismay of some of his coaches, Jeff also incorporated some of their wild tendencies into his play. He worked hard on his natural jumping ability by jumping rope with his sister Renee. Jeff hoped to play for the Wildcats someday.

In eighth grade he could touch the rim, virtually unheard of for a player that young. By the time he was a sophomore he could almost dunk. A year later, there was no question.

A home game that junior year with Madison was memorable for Jeff, but not for good reasons. "I thought we were pretty good, and here came Madison – a great team that ultimately would make it all the way to the state finals – to our place. I thought we would give them a run for their money," he recalled.

They didn't, though, and Madison - led by Mike Daliboa - won handily, beating us every which way but Sunday, 100-61. As he watched the Mohawks and their fans dance around the Springboro gym, Jeff cringed. Over the summer, he began to work harder and get better. He traveled the circuit of open gyms in his 1964 Chevy Malibu, playing against the best players in the area. He wanted revenge against Madison.

By the time his senior year came around, that ten-foot hoop in his father's yard was over eleven feet from the ground, and the green grass below had been pounded away into a dirt floor that continued to get deeper.

UK was still the dream. A successful senior season as a Panther, though, was a reality.

* * *

After three quarters, we had a 53-40 lead that felt pretty comfortable. Coach Hall stayed seated on the bench pretty much by then, which was always an indication that the game was under control. We poured it on in the fourth quarter, scoring another twenty-four points as Waynesville was sent whimpering home, 77-62. After the loss at Mason just after the first of the year, we had won four in a row in convincing fashion. Our overall record was 9-3, and now we were 6-1 in the FAVC, tied with Mason, with three conference games ahead.

Gary, as weak as he was from the flu, blistered Waynesville for 21 points, hitting ten of fifteen shots from the field. Jim Hough scored 20 points and Jeff 17. Brutey came up after the game and was especially pleased with the turnaround jumper, which he and Jeff had worked hard on through the years. "You mastered it tonight, Jeff. Good job." A comment from Adolph Rupp himself wouldn't have been any sweeter.

The next couple of months were going to be exciting. For us, anyway.

Brutey, meanwhile, walked home alone.

CHAPTER 34

Sure, Perry Mason looked impressive,
but who'd want to be a lawyer instead
of a pro basketball player? Put me in the
line-up with John Havlicek any day.
-- The career plan

TUESDAY, JANUARY 23, 1973

The legal term, borrowed from its Latin root, is corpus delecti. In its simplest terms, it says that a confession from an accused cannot be used unless there is independent evidence of the crime and the defendant's connection to it. Dad told Brutey it's what he had in mind when he spoke to Charlie and Jimmy the day before Thanksgiving. When his efforts to resolve the case short of trial had failed, he had no choice but to argue it to Judge Fedders.

The hearing on his motion to dismiss was scheduled to start at ten. Brutey arrived at the courthouse at nine, too nervous to go for his daily run and too disheartened to work for any period of time. The demons he fought on Christmas Eve had returned, and he was once again feeling worthless, even if his motion had merit. That didn't change the fact that Janet Spencer was dead and that he was responsible for killing her. It didn't make him innocent. He was tempted to plead guilty and have the judge put him in jail for the rest of his life; he was already in a mental prison anyway.

"How long will this last, Tom?" Brutey asked.

"An hour maybe. Then the judge will consider our arguments and give us a decision later."

CHAPTER 34

"Later? You mean it still won't be over?" Brutey didn't mean to make it sound like a delay would be Dad's fault. He was just tired, and frustrated. Finally, he sighed and motioned for Dad to lead the way into the courtroom. "Let's get this over with."

At ten o'clock sharp, P.B. Stockman entered the courtroom, dressed sharply in a dark navy suit and yellow tie. His bright white hair gave him a sort of angelic look. In all of his years as bailiff for the common pleas court, this was the most difficult case to be involved with. Like almost everyone who knew Brutey, he had mixed feelings about this case. Brutey was a great guy, but what he was accused of was horrible. "All rise!" he announced. "The Warren County Common Pleas Court is now in session, the Honorable P. Daniel Fedders presiding. You may be seated."

Brutey had heard that voice for years over the loudspeakers at the Springboro football field, and had regarded it as something legendary – like the voice of Walter Cronkite or Howard Cosell or Paul Summercamp. But on this day he wasn't comforted by the voice of P.B. Stockman at all. He sat at the defense table with his head down in a silent prayer. He wanted to run out of the courtroom, jump in his truck, and take off to wherever he felt like going.

And never come back.

"Mr. Prosecutor, is the state ready?" Judge Fedders began.

"Yes, your honor."

"And is the defense prepared to go forward, Mr. Kirby?"

"We are."

"All right. Call your first witness."

"The state calls Charlie Reedy."

Charlie lumbered to the witness stand in his uniform looking like a middle linebacker. He placed his hand on the Bible and took an oath from P.B. Stockman. He then positioned his gun belt and took a seat in the witness stand, which was off to Judge Fedders' right. Prosecutor Morris Turkelson then began with some standard preliminary questions, which he zipped through in rapid fire. Charlie was a Springboro police officer and he was on duty the night of October 27, 1972. He had received a dispatch to St. Rt. 73, just east of town, where he found the vehicle driven by Janet Spencer crashed into a telephone pole on the other side of the road, just as he had been told he would find. He was met there by Bob and Sandra Wrenn, who had been driving westbound into Springboro and had witnessed the accident, Charlie was told. Other cars had now stopped to see what had happened. Charlie described a situation that was as sad as anything he'd ever seen, particularly with two small girls in the backseat not aware that their mother was dead.

"Officer, did Mr. and Mrs. Wrenn describe the vehicle that caused this accident."

Dad interrupted. "Your honor, the defense stipulates to the written report prepared by the Wrenns on the night of the accident."

"Mr. Turkelson, do you agree with that stipulation?"

"We do. Rather than have the Wrenns appear before you and say what they wrote in their report, we agree just to present their statement. However, I would like to use their statement to support the actions of the officer."

"Mr. Kirby, any objection?"

"No, sir."

Let's get on with it! By now Brutey was ready to hyperventilate. He was given a notepad and a pen so he could take notes, but he didn't have the focus to do any of that. This was legal wrangling, stuff he had heard about on television but never dreamed he would ever have to experience. He was guilty and he knew it, but Dad had convinced him it was the state's job to prove his guilt, and not their job to prove his innocence. "It'll all work out, Brutey, you just have to be patient," Dad had repeated.

Brutey was out of patience. He wanted to return to a Saturday morning at the ball field, coaching kids, where they only thing that hung in the balance was winning or losing a simple game. But he didn't have that option. He would either throw himself on the court and risk going to prison the rest of his life. Or he tried to make the best of a bad situation and try to salvage what was rest of his life. This was pure torture.

Should he have turned himself in? He knew the answer, but that didn't make it much easier.

Mr. Turkelson established that the vehicle the Wrenns saw down the road from the accident, the one they presumed had run Janet Spencer off the road, was "most likely" a truck. He then established that Brutey Baker drove a truck. He also established that, according to county records, ninety percent of all truck owners were male. Then he turned to the most damaging evidence of all, the written and oral confession by Brutey. He waved the written statement in the air many times for emphasis, as if a jury were present and needed to see such a show.

CHAPTER 34

"Mr. Baker told you he was the one driving that truck, isn't that correct?"

"It is." Charlie said boldly.

"And he told you he had been drinking, isn't that correct?"

"It is."

"And because he was drinking, he was scared, and that's why he took off?"

"Yes."

"And when he gave you this statement, was he under the influence of anything?"

"No, he was clear-headed, sitting right next to Mr. Kirby, wanting to tell us what happened."

With that, Mr. Turkelson rested. Brutey wondered again what the point of this exercise was; his confession said it all, he believed. Surely P.B. Stockman was thinking the same thing, as was the family of Janet Spencer and everyone else who was watching that day. Wasn't it written all over his face? This was the longest hour of his life.

Judge Fedders looked up when Mr. Turkelson rested. He had been taking notes. He looked as though he had expected to hear a series of additional questions, and was surprised that he didn't hear them. He finally inquired of that further.

"Mr. Turkelson, do you have any testimony about the vehicle other than it might have been a truck? I mean, do we have testimony of a color, maybe a portion of the license plates identification, a tire mark on the roadway, anything like that?"

"No sir, nothing other than the testimony that it was a vehicle that might have been a truck."

The judge tried it again from a different angle. "What independent evidence do you have that the truck Mr. and Mrs. Wrenn saw was the same vehicle owned by Mr. Baker?"

"Your honor, he said it might have been a truck. That's our connection."

The judge lowered his head and absorbed the information he heard and considered what direction the case should now take. He had been the Springboro prosecutor before becoming common pleas court judge. Neither Brutey or Norma or anyone in Janet Spencer's family had ever met the judge personally, but they knew of him. He seemed like a pretty smart judge. Of course, judges get even smarter when they side with your position. Brutey was past the point of even caring.

"Mr. Kirby, any questions you wish to ask?" the judge asked.

"Yes, sir." He grabbed his notepad with his own set of notes and stood behind the podium in the center of the room. He had cross-examined Charlie a hundred times. He'd had lunch with him almost as many.

"Officer, do you know of any evidence, other than what Mr. Baker told you, that would indicate that he had been drinking that night?"

Charlie squirmed. "No, he said he had been drinking a six-pack in the car on his way home from Kings Mills."

"So there are no witnesses, no independent evidence of Mr. Baker's drinking other than what he told you, correct?"

Charlie hesitated before answering. He obviously didn't like his answer. "That's correct."

"And officer, can you tell me the overall effect that alcohol had on Mr. Baker that evening?"

"Well, it caused him to go left of center and kill that lady." Charlie stood up straighter in his chair with that.

"It had been raining that night, hadn't it?"

"A little."

"And the accident occurred on a portion of 73 where it curves to the right, where Mr. Lovely owns a farm, isn't that correct?"

"Yes."

"And, officer, you don't arrest people for DWI just because they drive left of center, do you?"

"If they kill somebody, I do."

Dad almost chuckled because he walked right into that one. He knew Charlie was always looking for that angle, too. "Setting aside what regrettably happened to Janet Spencer, driving left of center is not in and of itself a reason to arrest someone for DWI?"

Charlie reluctantly agreed.

"When you stop someone and suspect they've been drinking, you give them standard field sobriety tests before deciding to arrest them, don't you?"

Again Charlie squirmed. "Uh-huh."

CHAPTER 34

"Before you arrest somebody for DWI, you ask them to walk a straight line, stand on one leg, touch their nose with their finger, and say their ABCs, don't you? Stuff like that?"

Charlie murmured and nodded.

"You weren't able to do that on Brutey Baker, were you?"

Now Charlie was indignant. "No, because he took off on me. A man shouldn't be allowed to get away with that."

"It's not illegal to drink and drive, is it?" Dad asked. "What's illegal is to be *drunk* and drive?"

"Yes."

"And you don't know if Mr. Baker was drunk, do you?"

"No, 'cause he made sure I'd never know."

"You don't know if the alcohol caused him to drive left of center, do you?"

"Uh, no."

"Was he driving too fast?"

"I don't know."

"Reckless?"

"No."

"So, officer, your independent evidence of a criminal act is the vehicle went left of center, something that in and of itself is not something you arrest someone for?"

Another murmur.

"And the connection you have to Mr. Baker is that it might have been a truck, but it also could have been any other vehicle out on the road?

Charlie glared at Dad. Could it be these two were actually friends?

With that Dad sat down. Brutey knew that what just happened was beneficial to him legally, but he still wouldn't let himself go there. He still felt so guilty, so responsible. He was so sorry for what he did and the trouble he had caused. The judge asked if there were any more witnesses. The attorneys shook their heads, and, with that, the judge adjourned the hearing and P.B. Stockman called court to a close. Within a half-hour, Brutey was home, back in bed, too upset to talk to anyone and too frustrated to go back to sleep. Life was pure hell. There was no point to living.

The pain was just too great.

At noon there was a knock on the door. Norma answered it even though Brutey didn't want her to. When she opened the door, there stood Reverend Dawes, dressed sharply in a tan suit and blue tie.

Always right on time.

CHAPTER 35

Watergate? Vietnam? What's that about an oil crisis? A twelve-year-old's world revolved around his music, and the next game on the schedule. Go, Panthers!
-- The real world

TUESDAY, JANUARY 30, 1973

My first kiss came after school, long after the other kids had left, in a secluded little corner between the gym and the band room.

We were waiting for the bus that would take us to our game that evening at Little Miami. School let out at three o'clock, but our bus wouldn't leave until three-thirty. That gave us players a chance to roam the school a little, talk a little and laugh a lot, and stay loose for the game. Maybe we should have done homework, but there were other times for that. When the school day finished, the last thing I wanted to look at was a book.

What I did like looking at, though, was Serena Jacobs, a girl in my Math class and study hall. She just had that look about her. Long brown hair, a beautiful smile, and baby blue eyes that practically sang. I'd always been a sucker for a pretty face. And hers was as pretty as they come.

For months I'd sat near her in study hall. She would help me with Science, and I would help her with English. I never knew how nice a girl could smell. I mean, I had two sisters, and I'm sure they were clean, but I never got close to Jenny or Julie. You know, *close*. When Serena leaned over to take a close look at what I was reading, I could smell the fragrance in her hair. And there may have been a hint of perfume.

For about a month, I wondered if maybe she put the perfume on because of me.

When class let out that day, I went to my locker which was near my homeroom. I put my Science book away and then grabbed my coat and gym bag. Since it was game day, I was dressed in dress pants, light blue shirt and a yellow striped tie, which I always found confining but obviously made me look better than usual. Serena's locker was very close to mine. I noticed she seemed to be in no hurry getting out of the building. Soon it was just the two of us.

"What do you guys do until the bus comes?" she asked. She flipped her hair behind her left ear.

Usually I would get tongue-tied at this point, but on this day I was cool and comfortable. The words came easily. "We take it easy and get psyched up for the game," I said. "Some guys sit alone and meditate. Other guys sit in groups of three or four and talk about a particular strategy." This sounded so much better than saying we usually sat around listening to Kruer tell jokes. Serena seemed impressed.

"Here, I'll walk you downstairs," I said. I reached for her books and led her down the steps. Along the way, I had her talk about her family. I asked what music she liked and what she and her friends did on weekends. I cracked a few jokes, made sure I complimented her outfit, and also noted that her hair looked a little different lately, like she'd just had it done. I'm telling you, Joe Namath couldn't have made a better impression than I was making.

When we reached the bottom of the steps, we turned to the main corridor, and a bunch of my teammates were there. Yeah, that's what I was hoping for. I wanted those goof-offs to see me with such a pretty girl. I wanted them to look up, point and whisper, like – wow! Look at Kirby. I was king of the castle, let me tell you.

We turned left and walked past the cafeteria, making our way towards the hallway to the gym. It was beginning to snow outside, and Serena mentioned that her mom would be there in a few minutes to pick her up. She was going to the dentist that afternoon to have a tooth pulled. Braces were going on in a few weeks.

"I dread that because I'll just have a mouth full of metal," she said. "I'm sure I'll look stupid."

We stopped in the doorway to the band room. For some reason, no one was nearby. The gym was mysteriously quiet. One of the overhead lights was burned out, so the corner was quaint and cozy. And dark. Serena looked at me with her big beautiful eyes. I grabbed her by the hand, and then I put my right index finger on her lips. "Shhhh," I said. "You could never look stupid. You're beautiful just the way you are, and braces won't matter a bit."

Okay, that might have been another lie.

Serena smiled. She leaned forward, her eyes looking into mine. I could tell this was the moment I had always dreamed out. It was going to happen. I was alone with a very pretty girl and I was going to kiss her, on the lips, giving me an experience like no other. I'd seen Marcia Brady kiss Davey Jones on *The Brady Bunch*, and she practically fainted. I wondered if the same thing might happen to me.

I put my right hand on the back of her neck and drew her in. She felt so soft and warm. Our noses touched, and for a second there was a chuckle.

Then I planted the longest kiss –

"KIRBY!"

-- and for what seemed like an eternity we were locked as one. It was like a fireworks –

"KIRBY! NOW! Look at him, he's smiling so big."

And then suddenly she was gone.

Serena? I opened my eyes, and there were about ten guys from my team, all looking down and wondering what in the world I had been thinking about. I was confused, because I wondered what they were doing watching me kiss Serena. And where was Serena?

Oh, don't tell me.

"Hey, Kirby, you know you're going to wear yourself out just thinking about a girl like that," Coach Wilson told me. "Now get up, the bus is here."

I got up off the floor, and dusted the dirt off my good clothes. I fell in line with everyone else to get on the bus to go to our game at Little Miami. I know I should have been focused on the game. I should have been thinking about my particular assignment. But I wasn't.

Instead, all I could think about was how this day-dreaming thing just had to stop.

I was going to get hurt if it didn't.

* * *

After the awful, gut-wrenching experience in court, Brutey met with Reverend Dawes for more than an hour at the church. Brutey talked openly, and Reverend Dawes listened. This was not a time when Brutey needed deep spiritual insight on why bad things happen to good people, and how God is still with us, even when the world is caving in. Rather, it was a time for Brutey to talk and let loose of all the emotions festering inside him. When Brutey shook hands with Reverend Dawes and walked out into the winter air, he wanted to go to sleep for several years and wake up and find the whole situation as a distant memory.

By Thursday he began to return to normal, going to work and showing up at our practice, if only to watch. On Friday night we saw him on the sidelines of the varsity game. We were told Brutey wasn't coaching because he wasn't feeling well, and he would get back to coaching when he felt better. We never thought to question that statement. We were twelve, and we thought the Harlem Globetrotters played real basketball. And big league baseball was a game, not a business.

Coach Wilson didn't have a good feeling about our Tuesday game at Kings Mills. We practiced hard in the days before going there, running hard and working on defensive drills. He hoped that our minds were focused as we got on the bus that cold Tuesday afternoon. My mind was focused, all right, but not on basketball. It was still back there in that dark corner with Serena. It seemed so real.

Brutey was on the bus with us as we meandered our way to Kings Mills. He sat quietly up front next to Coach Grigsby, the eighth grade coach, with Coach Wilson in the aisle across from him. The bus traveled south on 741 to Mason, where it would take a left to go towards Kings Island Amusement Park. Brutey frequently looked back at the rest of us and laughed at the shenanigans that were going on. Kruer may not have been responsible for all of it, but he owned his share. He had me laughing so hard that I quickly forget about Serena. Our team was loose, and confident, and ready to play a good game.

The bus ride seemed to take forever, though. An ice storm hit just as we were about to leave school, but the forecast called for it to stop in less than a half-hour, so the coaches decided to go ahead with the trip. Normally it took twenty minutes to get to Mason; then going over to Kings Mills was another five minutes. But on this day it took us a good forty-five minutes to get there. By the time we finally we arrived it was four o'clock, only a half-hour from game time. We had to hurry.

As I warmed up, I pretended the pep band was playing the school fight song and every eye in the gym was focused on me. "Is he hitting tonight? Does his shot look good? We need Kirby if we're going to win tonight." Of course, the reality was my team would probably play better if I *didn't* play.

CHAPTER 35

"In here, fellas," Coach Wilson shouted. We all formed a circle around him near our bench. The cheerleaders were doing their "Hello" cheers to one another, and the officials gathered at mid-court to make certain of their assignments. The Kings Mills gym was a converted old barn that had rafters and a balcony, a portion of which was actually in play in one corner. It was a neat place to play.

"This is a big one. They don't lose here very often, so they're thinking they have us whipped before this game gets started. Everyone loose?"

"Not me, Coach," Kruer quipped.

"You're not playing yet," I snapped back.

"Oh, yeah."

This game was our ninth of a twelve-game season. We were 7-1, having whipped Waynesville, Lebanon, Madison, Clinton-Massie, Monroe and Little Miami after our season-opening victory against Carlisle. Our lone loss was the Thursday before at Lakota where we faced King Kong and his sidekick, Godzilla. The T-Birds had two guys who were taller than me and Mitch stacked together. Both were six-foot four, which was outrageous for a seventh grade team. We wondered if either one owned a driver's license. We were certain that one of them was starting a mustache.

Coach felt the game with Kings Mills was the toughest of our last three games.

"Let's go, boys! Play hard!" Brutey shouted from a distance, as our starters took the floor. "Todd Thompson, make sure you box out. And Mitch, take that outside jumper if it presents itself." He seemed like the same old Brutey.

Jerry Monnin won the opening tip easily and Kings Mills scrambled to get on defense. Mitch dribbled up court, flipped it to Shane, who then bounce-passed to Donny as he broke across the middle. He faked to his right, took two dribbles and banked a five-footer off the backboard, giving us a quick 2-0 lead. The rest of the quarter went just as easy and we led 14-4 as the second quarter began.

Coach Wilson substituted generously in the second quarter, so Kruer, Lance and I took over. We didn't play as well as the starters, but we still kept up a twelve-point lead at the half. By the time the fourth quarter came around, Mitch and Donny and Shane were done for the night. They sat the bench and while us scrubs played the rest of the way. When we finished we were ahead by twenty-four, our largest margin of victory all year. Coach Wilson breathed a sigh of relief; this one was much easier than he had thought.

I loved every second of it. We were Panthers, and we were winning. Midway through the fourth quarter I dove for a loose ball and went flying into the scorer's table, banging my head in the process. People gasped in horror and the game stopped momentarily to make sure I was okay. Coach Wilson and some of my teammates hovered over me asking me questions to see if I'd suffered major brain damage or something. Surely the cheerleaders had to have been impressed by all of that.

"Jeff, what year did Ohio become a state?" asked Coach Wilson, my Ohio History teacher.

"Geez, he wouldn't know that if he had the book in his hands," one guy quipped.

I heard some chuckling. "Okay, stay still, Jeff. Where did John Havlicek play basketball in college?"

I didn't miss a beat. "Ohio State, in the early sixties, with Bobby Knight and Jerry Lucas," I said quickly, rising to my feet.

The Kings Mills coach was astounded. "Maybe he's hurt more than we think." And everyone laughed.

Afterward, I planned to use my injury to try and make the evening complete. I could wear a Band-Aid on my head, or -- better yet -- some big bandage, and show the world that I was a really tough guy who could survive almost anything. Then I could surely get a certain cheerleader's attention during the eighth grade game. That, of course, might lead to sitting close to her on the way home, where we could talk and get to know one another. Who knew where that would lead? Maybe a kiss later? The thought of it petrified me, actually.

But it also thrilled me, too.

I planned to shower and dress quickly so I could get a good seat for the eighth grade game, real close to the cheerleaders. I rushed to the mirror to check the bruise on my head, and I was thrilled to see that it was still there, and I checked with Mike Woodward, our team manager, for the biggest bandage we had. Then I wrapped myself up like I'd just walked out of a war zone.

I had everything in place, perfectly.

* * *

Brutey spent the game standing along the far sideline. He hooked up with some old friends of his who lived in the area, and they talked about the old days when they played against one another. Brutey had scored twenty-five points against them one night back in 1955.

He loved being at our game, but he still had trouble watching. He longed to be in the huddle and on the bench, coaching. But his future was uncertain, in more ways than one.

Brutey was waiting on Coach Wilson when he walked out of our locker room. Behind them, the eighth grade game was getting close to tip-off. The guys on my team trickled by them one by one as we changed back into our shirts and ties.

"Anything from the Judge yet?" Coach asked him. "I know you've really been worried about that."

Brutey shook his head. "He said he would be making his decision in the next week or two. Trial has been scheduled for March, so he has to let us know pretty soon."

"Think he'll dismiss it?"

Brutey wondered the same thing. "I'm not sure. I haven't been able to keep my hopes up about anything. I go to work, do some scouting, and go to some ball games. But mostly I just stay home. This whole deal has got me tore up something bad."

Coach tucked the clipboard under his arm. "Well, let me know if there's anything I can do for you."

Brutey looked directly into Coach Wilson's eyes. He knew he had to get back to the game, but Brutey needed something from him. "Well, that's what I was meaning to talk to you about. I think what has hurt me the most -- aside from what I done -- of course, is that I haven't been able to coach. Mike, it's all I've known forever, and to just have it cut off like that has hurt me more than anyone will ever know. I miss it so much."

There was a pause. Coach Wilson understood, but the decision was out of his hands.

"Brutey, I …uh –"

"Mike, I know there's a coaches' meeting next week. All I ask is that you put in a good word. I've tried talking to Harry, but he's been so busy and I don't want to detract from what the varsity is doing. Just, please, if my name comes up, tell everyone I'm still interested. This basketball program has been such a big part of my life, ever since I was a kid dribbling basketball along Main Street on my way to school. It's my life."

The buzzer to begin the eighth grade game sounded.

"With everything that's gone on, I need to be coaching. I need to be sitting on the sidelines during games. I need to be in practice, showing stuff and running drills. Please."

Coach Wilson put his hand on Brutey's shoulder. "I understand. But, Brutey, I don't have much weight to throw around."

"You'd be surprised, Mike. Every little bit helps. Please."

The eighth grade game was now underway. Ronny Hart took a lead pass from Keith Crocker and we had a quick 2-0 lead. I took my seat next to Kruer right in the center of our cheering section, in a place where all of the cheerleaders would have to see me. The bandage on my head was unmistakable.

Coach Wilson put things in perspective for Brutey. "You know, there are a lot of people who are in on the decision on whether you stay with the program. Mr. Perez feels he has a say-so, which is what a superintendent is supposed to do. Then there's Mr. Clingman, and the same holds true with an athletic director. Then there's the school board."

Brutey grimaced. "I'm not sure Mr. Wade likes me very much."

Coach Wilson fired right back. "Like everyone else, he loves you as a person. But you have to understand, what happened that night, it not only affected you, it affected the whole program, the whole town really. And he's a man who's worked his whole life to make this town what it is."

There was no disagreeing with that. Brutey knew all of that was true, but he just held hope that there was a way he could stay on. He couldn't go through another season standing at the doorway to the coaches' room. He'd rather not show up at all than do that again.

"Thanks for your time, Mike. I'll let you get to the game."

* * *

Our eighth grade led by six when the first quarter ended. I still had not made eye contact with any of the cheerleaders, let alone the one I was most interested in. I was going to do something drastic before long if I needed to, and it looked like I was going to need to. But my head was busted open! What more did I need?

Just then Mitch and Shane sat down right behind Kruer and me.

CHAPTER 35

"Say, did you hear Donny's going to break up with Rhonda Riley?" Shane asked Mitch.

"He's got the hots for Debbie Balyo. Someone told me they talked last night."

"So now all the cheerleaders have boyfriends, huh?"

Right then I could feel my heart sink. I was looking my best, ready for the biggest step I had ever planned in my life. And now I was hearing the worst news ever.

Nooooooooooooooooooooooooooooooooooooooooooooooooooooo oooooooooooo!!!

A good brain injury went to waste.

I was never going to have a girlfriend.

CHAPTER 36

At the IGA, at the drug store, and
at the K&W, everywhere except
Mrs. Kuhn's class, the talk was
all the same –varsity basketball.
-- The town news

FRIDAY, FEBRUARY 2, 1973

The ruling on Brutey's motion to dismiss was expected near the end of February, Dad told Brutey. In the meantime, the judge would review the evidence and do extensive research of similar cases from around the state. Then he would carefully draft his opinion, knowing full well an appeal likely would be filed by the losing side. The filing of an appeal was something he couldn't control, because some people never want to stop fighting. But the outcome of the appeal he hoped he could control, so he carefully studied the material he came across. No judge has ever liked seeing his or her decisions overturned on appeal.

After another day of trying to forget his case, Brutey left work around four-thirty and arrived home shortly after five. It had been a great day and he was looking forward to the home basketball game that night against Clinton-Massie. Brutey smelled Norma's vegetable soup the second he hit the front door, and he planned to have a quick bite and change clothes before he would he would be out the door. Norma and the boys were already ready to join him.

"Finally made a sale on the Hilden account today," Brutey announced. "Big account. I've been working on that old man for four months."

Norma smiled.

CHAPTER 36

"You like seeing me happy, don't you?" he asked, watching her nod her head and smile again. "I tell you, I was in the car today up by the Mall. I had the radio on as I was driving south on 741 past the drive-in, and it hit me what Reverend Dawes was trying to tell me the other day. I can't control everything. Sometimes I have to just let it go and trust the plan that's been set out in my life. Everything will be okay if I do that."

He dove into his first big bite of the vegetable soup. The carrots and green beans came from the garden Norma had out back, and had been canned for safekeeping throughout the winter. The sirloin steak came from the IGA, which had the best meat around. Brutey loved Norma's cooking better than anyone's. Especially now.

"So you're not going to worry about the judge's decision? You were up half the night earlier this week stewing about it."

Brutey wiped the corner of his mouth. "Didn't do any good, did it? Besides, nothing's going to happen for a few weeks. I might as well do something productive, if I can."

"Starting with?"

"Starting with getting to the game early tonight and get these boys fired up. People are talking about them. They figure they can go places, like state. You only get one chance in life to do stuff like that; in two months it'll all be over."

"All right, then. Go change your clothes so we can go."

"Back in a flash."

Brutey changed into a dark blue shirt with a yellow tie. He wanted desperately to put on his blue Panther blazer but he thought better of it. Harry would shoot him, he figured. He wore a white belt and matching white shoes, his most stylish look. If he couldn't officially be part of the team, then he would come as close as he could. He put a little more Bryl-cream in as he combed his hair.

He swept into the living room and saw Norma on the telephone. Instantly, he knew it wasn't good news. She looked at him and closed her eyes. He knew it was my dad, with news – awful news. His heart stopped for a second.

"It's Tom," she said. "Judge wants us back in the courtroom."

"Why? Did he rule? Am I going to prison? Why go back if we've already had our hearing?"

Brutey took the phone and tried to grasp what Dad was telling him. The judge needed more information before he could rule. The case hinged on what the

Wrenns saw, or didn't see, and the judge couldn't make out their description clearly from the statement. So they had to appear in court. Again.

This meant another awful experience in the courtroom. And another delay. And probably another trial date.

This thing was never going to end. He was reminded of the awful memory of watching Janet Spencer's car run off the road. He could see the looks in the face of her parents. And he relived the awful experience of sitting in a courtroom, with Charlie Reedy testifying against him and Judge Fedders deciding his fate. *Damn, I hate this.* Why ever get my hopes up? They only go up so I can get shot down.

Brutey didn't say a word on the way to the game. He didn't say much else while he was there, either.

* * *

Though Brutey stood in a corner sulking, the atmosphere at the varsity game was more electric than it had been two weeks earlier. Old-timers said it was as crazy as it had been during the 1965 season. The varsity whipped Blanchester a week earlier in a dramatic, come-from-behind thriller, giving it four straight wins and putting it one step closer to the conference championship. *The Western Star* had a long story on Wednesday outlining all the scenarios that had to take place for us to win the championship. At the top of every list was for us to continue winning. The Diner crowd was positive that would happen.

At halftime of the exciting reserve game, the varsity players adjourned to the locker room to get ready. Boy, did I want to someday live that moment! Go in all decked out in cool clothes, and come out wearing a basketball uniform. Nothing was more awesome. Once dressed, Coach Hall huddled them together in front a chalkboard where he had written all the defensive assignments. He warned them about getting complacent. He cautioned them about undermining Clinton-Massie's talent. He ran through all the points Brutey had highlighted on his scouting report, but when Coach looked up, something wasn't just right.

Coach Hall could sense that his team wasn't all there emotionally. As he lectured about the finer points of the game, he looked out to a few blank stares and, with one particular player, total indifference.

"You fellas' think you're that good? Think you can just show up and win a ball game, just like that?" He snapped his fingers. "I'm telling you, don't mess around. Not with this team. Not now. Either you guys get your heads in the game, or be prepared to pay a big price." He asked if they understood, and in typical fashion they said they did. Yet when the game started, it wasn't so clear they had.

Clinton-Massie marched into enemy territory with its game face on. It jumped to an early lead, taking our crowd out of the game. We were shocked. *We* were the awesome Springboro Panthers. *They* were the forgettable Clinton-Massie Falcons. Who did they think they were? Didn't they know to just fall down and play dead? We came back and actually held the lead at halftime, 35-34. But Coach Hall was steamed. He spent the next twelve minutes giving a heated pep talk that more than once reiterated the phrase, "I told you so."

In the stands, there was a lot of uneasiness too. This team wasn't supposed to struggle against Clinton-Massie. Not at home. Not after we'd already won four straight. Jim Hough Sr. looked over at Bryan Howard and shrugged his shoulders. Then they got up and went to the concession stand to stretch their legs and get a cup of coffee. Mr. Hough, a former player himself and then coach at Springboro, had seen the scenario many times before. An underdog team got some early momentum and started playing a lot more confidently. After a while they felt they deserved to win. Such is the way that upsets can happen.

Was tonight that night?

So far it looked like it would be.

* * *

When the varsity was 5-3, having just been blistered at Mason, the team's fathers could have staged a rebellion. They could have openly criticized Coach Hall and pointed fingers at players on the team who were not playing the way they should. Such has happened on many other teams since the beginning of competitive sport. They could have done those things, and more, but they didn't.

Following the lead of Jim Hough Sr. and Charlie Harris, and others, some of the team's fathers took a more positive route and offered the team a steak dinner if it won the last ten games of the regular season. This was quite an offer. This was during the days the team had no pre-game meal – other than a burger and fries at the K & W or Frisch's -- and there wasn't a steakhouse on every corner. Lowell's was the nicest restaurant in town but hardly any kids ever ate there. The offer was an invitation to change the direction of the season, using positive methods.

In the games since then, the strategy had been working fabulously. But now, at halftime against a recharged Clinton-Massie team, it didn't look like the dads were going to have to pay up. Coach Hall lit into everybody inside the locker room. No player was exempt. And parents were outside wondering just what in the world they were watching.

Jim Hough Sr. remained confident, though.

"There's plenty of time left. We haven't played a poor half in quite a while, and they're entitled to that. A lot can happen to change everything in the second half," he said.

His words were spoken like he was a true sage. He had years of basketball experience. He was a player for Springboro back in the forties. Later, he played for the University of Dayton. Then he returned to Springboro to be a coach, which he did until he decided to become a principal. There wasn't an aspect about basketball that he didn't know. He and Mr. Howard settled back in the stands and listened to the pep band wail away as the players warmed up. Jim Jr., with sweat coming from his brow, looked hot from the top of the key. Meanwhile, Gary Patton swished jumpers from the wing.

As Mr. Hough predicted, a different team started the third quarter. This team was good. This team had a killer instinct. It was the team we had grown accustomed to. Jimmy hit eighteen-footers and Gary drove the lane. Gordy rebounded and Chuck swished baseline jumpers. Jeff hit turnaround after turnaround, much the same way Pistol Pete would do. And Clinton-Massie didn't have a chance. The final score was lopsided, 87-61. When the final buzzer sounded, Mr. Hough looked over at Mr. Howard. There was no shrug of the shoulders this time.

The steaks were thawing out.

* * *

Brutey spent the whole game in his typical spot standing beside the door to the coaches' room. Since the concession stand was in the opposite direction, no one walked by him there. He could still see the occasional stare and finger pointed in his direction, but by and large it was his place to focus on the game and the players he loved so much. During the two hours of the game, Brutey was free from any worries or the thoughts about the case that consumed him. He could be "Coach" again.

CHAPTER 36

During one point in the second quarter, Gordy Gregg chased a loose ball that went out of bounds right next to where Brutey stood. "Step around your man, Gordy! Use your feet!" Brutey told him. Gordy listened and the next time down the floor he took a bounce pass inside from Dave Collins and scored. Gordy gave Brutey the thumbs up sign as he ran back down the floor.

He had more suggestions during the third quarter Panther comeback. He told Gary Patton about a backside pick. He told Jeff Howard to take a short jumper instead of trying to force a pass inside. He sat back and watched the momentum turn around entirely, so much so that the starters left the game early in the fourth quarter. The rest of the game was like one big party.

"Five down, big boy, " Mr. Hough told Brutey. "Next weekend will be the biggest test." Brutey would be off the next night to Oxford Talawanda to scout Middletown Fenwick, one of Springboro's opponents the next weekend.

"We're playing so well, I can't see a problem," Brutey responded.

He watched the post-game celebration and hung around to see who led the team in scoring and rebounding. He told Norma and the boys to go ahead and drive home because he needed the long walk home all by himself. When the excitement of the game subsided, the sadness about his situation increased. He was reminded once again what he had done. He was confronted once again over the consequences he faced.

And now Judge Fedders wanted more testimony. That obviously meant he was leaning in the prosecution's favor and he wanted more testimony in the record to support it. He was going to get convicted, and they were going to send him to prison. For many years he would live in a four by six foot cell. He would lose his family, lose his job, and lose his chance at continuing to coach the Panthers.

The brisk, frigid air hit him the minute he stepped out the door. By the time he was halfway home, his face was numb.

He wanted anything to help escape his reality. Deep down, he knew that coming clean had been the right thing to do. He just didn't realize how hard it would still be. Boy, what he would give for a beer.

Spanning the globe to bring you

CHAPTER 37

the constant variety of sports...
the thrill of victory...and the
agony of defeat

-- ABC's 'Wide World of Sports'
In our living room every
Saturday afternoon

THURSDAY, FEBRUARY 8, 1973

"Do you solemnly swear or affirm that the testimony that you're going to give is the truth, the whole truth and nothing but the truth, so help you God?"

"I do."

"Please be seated."

Bob Wrenn was dressed neatly in dark pants, white shirt and blue and white striped tie. Brutey had never seen the man before, let alone ever talked to him. Now the man was on the witness stand in his case and had the power to send him off to prison in a moment's notice. What if he suddenly remembered the make and model of the car? What if he had a license number? What if now, more than three months after the accident, he suddenly had a vision of the driver of the other car and was able to testify to it? Surely Judge Fedders would convict him on the spot.

"Please state your name and address." Since the hearing had been scheduled so quickly, Morris Turkelson – the county prosecutor – was unavailable because he was in another trial. Roger Young, the first assistant, took his place. He stood tall at the podium, looking as confident as a Michigan grad was supposed to look in the courtroom. Dad took notes at the defense table, with Brutey at his right wearing his dark blue suit. Brutey had been told this would be a routine hearing, where Mr. Wrenn would flush out in person what he had already written in his statement, with no real surprises. Brutey didn't look at it that way, though. He likened it to actually playing a team who looked unbeatable on a scouting report.

"I am Bob Wrenn. I live at 40 Willow Drive, Springboro, Ohio." Brutey's heart sank. Willow Drive? Only good people live on Willow Drive. There's never any trouble there. No complaints. Only good, smart, law abiding-citizens. He looked straight ahead and tried to keep his emotions together. Good things happen to those who believe, he told himself over and over. God uses everything to make everything work out.

"Mr. Wrenn, did you have an occasion to be driving westbound on State Route 73 into the Village of Springboro on the night of October 27, 1972?"

"I did."

"You came upon the tragic scene of Janet Spencer lying dead in the driver's seat of her car and –"

"Objection. Leading the witness."

"Sustained. Mr. Young, rephrase your question."

The prosecutor stepped back from the podium, reviewed his notes and then cleared his throat before asking his next question. "Mr. Wrenn, did you see a vehicle in the vicinity of The Lovely Farm on that particular night, right where Janet Spencer crashed?"

This is it. This is where he says he saw me. He's going to do like they do on television, and stand up and point a finger at me. Then the whole courtroom is going to express shock, and I'll sit here with a spotlight on me and be exposed for the despicable person that I really am.

"No sir, I did not. I got up to the crash scene and I was so --"

There was an audible expression in the courtroom. But it wasn't the one Brutey had anticipated. Judge Fedders looked up. The family of Janet Spencer turned and looked at one another. Dad wondered if he really heard what he thought he heard.

"—I'm sorry, could you repeat yourself? Did you say you did not?" the prosecutor asked.

That's the question, all right. Did he really say that? He did NOT? How could that be? In his statement, he said he did. It was a vehicle. Maybe it was a truck. Maybe it was something else. Now he's saying he never saw the vehicle at all.

"What I saw, I realize now, was the back of a vehicle that pulled out of Home Street onto 73. It all went so fast, you know. I was so angry about that young woman's death and how it had to be somebody's fault. As people started showing up, I started hearing things people were saying. Someone said a truck had been flying down 73 and they had the guy stopped up ahead. I wanted to put two and two together in my mind, but I went too far. Later, I realized I hadn't told the truth. Telling one false story was wrong. I don't want to do it again."

The assistant prosecutor stepped away from the podium again and ran his fingers through his hair. He looked at the family of Janet Spencer. He took a moment before saying anything else.

"Your honor, I'd like a moment … to … to review…" He fumbled through some papers in a file. He found one piece of paper and inspected it carefully. The courtroom fell to a hush and all eyes followed the prosecutor. "Your honor, may we take a recess?"

Judge Fedders contemplated the question. He scratched his forehead as the courtroom fell silent for a very long time. This hearing was scheduled for one hour. A significant delay would cause later hearings to be delayed.

"I don't see the need for a recess," he said. "If, though, you believe you are being surprised by this witness, I will allow you to declare him as a hostile witness and cross-examine him."

"I can do that?"

The judge nodded. "It's in your rules of evidence. I'm sure they taught you that at Michigan. Maybe you even got a copy of the rules when you passed the bar exam."

"Oh, yeah."

The young prosecutor re-examined the piece of paper in front of him. It wasn't clear what the document was. Perhaps it held the answer to the predicament he faced. Or maybe he was just buying time.

"Mr. Wrenn. Why are you waiting until today to change your testimony?" The prosecutor's tone of voice was terser now. Mr. Wrenn was no longer his witness.

"I didn't wait until today."

CHAPTER 37

"Then why didn't you tell my office earlier?"

Mr. Wrenn didn't hesitate. "No one asked me. I called the Springboro Police Department once I got this subpoena and told the dispatcher that I wanted to talk to somebody, but when they found out what it was about they told me the case was being handled by the state highway patrol, and I had to talk to them."

The prosecutor repositioned his thick glasses. "So why didn't you contact them?" he asked.

"I did. But no one got back with me."

The family of Janet Spencer groaned. They had been warned prior to the case beginning that there could be some difficulties. That's why the plea bargain was discussed. But some members of the family, particularly Janet's brothers, had been pig-headed in that discussion, and didn't want to hear anything but a lengthy prison sentence being imposed for Brutey. No matter what it took.

Now it looked like the plea bargain would have been the smart way to go.

The young prosecutor did his best to repair the damage. "Do you know Mr. Harold Baker? He goes by Brutey, doesn't he?"

"Only by reputation. I don't know him personally," Mr. Wrenn said.

"Have you ever talked to him? Specifically, have you talked to him or any member of his family, or his lawyer in the last two months?"

"No."

"Has anyone threatened you or any member of your family to get you to testify in the way you are today?"

"No."

"So you didn't see any vehicle ahead of you? All you repeated was what other people were saying on the night of the crash?"

"That's right."

The young prosecutor stood and glared at Mr. Wrenn for what seemed like a half-hour. Perhaps it was an intimidation tool. Perhaps it was utter shock. He fumbled more through some papers in his file until finally he wrapped them all together in front of him.

"No further questions."

The judge turned to the defense table. "Any questions?"

"Of course not."

"Very well," Judge Fedders said, closing the file in front of him. "I'll give you my written decision in seven days. In the meantime, I'd like to see counsel in my chambers." P.B. Stockman dismissed the courtroom.

Brutey knew the motion had gone so much better than he ever could have expected. He was relieved that at least the felony would be dismissed so a prison sentence would be avoided. But he still carried his guilt with him, and he knew he deserved to be held accountable and punished in some way. That was the whole reason for coming forward in the first place. Now he felt Janet Spencer's family was victimized all over again.

"That's not necessarily true, Brutey," Dad advised. "We gave them the chance to be realistic. We tried to not put them through all of this. Her mom and dad understood our position, but her big-mouth brothers pushed the prosecutors into this. Now all that's happening is they have to deal with their own poor decisions. Let me go back and talk with the judge and I'll call you later. Until then, try not to worry."

Brutey knew that wasn't going to happen. "What's the judge going to do?" he asked.

Dad spoke with assurance. "He has to dismiss the felony charge. My guess is he's going to put you in the county jail for a while on the misdemeanor. I'll bet that's what he wants to talk to us about right now."

"Six months?" Norma asked. "Six months? Are you sure?"

Brutey interrupted. "Honey, it's nothing compared to what they're going through over there. Tom, just let me know when we do that. I'll be ready."

Funny thing was, the minute Brutey accepted going to jail was the moment he started feeling better. Even if it meant he wouldn't coach again for a very, very long time.

* * *

That night, our seventh grade team played our final game of the season. I spent all day dreaming of one last chance to be a hero. I imagined Mitch going down with an ankle injury as we trailed by ten points midway through the third quarter. A loss seemed assured. Everyone was depressed. Then, I would enter the game. I would hit three long jumpers the first three times down the floor. Then I'd steal passes and block shots, and before long we'd be up by ten with only seconds remaining. I'd get carried off the floor on my teammates' shoulders and, in an unprecedented move, I'd get asked to play in the eighth grade game as well.

Coach Hall would then immediately call me up to the varsity.

Such is the way of dreams.

But we did not trail by ten midway through the third quarter, and Mitch did not go down with an ankle injury. Instead, he dribbled like Curly O'Neal and he passed off to Donny like some sort of magician. He scored at will, and we easily took control of the game. And the more Donny scored, the more all the cheerleaders went crazy over him. One time during a timeout I was tempted to tie his shoelaces together.

With two minutes left in the game, I went back in to replace Donny, who had played a perfect game. He had scored fourteen points and grabbed eight rebounds, plus blocked a few shots. He was the guiding force in our easy win at Middletown Madison. He took a seat next to Coach Wilson, who wrapped him up in a towel and told him how well he had played. Then he sat back and watched Danny Kruer and I shoot ten times apiece in a frantic final minute.

The buzzer sounded. Game Over. Season over.

We were 11-1, successful by anyone's standards, and we laughed and cut up on the entire bus ride home.

"Wilburn, I'm not surprised you scored so many points," Shane joked, pointing his finger in Donny's direction. "You were guarded by a guy with one leg and half-blind. I'd have had thirty against that guy." He got a good laugh with that one.

"Yeah, yeah. Shane, you couldn't score thirty if they put you on the court all by yourself to shoot lay-ups," Donny shot back.

"I'll show you tomorrow at the park. Me and you, after school."

"You never learn," Donny said. One thing was for certain, the rest of us would be there to watch.

Amid the laughter and the chatter, I was already looking forward to the next season. I was determined to work hard every day, dribbling my basketball to and from school, and spending endless hours at the park shooting jumpers. I was going to run miles. I was going to lift weights. My first year as a Panther was over, and I was more determined that ever to accomplish the dream I always had – to play on the varsity. In front of a packed house. With newspaper reporters documenting my every move.

When we returned to the school, Coach Wilson pulled us aside in the gym. He knew it was late and some of us had tests the next day. But there was stuff he wanted to say. One by one we filed in and took a seat. Danny was seated next to me, quietly taking in the scene and reflecting on our experience. Mitch and Donny were on the other side of me; Tim Thomas was in front. Ricky Baker was right behind me.

Brutey was off to the side, with his head down. He hated to see this season end.

There was no cutting up now. The reality sank in that a great experience had come to an end. There was joy and sadness all at the same time. Coach stood in front of us, his tie loosened. He was holding the same clipboard he'd carried around on the day we had try-outs. Since we were all so quiet, he didn't waste any time.

"I wanted to tell you how much I have enjoyed this season," he began. "You've shown yourselves to be good basketball players, but more importantly, you've shown yourselves to be good kids. It's been a pleasure getting to know every one of you the way I have."

The gym lights were off, but there was a glow emerging from an area just off the locker room. In the shadows I could see the backboard and hoop at the north end of the gym. It hardly seemed like the same place that was so alive and crazy when the varsity played there.

"Take this experience this year and remember it. You won't have many opportunities to live your lives without a lot of worries, where your main focus can be on playing ball. So enjoy this while you can. But I want you to learn from this year, too. Every one of you can become even better players. And you get better by practicing – shooting free throws on your own, working on your ball handling on your own, playing pickup games as often as you can. Don't wait until next September; practice throughout the summer.

"You've seen how success comes from hard work and discipline. I know I've been hard on you sometimes. But you've also seen how much fun you can have from winning."

The gym was as quiet as I had ever experienced it. Coach Wilson stepped up to the first row of the bleachers to make his final point.

"Build on this. Use this experience to become better players. Use this experience to become better kids."

I looked around briefly. Everyone else was as moved by Coach's words as I was. I was ready to start practice for next year right then and there.

"You've represented your school well. You should be proud of what you contributed to this program. Right now the seniors are getting all the attention. But one day it will be you guys.

"Thanks, guys. I want to thank each one of you."

And with that we huddled one last time, dressed in our ties and our jackets. We each put our right hand in the middle, and on three we all shouted in unison: "Hustle."

For once, Danny Kruer was speechless.

Brutey, meanwhile, was crying. This was an ending for him in more ways than one.

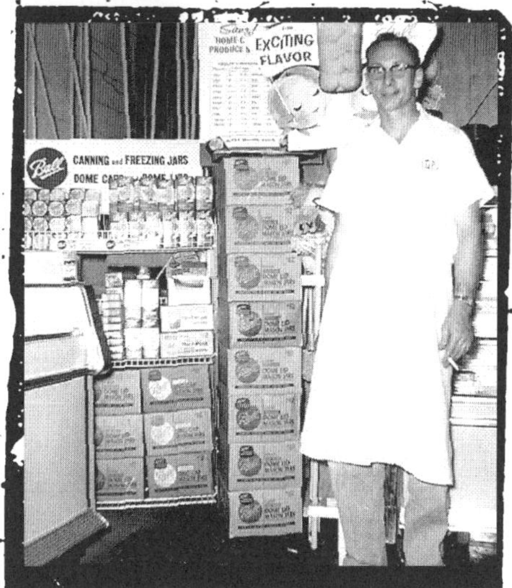

On Friday nights, the town would cheer for Dave Collins, Jeff Howard and Gary Patton, seniors who each played three sports. On Saturday mornings, it would do the weekly shopping for groceries at the IGA, which was opened by Homer and Lillian Preston in 1958.

CHAPTER 38

Simon sing "You're So Vain," which
was one of our favorites – just
who is she singing about?
-- The dilemma

SUNDAY, FEBRUARY 11, 1973

After a church service that comforted him and assured him more than ever that he had been right to turn himself in, Brutey went home to clean the garage, while Norma went to the IGA. The boys were out of peanut butter and she needed carrots and peas for another batch of vegetable soup, which she would spend the afternoon cooking. It was a clear day, but cold, and customers were bundled up as they mingled their way through the aisles. Norma passed by the aisle that displayed all the alcohol and she was glad she no longer had to buy Weideman beer for Brutey. Those days were gone.

As always, she did her best to watch what she spent. A loaf of bread was up to thirty-nine cents, and a gallon of milk was getting close to a dollar. She read labels and evaluated the cost of various products, deciding on an item only when she was sure she was getting the most quality for the best price. Apples were cheaper when purchased by the bag, and breakfast cereal was cheaper when it contained no sugar. Ricky and Larry often told her they were tired of oatmeal, and they joked that their heads were going to turn into a pile of mush, but she told them they were going to have to get over it. Heart problems ran in the family. And oatmeal was cheap.

Who knew how long their money would last?

As Norma passed by the cookie aisle, she heard a voice from off in the distance. "Hey, you tell that no good husband of yours I'm mad at him." Norma was startled by the shout from the other end of the aisle. It was Homer Preston, the owner of the IGA. He was doing a little shopping of his own, but probably not for himself. Norma figured he was putting together another cart of groceries for a needy family on East Market Street, as he often did. Homer barked a lot when he talked, but he was harmless.

"Why's that?" she asked, smiling.

Homer placed several cans of soup in his cart. "Why's that? 'Cause he ain't come and seen me in a while, that's why. Who's he think he is anyway, the president? Tell him I'm here every day, twelve hours a day, and I ain't asking too much for him to stop in once in a while. We can have a cup of coffee. Then I can make fun of that fat old head of his."

Norma chuckled. "Okay, I'll tell him. He's just been going through a hard time right now."

"Hell, I know that. Why don't he come to me for help?" He put some saltines and cheese slices in the cart.

Norma picked up a head of lettuce and inspected it. "It's not his style, Homer. You know that. He'll probably tell you our phone is still connected and you could have called him if you wanted to help."

Homer grunted. "Maybe I'll do that. Then I'll come over and kick his ass."

"I'm sure he'd like that."

She appreciated Homer's heartfelt concern. His interest in the people of Springboro was a big reason the IGA had become as successful as it had. In many ways, it was as much the nerve center of town as the school or the K&W was.

She moved through the fruits and vegetables. She then looked at the cleaning supplies. She picked up some detergent, some dishwashing soap, and some Comet. When she got home the boys would sing their made-up Comet commercial all day long and then make jokes about the Mason Comets. It happened every time. *So get some Comet, and vomit, today.* She smiled for the first time all day.

The court case was terribly hard on Brutey, and every day she listened to him and offered a word of comfort. She'd give anything to take away his pain. But what was equally difficult was what she was going through, for she had to endure stares and pointed fingers, too. She knew there were phone calls passing all over town about the latest juicy gossip about the situation. And she could hear the whispers around her. As a result, she spent many mornings crying in bed, and many afternoons hiding as she did errands around town. She never said it, but she felt she was a victim every bit as much as Janet Spencer and her family was.

She turned into the frozen foods section and stopped in her tracks. She wanted to abruptly turn around, but that would have been too obvious. Right in front of her was Mildred Williams, a woman who never said a positive thing in her life. She was a member of the PTA and the Mother's Club, and she led the ladies auxiliary at the Methodist Church, but Norma found her to be one of the phoniest and rudest people on Earth. There was no escaping her now.

"Why, Norma Baker, how are you this lovely day?" They were face-to-face in the aisle, their carts in front of them. "I was just leaving church when several of the ladies started a conversation about you."

Norma pretended not to care. "Oh, really?"

"You know, I was so thrilled to hear that court went well for you the other day. But it's a shame that some people don't feel that way," Mildred said.

"Some people. What do you mean?" Norma asked, crunching her brow. *I hate this lady. I hate her sooo much.*

"Well, some people have started a petition to make sure Brutey never coaches again. We, er, um, *they* don't want a murderer coaching our children."

Norma couldn't believe what she was hearing. "He's not a murderer," she said. "He had an accident. He made a mistake. And he decided to come forward when he had a chance to stay quiet about it forever." *I'll show you murder in a minute if you keep talking.*

"Yes, I mean, he had that accident where that poor woman with those little kids died. Some people just don't think that's a good role model."

Norma decided to quit talking to Mildred Williams. It was clear the woman had started a petition and was soliciting people from all over town to be part of it. And she didn't have the guts to tell Norma directly that she was behind it.

Norma walked away without saying another word.

She quickly paid for her groceries and drove straight home. As the boys sang and giggled all afternoon in the living room, Norma went into her room and slammed the door. When would this ever end?

* * *

Brutey spent the afternoon at the high school watching game films with the other basketball coaches, which was a welcome diversion. Since he had scouted Mason the night before, he missed Springboro's game at Fenwick, which he'd heard had been a great game. The coaches watched and took notes, and reviewed game film with a critical eye towards finding some way to improve the team. Amid all of that seriousness, though, they often found something to laugh at, like an official's stupid call, or a fan in the stands picking his nose. For Brutey, it was as fun as a night on a barstool at Ron's Pizza used to be; only no alcohol was involved. He so loved being part of this group, and he hoped to be part of it for a long time to come.

The Panthers won both games over the weekend, thanks to the combined effort of all the players. But clearly the play of one particular player had been most brilliant of all. Gary Patton, whose home number of twenty-two reflected his personality, was explosive, fiery and prone to get scorching hot in a moment's notice, and that had never been so true than that particular weekend. He played loose and enjoyed every minute of every game, which was why all the coaches loved him so much.

Gary was the guard opposite Jimmy Hough, and for that he never got his share of individual attention or recognition. But like his cousin Jeff Howard, he was talented enough to be a standout anywhere else he may have played. Gary was excellent on defense, great at moving the ball on offense, and was deadly from the perimeter. He scored easily from what would be today's NBA three-point range.

For every game, Coach Hall could count on Gary for a good, solid performance. And, occasionally, he performed heroics.

In the first of Springboro's two games that weekend, an easy victory at home against Kings Mills, Gary sparked a spurt of thirteen unanswered points in the third quarter, giving us a fourteen-point lead that the Knights never recovered from.

But Gary's biggest heroics came the next night at Fenwick, a small Catholic school in Middletown that had good players from a cross-section of the whole area. Though only a Class A school, Fenwick was always tough to play. They were talented and spunky and as a result…no one liked Fenwick. Its gymnasium was like a snake pit, loud and hostile because it was inhabited by exuberant and generally obnoxious fans. It was hard to win there because no one felt they got a fair shake there. And from all indications, Fenwick was just fine with that perception.

CHAPTER 38

By the end of the first quarter, we were getting blitzed pretty badly and the flurry continued from there. Fenwick led by ten at one time. But we fought back. By the end of three quarters we were still behind by four, and had the officiating been any better, we probably could have been tied. As the teams drank water and rested in preparation for the last quarter, Coach Hall turned his total focus on the two officials and their sloppy calls.

"They couldn't have cared less; they didn't even look at me. Watch this, I'm yelling and this guy's walking away from me," Coach noted as the game filmed rolled on. It looked like the seven-game winning streak was coming to an end. There would be no steak dinner.

But our team kept pushing anyway. Gary hit a jumper and closed the gap to two. Later Dave Collins scored a bucket to bring the game even. It stayed that way, back and forth, until Fenwick took a two-point lead with under a minute to play. That gave us a chance at one final shot, and by now everyone in the entire gym was standing. Jim Hough dribbled up the floor and threw a pass inside to Chuck Mockabee, who was blocked inside. He passed outside to Jeff Howard, who looked for the shot but found nothing. He quickly passed to Gary on the left wing who found an opening. He fired amid two Fenwick players who were quickly closing in, missing the mark. It was painful to watch and the Fenwick fans exploded in joy, running on to the court and taunting the Springboro crowd.

But there was a whistle. Gary had been fouled in the process of shooting, sending him to the free throw line with only seconds left. He got two free throws to tie the game.

He had spent hours and hours practicing free throws through the years. On summer nights he shot them alone; at practice he shot them surrounded by his teammates, oftentimes at the end of practice during a drill that required more running for each missed free throw. He had his routine and confidence in his ability.

But these free throws were harder than most. Not only did he have six hundred frantic Fenwick fans screaming at him, but he had been hurt by the foul. His right hand pulsed in pain. "He had a hard time even holding onto the ball," Coach reported.

Still, he dribbled, took aim and fired. His first shot was good. "Nothing but net. A perfect shot," Coach commented.

That left one more shot, with us still trailing by one. He grabbed his right hand with his left and squeezed, trying to numb the pain away for one more shot. Once again Gary toed the line and completed his pre-shot routine amid the screaming and taunting. All eyes were watching and all fans were on their feet. He hit the second shot, too.

The game went into overtime.

By this time, the Falcons were out of steam and their fans were devastated. The Falcons had nothing left in the overtime. By game's end we had whipped Fenwick pretty good, 81-76, for their eighth win in a row.

Coach turned off the projector and filled in some of the post-game events. The Springboro fans couldn't believe they'd made such a turnaround in such a difficult place to play. One dad mocked having a heart attack. A mother was in tears. Downstairs in the locker room, the players acted as though they had just won the world championship. It was hard to figure out what they were happiest about – the eighth win, the overtime excitement, of the simple fact and beating Fenwick on its own floor. "It's always a huge win there," Coach said.

Brutey wished he had been there, on the bench. He wanted to build confidence and shout directions. He wanted to do more than scout on game night and watch film the day after.

He wanted his old life back.

This was what life was all about.

Coach closed the meeting with a call for perspective. "Gentlemen, we're getting to crunch time," he said, turning to the chalk board. "If these kids continue to play like they are now, we can go places. But they have to know that the road gets tougher the farther we go. And they can't start looking too far ahead. Our focus now is Little Miami, who's always tough at their place. Then we have Mason and everyone here knows how much we owe them."

There was no debate there. An intense dislike for Mason was an unspoken reality.

The coaches closed their notebooks and readied themselves to get back out in the winter cold. The meeting was over and their plan was in place. After a hard week of school and then a busy weekend, it was hard to believe a new school week was upon them already. Each of them needed to get home to get some rest.

Coach Hall stopped Brutey on the way out.

"You doing okay?" he asked.

Brutey hesitated. "Yeah, I guess," he said finally.

"You know, it's a damn shame what happened. It's a damn shame for everybody." Brutey acknowledged the comment and agreed. There was nothing more to be said.

They opened the outside gym door and were brutally greeted by the cold, howling wind. It had blown off the snow that had covered their cars during the short time they were in the building. Brutey decided he wouldn't push for a discussion about a permanent coaching position until long after the season was over.

Somewhere, Mildred Williams was smiling at the thought of that.

Myrtle Reedy never missed a Springboro sporting event, earning her the nickname as a Springboro "Super Fan." She was among many, like eighth grader Gary Cushman, who enjoyed a thrilling '72-'73 basketball season, one that ended with Gary Patton, Coach Harry Hall and Jim Hough celebrating a conference championship.

CHAPTER 39

She doesn't know much about football, but she sure can catch a pass.
-- Mr. Vince Ross, Springboro H.S. Principal

Saturday, February 24, 1973

The envelope was white and inexpensive, obviously printed on standard stationary. What set it apart was its return address in the upper left hand corner. "Warren County Court of Common Pleas" it read at the top. And just below it, in smaller lettering, were the words "Judge P. Daniel Fedders."

My dad sat in his office cleaning up some files and making some phone calls, his typical thing on a Saturday morning. The secretaries were off, and casual attire ruled the day. He zipped off his jacket and settled into his desk chair, staring at the envelope that was on top of the stack of papers on his desk. Surely it contained Brutey's fate.

He thought about how, in the criminal justice system, one piece of paper often carried such incredible significance. If it contained words like "overruled" and "guilty," he had a client who would likely face a prison sentence. If instead it had words like "sustained" and "insufficient evidence," he could breathe easier knowing a lesser punishment was coming. It almost didn't seem right that one man had such power. But that's the system.

The uncertainty of a court's judgment never got any easier. Dad had been through some terrible battles. Watching a jury fill into a courtroom to render a verdict remained one of the most difficult things in life to endure. Reading a judge's decision wasn't much easier.

He tried to make out some of the words before opening it, to get a preview of what he was about to read. But the paper was too thick. He could see the judge's signature, but nothing else. At twelve minutes after ten, he figured there was no sense putting off the inevitable. He opened the envelope.

* * *

Brutey was at Dutch's Barber Shop at that moment, getting his hair cut. The plaza was alive with women headed for the grocery and men headed to the hardware store. Sam Fish, a longtime local farmer, and his son Nelson were in Dutch's too. They talked about stories from long ago, and about the basketball team, and especially about the rapid development of Springboro.

"When I was a kid, there wasn't anything around these parts," Sam Fish said. "Look in any direction, all you'd see was farmland. Stand outside on a sunny summer afternoon, all you'd hear was the wind blowing through the trees. This town was small, I tell you."

Mr. Fish's father had come to Springboro in the twenties to be a farmer, and Mr. Fish followed in his father's footsteps. He loved the land and nature. He loved the simplicity that small town farm life allowed.

"They're building more houses up there in Tamarack," Dutch said. "Did you fellas hear that?"

Mr. Fish grimaced. "Yep. It's getting bigger and bigger up there. Before long they'll be everywhere," Mr. Fish said. "Brutey, seems to me you ought to be buying a place up there."

Brutey chuckled. "You're kidding me, right? When did I inherit a million dollars? Only the rich folks live up there. Sam, maybe you should start your own subdivision with all that land you've got."

Now it was Mr. Fish's turn to chuckle. "It ain't happening. When we were kids, there were – what? – four or five hundred people in this town? Then in 1960 about nine hundred. Crimany, we're up to two thousand people now, mostly because of Royal Oaks. We don't need any more subdivisions around here. The place is as big as it needs to get."

Brutey nodded his agreement. Before long they were talking about the latest development in the Watergate scandal, and then a comment or two about when the troops should leave Vietnam. Then they took turns telling some raunchy jokes. Brutey found himself smiling a time or two and really appreciated it. The conversation took his mind off of what he was really worried about – his case. He hadn't slept well the night before, and he was mad about that. He was determined not to worry, and yet the thoughts seemed to creep into his mind at times when he least expected it. He was mad at himself for not keeping that under control better.

But Mr. Fish was just the guy he needed to spend time with, and Brutey regarded it as a stroke of luck to run into him here at the barber shop. Mr. Fish was a good man, and a good friend.

"We whooped on Mason pretty good last night, huh Brutey?" Mr. Fish commented. "Jumped on 'em right from the get-go and never let up."

"They had it coming," Brutey said, shaking his head. He couldn't remember the last time the varsity played with such intensity. Everybody played hard. Everybody was emotional. Though the conference crown was already locked up, there were other factors that made this such a big game. It was the last home game ever for the seniors, for one. And it was also against Mason, the team that ended our season the year before and then beat us earlier in the season at their place.

"I saw fire in the kids' eyes. They wanted to end their career here with an obliteration of Mason."

"They sure did that."

"The Howard boy was ready to dunk it, if given half the chance, did you know that?" Brutey offered. "Jeff's been dunking for years in practice, but he didn't dare do it in a game 'cause he knew he'd get a technical, and he knew Harry'd yank him from the game."

"Yeah, but it was his last home game."

"That's why he was gonna' do it. Didn't get the chance to, though."

Dutch finished up his haircut. Nelson took his turn in the barber's chair, and Brutey commented on how tall Nelson was getting. "Nelson, you guys gonna' whip Mason like that some day? You have to keep it going, man. I know you have the game to do it," he said.

"Yes, sir."

"Good boy."

Brutey and Mr. Fish had gone to school together, played ball together, and now had raised their kids together. Mr. Fish grew up on a farm off Lower Springboro Road, and played basketball and baseball through high school, even playing in the band for a while. He had dated Barb Arnold all through high school, and they married in 1957, initially living in a small white house on Main Street across from what is now the Brass Pig, which is now known as Magnolia's On Main.

Nelson was born in 1959, and daughter Linda – who is my age – was born a year later. They moved to the apartments on West Mill Street, next to the taxidermy, in 1965, where one of their neighbors was Gerald Saunders, who was the varsity basketball coach at the time. Son Danny was born in 1962 and youngest daughter Leslie was born in 1968.

Mr. Fish and Brutey saw one another at ball games and school open houses. They also worked at the same company, though in different divisions. Away from work, Brutey got into coaching, while Mr. Fish continued with his love of farming. At one point he farmed eight hundred acres. In 1972, Mr. Fish moved his family to a home on Lower Springboro Road, where they owned various livestock, including horses. Linda, when she was only twelve years old, would often ride her horse down Lower Springboro Road all the way to the Wade family farm on Factory Road so she could attend 4-H meetings with Ralph Wade.

As Dutch finished up with Brutey, the front door opened, and in walked a new customer, someone they'd never seen before. A man in his thirties pushed a boy of probably ten or eleven in a wheelchair. The man wore a John Deere hat. The boy talked about the college basketball game that would be on later that afternoon, UCLA and Stanford. His face lit up when he talked about Bill Walton. "Tell you what, Dad, if he doesn't score thirty points, I'll buy the ice cream."

All Brutey noticed was the wheelchair.

The dad agreed with his son. They joked back and forth while Brutey paid his tab and Dutch prepared to cut Nelson's hair.

"I'll be with you in just a minute, sir. Let me finish up with this young man over here."

"No problem."

It was the last thing Brutey needed to see. He didn't know why the boy was in a wheelchair, and he sure wouldn't ask. But his active imagination gave him a reason. Probably a drunk driver not paying attention. He slammed into the boy's car, crushing his pelvis, leaving him a cripple for life. And now a kid wasn't able to play basketball ever again.

Just like Janet Spencer would never hug her kids again.

He had hoped to stick around talking to Mr. Fish and Dutch. There were a thousand other topics they could have covered. But just like what happened when he first woke up that morning, the thought of his court case flooded his thoughts.

The sight of the boy was too much for him. So he said goodbye and took off for home.

He barely noticed the people milling around the plaza. Brutey jogged home wishing he could just keep running, all the way to Florida or wherever, and start over someplace else.

He found Norma on the telephone as he walked in the door. It was my dad. The judge's decision had come in the mail that morning, and he wanted them to know the news right away. The good news. Excellent news. This was cause for a celebration of sorts, she said.

Norma was so thrilled. "Here, I'll let you talk to Brutey."

Instead, Brutey held up his right hand. "Tell him thanks, but I'm not feeling very well."

"But, Brutey, you won!"

He stood in the doorway, his lips pursed as if ready to say something, but he didn't. Instead, he waved her off and turned around.

There would be no celebration. Instead, he retired to the bedroom for the rest of the morning. He never told Norma about the boy at the barber shop. There was no winning in what he had done, no matter what happened in court. There was no feeling good, only varying degrees of feeling bad. Despite the news from the telephone call, it was probably his worst day yet.

And, on the horizon, he still had a day he would walk into the county jail. When it rained, it poured.

* * *

We saw Brutey jogging through the plaza that day on his way home from Dutch's, and we were surprised when he did not turn and wave at us. The whole gang of us guys had met at the basketball court behind the Jonathan Wright, and after three games we were hungry. The Diner was busy as usual, and we all squeezed into a booth to drink milkshakes and share a massive plate of French fries. The squishing sound in the background must have been the sound of our arteries clogging.

"Man, we spanked you the way Billy Harrison got spanked yesterday during study hall," Turkey said.

"Oh, man! Did you hear that, too? I was upstairs in English class. I guess that's why Mr. Ullum left the door open."

"They always leave the door open when someone gets cracked."

"Hefflin lifted him off the ground with the third one, too," I said, wincing as if the pain had actually been inflicted on me.

"Did you see it?"

"Nah, but I heard him moaning."

"Guess he won't be smoking cigarettes in the bathroom anymore," Turkey said, chomping on a French fry.

"He won't be doing much of anything anymore," Lance said with a chuckle.

"Me either," I said. "I don't ever want to get cracked. Some people don't think the schools should ever do that, but it works."

"Makes me behave, that's for sure," Turkey added.

"What you do isn't exactly 'behaving,'" Lance joked. "You just have all the teachers fooled."

"I'm lovable. What can I say?"

We attacked the plate of fries, and within minutes they were gone. We were like a bunch of piranhas. There was the usual chatter about the games we'd played that morning, plus the varsity game the night before. Plans were being made to go to the UD Arena Tuesday for the tournament game.

We finished our milkshakes and slid up to the counter to pay Evalyn what we owed. Turkey predicted a three-game sweep in the afternoon set, and Lance laughed at him. Donny and Shane were coming that afternoon, so the jawing would definitely go up a notch. None of us had a anything else to do the whole day.

There were two doors to Bennett's Drugs. The left door took you inside the store, where near the back The Diner was located. The right door was the exit door, and the counter where Evalyn worked was directly beside that door. There was a long wall that separated the two doors, so if you walked in you never saw who was at the counter ready to walk out, and vice versa.

Just as we were walking out, I realized I had left my basketball back in the booth we'd been sitting in. "Go on ahead," I told the guys. "I'll be there in a few minutes." I'm not sure why I bothered to say anything. Not a one of them turned around to acknowledge that I was talking. They still wouldn't notice I was gone until the game got ready to start.

I was the same way, though.

A girl my age was at the cosmetics counter when I walked back. She was a new girl in school, very pretty. I didn't know her very well, though, because she was only in one of my classes – Science class, of all things. Her first name was Kim, and her last name was Terrence or Terron, or something like that. Her family lived on Factory Road. She had a brother who was confined to a wheelchair after he crashed a go-cart about a year ago. I would have given anything to have the courage to say hi and start up a conversation with her. But since I didn't, of course, I slipped by her without a word.

Of all days not to have a head injury. Or be in a dirty football uniform. This would have been perfect situation.

Surprisingly, she noticed me, though. And after I retrieved my basketball, she was waiting on me.

"Hi." She had long blonde hair and blue eyes. She always seemed to have a smile on her face, as she did at the moment. I think they'd moved here from California.

"Uh, hi." I was such a dork. *Can't you ever think of anything witty to say?*

She wanted to know what I had been doing, and she told me she was picking up some things while her dad and brother were at the barber shop. She spoke easily and confidently, so I let her do most of the talking. She was as nice as she was pretty.

"So do you like it here? In Springboro, I mean?"

"Everybody's been so nice and I just love the teachers, especially Mrs. Kuhn. Don't you just think she's fascinating?" I had a lot of words for her, but fascinating had never come to mind.

"I'm going to a birthday party today. Seems like there's always something to do around here – I love it! And, hey, I heard about this talent show they're having at the school next Saturday night."

Man, she was pretty! Was she really talking to me? I turned around to look behind me just to make sure. "Yeah, I heard something about it. A lot of funny people will be in it."

"Sounds like fun. You gonna go?"

As it turned out, my social calendar wasn't exactly full. Unless there was a scheduled ball game, I never knew from one minute to the next what I was going to do.

"I think so. Yeah." This sounds like an awesome opportunity!

"Great! Maybe we can sit together."

I looked at her like her hair had suddenly caught fire. What did that mean? Was that like a date? "I'll look for you."

"Yeah. Okay. Sure."

Just then her dad and brother walked in looking fresh with new haircuts. And I realized I was late for the games at the school. She said goodbye and I said I'd see her later, and I spent the whole rest of the day realizing I was going to have a date the following Saturday night. And she was pretty! And she liked me!

I flew back to the Jonathan Wright and re-joined the game. I outscored, out rebounded and outplayed everybody the rest of the day. It's like I was Walt Frazier and Lew Alcindor all wrapped up into one.

No one had a clue as to why I was suddenly so good.

CHAPTER 40

Blue and white, you're outa' sight
Hey, Hey, Hey
Blue and white, you're outa' sight
-- Panther cheer

SATURDAY, MARCH 3, 1973

As soon as final buzzer sounded and the players all collapsed to the floor, predictions were being made that it was the single-most exciting, thrilling and thoroughly enjoyable game in the history of Springboro athletics. It had everything – magical plays, suspense, reckless hustle for loose balls and a wild chaotic crowd that cheered on every move.

It came in a second-round tournament game we played at the University of Dayton Arena, a futuristic, state-of-the-art glorious structure north of our town that was only a few years old at the time. In the week leading up to it, we had thoroughly annihilated Mason in the final home game of the season, thus solidifying our status as conference champions, and we had whipped Oakwood in the opening round of the tournament, setting up the second-round thriller. Our opponent was Twin Valley South, a small school in rural Preble County that had been decent throughout the regular-season, but was not expected to be a match for us. All we had to watch out for was their hot-shooting guard, Dale Spitler.

From the beginning, the game was fast-paced and action-packed. We scored, they scored, we'd go on a run to get a lead, and then they would fight back. Coach Hall worked players in and out masterfully, trying to keep everyone fresh in the run-and-gun atmosphere.

When it was over almost three hours later, players fell to the floor in exhaustion.

Our team, the Springboro blue, was able to raise its hands in victory. The celebration that followed resembled an Ohio State victory over Michigan. Maybe it was bigger. It was pandemonium. Players hugged one another and fans high-fived and shouted their joy. Myrtle Reedy, the super fan who had attended every game for years, shook her head and said she had never seen anything like it. Ralph Wade, the unofficial mayor, proudly proclaimed it the best game he had ever seen.

I couldn't believe I'd actually witnessed such an awesome game. I was at the game with Roger Woolery and his dad, and I was so pumped with adrenaline the whole time, experiencing each play as though I were personally involved. I was thrilled that our season would continue.

The celebration continued out into the parking lot, then back into town. Parents went to The Diner and kids went to the K & W, where they relived every moment, every play and every turning point. Every player was praised, no one was left out. Gary got hot, Gordy got physical, Jeff and Chuck and Dave hit clutch shots when we needed them. What an effort, what a game. This was one for the history books.

But there was one player who received special attention in every conversation. For years he had been a team leader and a top scorer, and against TV South he was all that and then some. He was known throughout town simply as "Jimmy."

* * *

Jim Hough was shooting basketball for as long as he could remember.

With his dad, Jim Hough Sr., being the varsity basketball coach until 1962, six- and seven-year-old Jimmy would go to practices with him, shooting a volleyball because it was small enough to fit his hands. His dad resigned from coaching to become a principal in the school district, but Jimmy continued to play. The Hough residence was on Elmwood Drive, which was right around the corner from the high school, making the outside courts there available to him on a daily basis.

Jimmy worked hard to hone his God-given talent; his dad was always there to give him pointers.

He was ten when the '65 team of George Burkhart, Bob Mockabee and

CHAPTER 40

Mike Blevins turned the town on its head by going to the state finals. Jimmy went to every game and was mesmerized by its talent. The next day, he would go to the high school courts and imagine a day when he was in an important game in a Springboro uniform.

He was a seventh-grader when Coach Hall came to town to coach the varsity. Jimmy's coaches that year were Ted Hall (no relation) and Brutey. He quickly established himself as a team leader and a proficient scorer. Playing with Gary Patton, Jeff Howard, Rod Dillon, Dave Collins and John Mockabee, they went undefeated. They lost one time the next year as eighth graders. Then as freshmen they had another outstanding season.

But after his freshmen year, Jimmy reached a crossroads with another love in his life – football.

He loved it as much as he did basketball, and he was as good at it, too. He had played quarterback on the Charlie Harris' traveling teams, then played junior high ball. He didn't play as a freshman, though, in large part because he wanted to focus on basketball. He went to every game, though, and instantly regretted his decision.

In the spring and summer of 1970 he had two big conversations with head football coach Don Ross, both of which helped him decide which direction he should take at the crossroads.

At the post-season basketball tournament in February 1970 Coach Ross approached young Jim, who was then a freshman, as they were walking up the steps of the UD Arena after the season-ending game. Coach put his arm around him and offered words of encouragement. "You know, if you work hard enough this summer, that can be you out there next year," Coach said.

The comment meant a lot to Jimmy because that was exactly his hope and goal. Over the summer he spent his evenings traveling the outdoor court and open gym circuit, playing against the area's best competition and continuing to get stronger and better. Starting for the varsity became more than just a dream; it was a reality.

Still, the love for football tugged at him. He'd played it his whole life, and missed it terribly when he didn't play the year before. So, while he played basketball every night all summer long, he spent his days throwing footballs to his neighbor Kim Zech, a wide receiver who was a year older.

When the beginning of practice rolled around, he went through the grueling two-a-day practice sessions that all varsity squads go through. He was assigned a number. He was given a position and a slot on the depth chart. And then one day he was summoned for the second of the two big conversations with Coach Ross.

It was a blistering mid-August afternoon after practice. Jimmy was drenched in sweat, exhausted from the day's practices and nursing a few aches and pains. Coach Hefflin told him he was wanted in the coaches' office, where he went before showering or removing all of his pads. Coach Ross greeted him warmly and then shut the door. "You know, Jim, you're a good football player. You're smart, you've got a good arm, and there's no doubt you could help us at quarterback."

He hesitated, allowing his next words to have the intended effect.

"But if you get hurt playing football, they'll run me out of this town." In other words, he was more talented – and more needed – as a basketball player.

Springboro was, after all, a basketball town; football was still in its developing stages.

So Jim Hough quit the football team before the regular season began.

He started on the varsity basketball team his sophomore year, quickly showing how he was like a coach and quarterback on the floor. He knew where everybody was and where they were supposed to be. Though the Panthers were not very good that year, Coach Hall and Brutey and The Diner crowd and everyone else for that matter knew what was coming. The young players would get older. And as they got older, they would get better. And that meant more wins. Jimmy was the undisputed leader through it all.

As a junior, Jimmy was the team's leading scorer and an all-conference pick. He enjoyed having his classmates back with him on the floor – Gary, Jeff, Gordy, and Dave Collins. And Rod Dillon played on the varsity that year. There were many thrilling moments – big games, and lots of wins and lots of attention. And there was also a scare. Midway through the season, in a conference game at Little Miami, Jimmy dove for a loose ball midway through the second half. When he hit the floor, he hit a metal hook-up embedded into the floor that was used for volleyball nets. When he looked up, blood was everywhere. It looked like he was done for a while. But tests were done and stitches were inserted, and for a few games he wore a bandage on his forehead. He stayed in the lineup and continued scoring.

I wore a similar bandage when I practiced alone at the park.

The season-ending losses to Mason stung because they made the season end on a sour note. Though they finished with a respectable 13-5 record, they had hoped to go farther in the tournament. That hurt proved to be a motivator over the summer, though, with more and more rounds of open gyms and big games against college stars and area top players. The hard work paid off, too, because the team hit the ground running in this senior season. Aside from the hiccup with three tough losses on the road against tough teams, the momentum continued.

After the win at Fenwick, a game in which Jimmy scored his 1,000th point in his career, the conference championship was sewn up with a victory at Little Miami. Mason came to town for the season-ending game, and the Comets didn't have a chance, getting blown out by more than twenty-five. As always, Jimmy was a steady contributor in points, assists and heads-up defensive play.

The Panthers easily won their tournament opener against Oakwood, which had Dave Stuckey in the starting lineup. But then Jimmy saved his best for the second-round game against South. He had eighteen points by halftime, and then hit shot after crucial shot during the chaotic stretch to the finish. The lead changed hands no less than twenty times. The Arena rocked. Jimmy fouled out with less than a minute to go, but by then he had scored 39 points, a season high. When Jeff and Gary and Gordy led the way to the 104-98 victory, in overtime, no one forgot the guy who got them there.

Coach Hall talked at length about his star guard in the press conference afterward. Newspapers highlighted his every move and accomplishment. And the town practically anointed him as something just short of royalty – the man who led the varsity, the man who could take us back to the state tournament, and this time come home a winner.

Jimmy. Just say that name and everyone knew who you were talking about.

They say the cream always rises to the top in the biggest game of the year. That was never truer than in this one.

* * *

The District semi-final game against Madison was five days later, on Wednesday night, and though it was not the scoring fest the TV South game had been, it was just as thrilling.

We led by only a point with fifteen seconds to go. Dave Collins, my neighbor who caught many passes during football season and was also the ultimate sixth man for the basketball team, was fouled, giving him two free throws. A miss of either or both shots still gave Madison a chance. And Madison was feeling a miss was a virtual probability, since a struggling Dave had shot six free throws that night and missed all six.

His seventh of the night, though, was perfect.

Our lead was two.

Dave had been the big brother I never had. His family lived on Walnut, behind our street, and I spent a lot of time at his house hanging with his younger brother Brian, who was on my baseball team. Through the years I'd been to Dave's football, basketball and baseball games all over. He was not a big guy, only five-nine, but he was gritty and determined. As he stood at the free throw line in the center of UD Arena for perhaps the most important shot of his entire career, I could barely watch. I closed my eyes and decided to listen for the crowd reaction.

Boom! Our cheering section exploded.

We knocked off mighty Middletown Madison, the state runner-up from the year before. And that brought on as much of a celebration as the TV South game had. It set up the District finals game on Saturday against Dayton Jefferson.

The games made headlines in all the local newspapers, with large stories and pictures. Having won thirteen games in a row, the team had the confidence and momentum it had worked hard to achieve over the last year. None of them could go to school or the supermarket or to church without someone initiating a conversation about the Jefferson game.

A District championship was a lofty but nonetheless reachable goal. Then there were the Regionals. If they were lucky, then they could go on to the State tournament just like their predecessors eight years earlier.

On that Saturday they played Jefferson, the team met at ten o'clock at the school. Coach Hall held a brief meeting, encouraging them to stay focused on the game at hand and not look ahead, as was so tempting to do.

"Our goal this year was to make a splash in this tournament," he said. "After losing in the first round last year, we wanted to make up for that disappointment. The good news is that we've done a little of that, and you can hold your heads high and know you've made this town proud. The bad news is that it gets harder each step here on out.

"Jefferson's got some big boys, and they're quick. We're going to have to play the best game of the year today. When you get on that bus, the game has started. I want you focused, I want you ready, and I want you to act like winners. Because that's what you are."

They loaded up on the team bus and began the twenty-minute trip to the University of Dayton Arena. They pulled out of the school parking lot to the cheers of some locals who had their cars decorated and were going to lead a caravan of other supporters to the tournament. The bus roared up Main Street, past the bus garage, past Dick Chenault's house and past the K & W.

Soon, they were gone.

* * *

There was more bad news that night. I attended the talent show, dressed as nicely as I could. I watched Kip Zech, Kim's younger brother, bring the house down with his mimicked version of *I Am Woman*, by Helen Reddy, which had become sort of a theme song for the women's movement at the time. Kip was dressed as a woman and his biggest laugh came during the line …"and look how much I've gained." He grabbed his make-believe breasts as the crowd roared. In that respect, the night had been a good one.

But the bad news was that I looked around all night for Kim Tooley or whatever-her-name-was, but she never showed.

When I saw her at the school on Monday she told me she'd been invited to a party and forgot all about the show. By the next day she was walking to class with Tim Campbell.

I was destined to be single forever. I'd had my plans all through the school year to try to hook up with any one of a number of girls, and either I was too chicken or the situation never did present itself. This Kim girl looked like she was best candidate yet, and even that one went down the tubes.

But there was room for some consolation. Turkey told me she had bad breath anyway. And this time I was inclined to believe my friend. What a great guy, that Turkey.

CHAPTER 41

You help me along, making me strong
Oh, give me the beat, boys, that free
my soul, I want to get lost in your
rock n' roll, and drift away
-- The troubadour
Dobie Gray

FRIDAY, MARCH 8, 1973

After P.B. Stockman gave the order to stand, Judge Fedders entered the courtroom holding both the file and the fate of Brutey Baker. He would accept a guilty plea from Brutey that morning to leaving the scene of an accident, which was a first-degree misdemeanor. That meant he could sentence Brutey to six months in the county jail. It also meant that he could put him on probation, order him to do community service and also suspend his driver's license. He deserved at least that much for what he did, no matter what the concept of corpus delecti did to this case.

Janet Spencer's husband and their two little girls sat in the front row. John Spencer wore a blue suit and striped tie, the same suit he wore at Janet's funeral. He still wore his wedding ring, too. The girls each wore Sunday-school dresses with charms around their necks that had their mother's picture inside. In many ways, this day was far worse than the day Janet was buried, because now they had to look at Brutey. John had heard all the positive qualities Brutey possessed, but none of them mattered. He still hated the man.

Janet's parents were on the other side of the girls, with Hazel sitting closest to the girls. Behind them were Janet's brothers and their wives, then a few uncles and cousins. They had all been warned by the deputies that outbursts were not to be tolerated. A single wayward comment would get them all tossed from the courtroom. The two brothers heard that and shrugged their shoulders. They were getting the final word on this, somehow.

P.B. Stockman told everyone to take their seat. The judge flipped open the file in front of him.

"This is case number 72-CR-473, the State of Ohio versus Harold Baker. We're here today for a plea and final sentencing, the Court having previously granted the motion to dismiss on the felony charge of involuntary manslaughter." One of Janet Spencer's uncles grunted at that comment, which the judge heard but let pass. This time.

"Let the record reflect the state is represented by Mr. Turkelson. Let the record also reflect that Mr. Baker is present and represented by Mr. Kirby. Gentlemen, is there something that is to come before the Court this morning?"

Brutey sat at the defense table next to my dad. Unlike the previous hearing, there were no papers strewn about. He did not have a notepad in front of him. Instead, he knew this was the day the family got a piece of him and he went to jail. He knew their sentiments and he knew what the judge was likely to do. He was ready for all of it.

Mr. Turkelson stood up. "Yes, sir. It's my understanding that the Defendant will be entering a plea of guilty to the remaining charge, your honor. The state recommends the maximum penalty."

"We'll get there in a minute, Mr. Turkelson. Thank you." He shuffled around some papers. "Mr. Kirby, does your client intend to plead guilty this morning to the misdemeanor?"

My dad stood up. "If it pleases the court, the prosecution and defense have made an agreement. We will not appeal the ruling that keeps the leaving the scene of the accident charge, even though we believe the corpus delecti cannot be met. In return, the prosecution will not appeal your ruling dismissing the involuntary manslaughter charge."

Judge Fedders looked down at the file for what seemed like an hour. He wanted to make sure everyone clearly understood what was being discussed, and whether he would go along with it. Finally, he looked up over his horn-rimmed glasses.

"Mr. Turkelson?"

"That is our agreement, your honor. The state recommends the maximum penalty."

"Yes. So I hear."

Brutey and Dad then stepped up the podium in the center of the room. The judge went through the remaining charge and its maximum penalties. He then went through the rights that Brutey waived by entering his plea of guilty. He had the right to a jury trial, and the right to require the prosecution to prove his guilt beyond a reasonable doubt. Further, he had the right to cross-examine witnesses who would testify against him, and the right to present witnesses who could testify in his favor. Lastly, he had the right to remain silent, and no one could make him testify if he chose not to.

"Do you understand the rights you're giving up, Mr. Baker?"

"I do."

"And do you understand the potential penalties I can impose, beginning today?"

"Yes, sir."

"Very well. And to the charge of leaving the scene of an accident, how do you wish to plead?"

Brutey turned to my dad, who whispered something in his ear. Then, in full voice, without a hint of reservation, Brutey said the word: "Guilty." The judge then asked him to sign a form that said, in writing, exactly what had been discussed there in open court. Brutey found it difficult to sign his own name. He was as nervous as he could ever remember. The form was handed to P.B. Stockman, who in turn handed it to Judge Fedders. Though the judge had seen this form a million times, he held it up and inspected it closely. The record needed to be clear that Brutey Baker entered this plea freely, intelligently and voluntarily.

Behind Brutey, Norma sat quietly in the chair next to where Brutey had been sitting. As the judge inspected his plea form, he turned around and made eye contact with her. Then he mouthed the words, I love you.

"Mr. Kirby, any reason that we should not get into the matter of the sentence today?"

"No, sir. Mr. Baker is prepared for that today as well."

"Very well. What would you or your client like me to know about this situation?"

CHAPTER 41

Like most lawyers, Dad took this as an invitation for him to go first. He pointed out that Brutey was thirty-four years old, a graduate of Springboro High School and a fifteen-year employee of NCR, where he was a salesman. He'd been married to Norma for nearly fifteen years and they had two sons, Larry, an eighth grader, and Ricky, who was in the seventh grade.

"He is remorseful about what happened, Judge. He wishes to apologize to the family of Janet Spencer. He knows that it was he who caused the accident that caused Mrs. Spencer's death. He knows that nothing he can do or say will ever bring her back, or ever heal the pain her family must feel.

"But as strange as it may sound, he deserves some credit. There was a time when the Springboro police, the state highway patrol and the sheriff's department had no idea who caused this accident. There were no eyewitnesses and there was no physical evidence. It's very possible Brutey could have gone to his grave carrying his secret. No one would have ever known. No way would he have been caught.

"He is a spiritual man who has been affected by the teachings in his church, and as a result he wanted to do the right thing. So he came forward to take responsibility for his actions, and had he not done so there may never have been closure for the family. That's huge, Judge. You get people in here who confess after the finger has been pointed in their direction. But you don't often get it this way. He deserves some credit for that."

Dad stopped momentarily to let that thought sink in. It's not wise to make the victim's family feel bad in most situations, but Dad felt Janet's family needed to hear that. The fact there were no outbursts as he said it told him that he had done the right thing.

Then he moved on.

"He told the police why he took off, which was because he had been drinking. But another point has to be made here. There's absolutely no proof that he was intoxicated when he took off. He had been drinking, yes, but at the most had two beers. That's not enough for him to be DWI. An involuntary manslaughter may have never stuck anyway, despite what the prosecution and the family might have you believe. It was wrong, yes, but not to the extent they would have you believe."

Still no outbursts. He slowed down for his final point.

"Judge, since October 27, 1972, the night of the accident, he has quit drinking altogether and has started going to church. He doesn't hang out in the bars after hours anymore. He has become more focused on what is really important in life, his family. I want you to know he will carry his guilt with him for the rest of his life. You can put him in the county jail for a little while, but he will be in a mental prison forever."

Dad put his notes away. He took a deep breath and then grabbed Brutey by the shoulder.

The judge then asked Brutey if there was anything he wished to say, something Brutey had thought about for more than four months. As uncomfortable as it was for him to speak in public, he knew he had to say something. He had to publicly acknowledge his actions, and apologize. Everybody had to hear it from him. He spoke to the judge without any prepared notes.

"Judge, what I did was wrong, very wrong. And while I don't want to go to jail today, I'm prepared to do that if it will in some way ease the pain of Janet Spencer's family. By going to jail, the discomfort for me and my family will only be temporary. But what they have to go through will last for the rest of their lives. "

Then Brutey shocked everyone.

"Judge, if there is one thing in this life that I have always done with passion, it's being a coach. I was fortunate enough to play basketball and baseball back when I was in high school. I was motivated to become a better person by some very fine coaches at Springboro, and I wanted to be the same kind of influence on the kids who followed me. And over the last ten years I've come awfully close to a lot of great kids, and hopefully I showed them a thing or two.

"But I'm willing to go to jail today and forego any coaching opportunities for a while. Maybe forever. I can go today and I'll miss the rest of basketball season, then all of baseball season and probably all of football season. That may not sound like much compared with the loss of a life, but the point I'm trying to make is, coaching these kids in Springboro has become my life. And if that's taken away from me, even for a while, that will hurt me as much as death. I will accept your decision. I know God has forgiven me, and I know everything happens for a reason. I leave it up to you."

There was some whispering from the side of the courtroom where Janet Spencer's family sat. Meanwhile, Judge Fedders pulled out a manila folder that contained nearly a hundred letters. All were character letters from Springboro residents. None condoned what Brutey did on the night of October 27, 1972. But all of them praised the character and the influence of a man who, except for those awful fifteen minutes, had been one of the best people around town.

CHAPTER 41

"I have read these letters, Mr. Baker, and it does seem that you've been the model citizen of Springboro your whole life. Here's a letter from a former player who learned as much about life as he did about football from you, he says. And here's a community leader who says you have sacrificed much to make Springboro a better place. All of them see a difference in you since the night Janet Spencer died. Some of that difference is positive – you are more focused on what is important in life and more attentive to the needs of your family. Some of them indicate sadness about you, like a part of you died when Janet Spencer died."

He then lowered his head, again allowing the information to fully sink in. This pause was much longer than any of the others.

"Mr. Turkelson, you have made it abundantly clear that you are asking for the maximum penalty. Do any of the family members wish to be heard?"

Yes, he said, there were two. Janet's brother introduced himself as Merle Richmond and he told the Judge how the family had been changed forever. "Our normal will never be normal again," he said. "We had to go through Thanksgiving, Christmas, birthdays and anniversaries without Janet, and I don't think we'll ever recover from it. My father here has been depressed ever since the accident. He can't eat and can't sleep. And every day he's got to pull out of his driveway and look next door and see Mr. Baker living in that house with his own family. It's just not fair. If you ask me, he don't deserve to live. But if there has to be punishment other than that, I think he should get the maximum allowed by the law, just like the prosecutor said."

The second speaker was Janet's uncle, Ralph Miller, a man who was brother to Janet's mother. He said pretty much the same thing, detailing the hurt and anger the family sustained because of Janet's death. "She was such a beautiful little girl, Judge. She was so nice to everybody and she gave her whole life to these little girls. Anybody who takes that away has to pay for it. Six months is the least he should have to do." Then he snarled at Brutey and sat down. Brutey looked at the floor.

As Judge Fedders reflected on what he had heard, he heard some movement near Janet Spencer's parents. He looked up to see her mother, Bible in hand, standing up and raising her hand. "Judge, may I say something, too?

Judge Fedders nodded his head in agreement.

Hazel Richmond walked slowly to the podium, adjusting her glasses in the process. She had known Brutey and Norma for more than ten years since they all became neighbors. The Baker boys were like sons to her. Janet was like a daughter to the Bakers.

Brutey just knew she would let him have it most of all. He rubbed his eyes and braced himself.

"Judge, I loved my daughter with all my heart, and I miss her terribly. She was so sweet and so young and so full of life. She was way too young to die." She paused as she fought back tears. Her voice began to tremble.

"But I'm here…to tell you…that I don't hate Brutey Baker. I may hate what he did, but I don't hate him. He's a good man who's done his best to live his life, raise a family and be a contributor to our community. All of that can't be wiped away because of one mistake. I can't condemn a man who has a heart as big as his.

"I have to forgive him – we all do -- and move on. Someday, all of us may get there. I certainly hope so. But until then, I wanted you to know, and I wanted Brutey and his family to know, that I know that what they are going through is difficult, too. My daughter loved him, and he loved her too." She couldn't finish the rest of her thought.

Some of her family wept, while others looked at her in disbelief. Brutey hugged Norma and both of his boys. The judge declared a brief recess. Court would resume in fifteen minutes.

* * *

The actual sentence was anti-climatic because the mood in the courtroom had changed dramatically. Brutey's family felt sorry for Janet's family, and vice versa, expect for Janet's brothers. Brutey and his family were braced for the full six month sentence. The family of Janet Spencer had to realize that no sentence would bring Janet back.

Brutey was sentenced to five months in the county jail. The remaining month was suspended on the condition that, for one year, he spent his weekends volunteering in an emergency room. He was also required to undergo alcohol counseling and provide the court with a copy of his progress every three months for the next two years.

"This means you won't be connected with the athletic program at Springboro for more than a year," the judge said. "If they want you, they'll wait for you. I'm giving you this sentence to deter the public from any further episodes like this one. The rest is up to you."

Brutey nodded.

The judge left the courtroom and P.B. Stockman banged the gavel. "All rise." Brutey was put in handcuffs and quickly whisked away to the county jail. His first night in jail was the first night he ever spent away from Norma and the boys. His third day was the day of Springboro's tournament game against Jefferson in the District finals. He spent the time alone in his cell reading his Bible, barely giving the game a second thought. He found the next day that Springboro had lost.

Suddenly, that didn't seem to matter, either.

CHAPTER 42

Batting first, playing right field

Pete Rose!..........Rose

--The voice,

Reds announcer,

Paul Summercamp

Saturday, June 2, 1973

The basketball was stashed away into a corner of my bedroom closet, next to my football cleats. Having dressed in my all-cotton baseball uniform, with IGA on one chest pocket and the number sixteen on the other, I reached for baseball glove and my new 33-inch bat. Our first game was that afternoon against the Yankees, no less, and we were expected at the ball field in a half an hour.

I yelled at my brother John, who was a new pitcher on our team, to hurry and get ready. Joey had written "Red" in bright red ink on John's baseball glove and they were wailing away on each other upstairs. Mom was on her way to break up the melee.

I took off for the park all by myself.

It felt good to be on the baseball field. I loved being in the dirt, with my cleats dug in, hearing the chatter. The lines on the field were bright white and unscathed. The baseballs were brand new, and our uniforms were so much spiffier than the T-shirts and sweatshirts we practiced in.

It was going to be a great season. I loved baseball.

There would be one major difference, however. Brutey would not be coaching this season, as he had done in every other baseball season I'd ever played in. It was weird to think about going to the park, where we could smell the hot dogs and listen to the chatter of players on the field, and not see Brutey in the third base coaching box, encouraging his batter to keep his hands back and hit the ball on a line drive.

Instead, Brutey was in the middle of his jail sentence. He spent his days lying in his bunk and reading, anxiously awaiting that late summer day when Judge Fedders would finally release him. Norma and the boys saw him on Wednesdays and Sundays, and they were surprised that he never talked about sports. He had said in open court that he didn't deserve to be part of the games anymore, and it was evident that he still felt that way.

Still, Ricky wished his dad could have been out to watch our game.

With two outs in the bottom of the seventh, we trailed by a run against the dreaded Yankees. I was standing on third base and Lance was on second. My brother John was at the plate, a ball and two strikes against him. Shane Hatfield, looking as fierce and intent as ever, was pitching. He had been masterful ever since he entered the game, striking out five straight, making him as invincible as Nolan Ryan or Vida Blue. But all of a sudden he found himself in trouble. After I walked on four pitches, Lance lined a double up the right field line. I was the tying run, and Lance would win it. All we needed was for John to hit a single.

"Let's go, John, you can do it," Coach McGraw yelled from the third-base coaching box.

"Come John, come John."

My mom and dad were in the stands, barely able to watch. My sisters, meanwhile, ran to the concession stand for a Popsicle, totally oblivious to the situation, as girls usually were when it came to important things. From third base I dug my cleats in the dirt and prepared to steal home if a ball ever got past their catcher, Todd Thompson.

Shane threw a hard fastball, low and on the outside edge. It was a good pitch, his bread and butter. But from the moment he threw it, John was in perfect rhythm with it.

He laced a hit right over Andy Muldowney on first base, landing in front of Kevin Watkins. Our cheering section erupted and John ran hard to first base. I scored easily and Lance came moving strong right after me. The play was close, and Lance and Todd Thompson collided, causing a cloud of dust to rise above the field.

The umpire's call seemed to take forever. It was so close.

"Safe!"

We'd won. We'd beaten the mighty Yankees and finally gotten some revenge on Shane Hatfield. John was congratulated by everybody and walked around the rest of the night as a hero. The post-game Pepsi was colder and sweeter than any drink we'd ever had before.

Later, I overheard Donny and Shane talking to one another as they sat in the stands together. The next game was already underway.

"He hit a good pitch," Shane said. "Nobody's hit that pitch all year."

"Hmm," Donny said, looking away.

"What? You think it was a bad pitch?" Shane said, hitting Donny on his right arm.

"Let's just say it's not the pitch I'd have thrown."

"Oh, I suppose you could have done better. Is that it? Now you want to tell me what pitch I should've thrown?"

"It's just that everybody knows he can't hit the inside pitch. I'd have thrown it right on the inside corner, as hard as I could, 'cause here's what would have happened. He'd have swung, but the contact would have…"

That conversation had no ending in sight.

In better days, Brutey would have loved it.

* * *

As the school year wound down, the weather grew warmer and the grass was a luscious green. The trees along Main Street were in full bloom, and the shadows covered the front entrance to the K & W as the sun fell behind them. Efforts were underway to make Central Avenue a four-lane highway. Discussions were being held at town hall to determine whether we needed a second traffic light. My thirteenth birthday was two months away and my mom was grieving over the idea that I would be a teenager.

Charlie Reedy and Jimmy Beavers continued to police the streets, and Ralph Wade continued to lead efforts to make Springboro schools a place of excellence. Eleanor Cushman and Myrtle Reedy were seen at the varsity track meets, and they were already planning their schedule for the fall sports season. They worried that the next football team may not be as good as the last one, since so many good seniors graduated.

I actually came to really like Mrs. Kuhn and Science class. Funny what happens when a student actually pays attention. Because I understood what she said, I came to like the subject matter better. And I got good grades. More importantly, I never experienced another public humiliation in her class for daydreaming.

As for English class, well....I never did develop a love for writing essays.

Throughout the spring, Jeff Howard was high-jumping for the track team, and Jim Hough, Rick Black and Rod Dillon led the golf team to a conference championship. Meanwhile, Gary Patton, Darrel Duncan and Dave Collins played baseball. All throughout the spring the guys cruised through town in their cars, listening to the radio, enjoying the warmth of the spring air and the freedom that comes from being a high school senior who was counting down the days to graduation.

That graduation came on that Saturday afternoon, when the threat of rain forced the ceremony to be moved inside to the gymnasium.

That's where one of the greatest classes in the history of Springboro said goodbye.

The students sat on the gym floor in chairs that faced the podium on the stage in front of them. The superintendent, Ray Perez, sat with the board of education. Ralph Wade was to his right, and next to him were Lowell Hayes and Bill Crocker, and then P.B. Stockman. Across the way were high school Principal Vince Ross and several members of the faculty.

Everyone stood for the pledge of allegiance, and then Mr. Ross said a few words. Mr. Perez made a declaration of how proud the school district was of the graduating seniors, and then he introduced the president of the senior class, Dale Midkiff.

Dale stood proudly before his classmates for the final time and gave an opening speech that looked back fondly on the years they had had together. He told stories of second grade with Mrs. Simpson, and seventh grade doing experiments in science class. There were plenty of good times and lots of memories, ones they would all remember for the rest of their lives, he said. Then he introduced Jim Hough.

He reminded his classmates that while the past had been great, the future was now on the horizon.

"From this day forward our lives will change dramatically," he said. "Some of us will go on to college and have a future as a doctor or a lawyer or an accountant.

Others of us will move on to a form of business and begin making money and buying homes. Soon after that will come marriage and kids and events that may take us to all parts of the country. When we gather together at reunions many years from now, it will be interesting to see the many changes in all of us.

"But in spite of what may happen in the years to come, we all share a common bond. We are the graduating seniors of the class of 1973, something no one else can ever say. We share memories of study halls and English papers and after school trips to the K & W. We have proms and school plays and athletic events that we will always remember. But above it all we have the friendships that have been years in the making. Though we may be separated by distance and circumstance, we will have those friendships that will always keep us together.

"My fellow graduates, I wish you well."

When the applause subsided, the band played the school fight song as the graduates filed out one at a time. They turned to hug one another, and then parents jumped out of the bleachers to join in the celebration.

Norma Baker sat in the back row, sobbing. Brutey would have loved this moment, too. Suddenly she felt like it had been an eternity since Brutey had gone to jail.

* * *

I was probably the last one in our house to go to sleep that night. I was up late thinking, wondering about the upcoming summer festival and baseball season. A brisk summer breeze whistled through my bedroom window, sounding a little like a train off in the distance. Otherwise, our house was so quiet with everyone sound asleep, and before long I too was lost in a deep sleep.

The Springboro Panthers were playing for the Class AA state championship at St. John's Arena on the campus of Ohio State University. After losing two of their first five games, Coach Harry Hall made the unprecedented move of bringing up an eighth grader to his team. Since then, Jeff Kirby has averaged more than thirty points a game, and since then, the Panthers have won twenty games in a row.

There's a capacity crowd in attendance and Myrtle Reedy, the Springboro "super fan," is sitting right behind the Panther bench waving a banner…

I was twelve years old. I may have lived in a small town, but I had big time dreams.

CHAPTER 43

Jenny, I don't know if Momma was right or if, if it's Lieutenant Dan. I don't know if we each have a destiny, or if we're all just floating around accidental-like on a breeze, but I, I think maybe it's both.
-- The theology of Forrest Gump

LIFE THROUGH THE YEARS

1973 TO PRESENT DAY

The Springboro class of 1973 moved on to college and their new families and their careers, and the town continued to grow. The green space that once existed north of town all the way to the Dayton Mall gradually disappeared, until it became a big four-lane highway with development on all sides. The same was true west of town all the way to Franklin. And along the way the farmlands were chewed up and split apart and made into subdivisions, making Springboro the near-metropolis that it is today.

Brutey was released from the county jail on a hot September Friday afternoon, and he returned home with little fanfare. The family of Janet Spencer had already moved out. The other neighbors didn't even acknowledge him as he stepped out of the car. He took a long, hot shower, ate a quiet dinner with Norma and then retired to the back porch to drink lemonade and try to put some perspective back in life.

"What's done is done," he said. "I have to be a man about this, and go about the work that I have in life. That means being a good husband for you, and being a good father to our boys, and going to work everyday so I can provide for all of you. To do anything more won't bring Janet back."

Norma reached over to touch Brutey's hand. She had worried about his sanity once the jail sentence was finished. Would he be depressed and become a recluse, or would he realize that there were many years left in his life and that he still had things he could accomplish? At least in the few hours she had had him home, he seemed resolved to finishing what he started the moment he decided he had to come clean over what he had done.

People have done worse things.

People have had harder circumstances to endure.

Brutey said those things over and over to himself, figuring that after a while he would actually believe them to be true.

"Honey, I'm here for you, no matter what," Norma said. "There's a difference between being a bad person and a person who does a bad thing. You're a good man, Brutey. I'm lucky to have you, and so are the boys. Your job now is to be here for them."

They sat quietly as the sun began to fall below the maple trees at the far edge of their property. The heat of the summer was quickly turning into a cool evening, which brought an abrupt chill. Brutey soaked in the quiet peace of his own backyard, and mentally he focused himself on returning to as normal a life as he could. He would take it one day at a time.

Just then he was abruptly thrown from his chair.

In the distance, he could hear the sounds of the Springboro marching band, with P.B. Stockman announcing their playing of the national anthem. In a few minutes, starting lineups would be announced and the new football season would be underway.

He hung his head as the memories quickly came rushing back. Maybe there would be a day when he would go back to the games, but tonight wouldn't be the night. No, not tonight.

It was still too hard, and way too early. He wasn't ready to be pointed at, gawked at and talked about behind his back. He missed the game, and he still loved all the players, but his presence would likely be more of a distraction than any help to them. His coaching days were done.

He excused himself and walked inside the house, where he sat in front of the television with the volume so loud that he could not hear the sounds from the game nearby.

Maybe someday he'd go back, but not tonight.

Definitely not tonight.

* * *

He stayed away for the better part of two years, but once he started back, he was there for everything. Brutey was in the stands when ABC-TV came to Springboro in the winter of 1978 to do a documentary on the girls basketball team in general and on Amy Tucker in particular. He also followed that team all the way to the Class AA state finals, where it lost a heartbreaker. He loved that a great group of hard-working girls was so successful, but Brutey especially loved the fact that Coach Don Ross, who was four years removed from leading the varsity football team, was the coach that led them on their magical journey.

He was also along the sidelines when the 1982 football team, coached by Bruce Smith, accomplished Springboro's first-ever undefeated football season. He often told people that while Greg Baker was the undisputed leader of that team, he had plenty of help – Johnny Bryant and Matt McGrew were also awesome running backs, and quarterback David Tibbitts was a deadly passer to the likes of Jim Denney, and the defense was a violent force all through the season. He believed that McGrew's 55-yard touchdown run in the Monroe game was perhaps the most pivotal play of the entire season, because it turned the tide in the third game of the season and propelled the Panthers the rest of the way.

He was there through countless girls' games coached by Rick Creager, and was there when Troy Holtrey made his coaching debut in what has become a very successful and illustrious coaching career. Like everyone else in Springboro, he watched '86 graduate Brad Lamb play in the 1991 Super Bowl as a member of the Buffalo Bills. And he loved watching Adam Dillon run a football in the '99 season and further enjoyed Jake Ballard and his band of tenacious teammates who went undefeated and into the state playoffs in 2005.

He sat and he watched and he grew comfortable again in assessing talent and pointing out where they could become even better players.

But he never asked to become a coach again.

There were times he waited for someone to ask him, but as time passed and the athletic program changed hands, he found that he was less and less familiar with the people who were in charge. By the time Jake Ballard hung up his cleats, Brutey was nothing more than a by-stander in the stands. He was not regarded as a pioneer who helped build the program into what it is today. He slowly accepted that reality and came to realize that he had had his fifteen minutes of fame.

Norma, however, could tell that Brutey was becoming increasingly restless. He was succeeding at work, and they had moved from their ranch-style home on Market Street to a three-bedroom split-level in Greenleaf Village, which had a three-car garage and a fully finished basement with a built-in movie theater. The boys were grown, and they had children of their own, and Brutey spent time going to their games as well.

It wasn't enough, though. Norma could tell.

"I'm fine," he'd say.

"You sure?"

"Sure, I'm sure."

And she would go back to reading the paper, knowing full well it wasn't enough.

Through the years, Brutey changed considerably. He stayed away from alcohol, which meant no more late-night carousing in the bars. He helped Norma around the house and he was attentive to the boys and the grandchildren. But he didn't laugh as much as he used to. He didn't call on any friends and never did anything, aside from go to ball games. He adopted a favorite chair in the den, and he spent most of his days and nights sitting in it, flipping the channels.

The world was getting bigger, and meaner, and more complex, and Brutey didn't like it. Norma had learned to leave the room when the news came on, since it was sure to evoke a tirade about Brutey's views about the government, or politics, or the world in general.

She prayed every night for Brutey to find some interest that would change the direction of his thinking. She hoped that an old friend would call, or some new hobby would develop. There had once been a time when she considered a divorce because he had been so involved in so many things, and so attracted by the public attention his way. Now he was just the opposite. And in Norma's mind, this was worse.

"I'm fine," he'd say again.

CHAPTER 43

"You sure?" she would ask again.

"Sure, I'm sure."

Hmmmm.....

What saddened Brutey most of all through the years was to see his friends pass away. It seemed there was a phone call or an item in the paper every week. He'd gone to funerals for Ralph Wade, Jim Hough Sr., Vince Ross, Neil Clingman, Lowell Hayes, Charlie Reedy, Junior Dillon and Cotton Orsborne, just to name a few. At each one he was reminded of how short life can be, and how difficult it was while it lasted. It brought back memories of Janet Spencer's death, and how the accident that caused it actually took two lives – hers and his. In a twisted way, he often wondered if she got the better end of the deal.

Then, most recently, Brutey read about the death of Brian Keaton, a kid who played on one of his first junior high football teams back in the sixties. Brian was a good player whose career had been cut short by a knee injury in a game at Little Miami. What Brutey didn't know was what happened to Brian after high school, when Brian went to college and then moved away. The paper said he worked for The Life Project, a non-profit organization in Southern California, but it didn't say what kind of work he did.

The memorial service was on a Tuesday at the Springboro Christian Church. Brian's mom had remained a member of the church, and Reverend Dawes certainly remembered how Brian was so active in the youth group when he was a kid. So he was more than willing to share a few words at the service.

Brutey sat in the back row, away from Brian's wife and children. Some of Brian's former classmates and teammates were also in attendance, and Brutey enjoyed seeing those guys again. He was glad to see that the boys moved on to be solid people, with good jobs and wives and children to care for. From what he overheard, Brian had done very well for himself, and his death was a tragic loss to all his friends and family. He was only 49 years old.

Reverend Dawes stood tall in the pulpit at exactly eleven o'clock. Though he was retired from full-time ministry at over eighty years of age, he still had a commanding presence. He quoted Jesus' words from Matthew 18:3 and then he went on to give a detailed history of the life of Brian Keaton: Born and raised in Springboro ... from which he graduated in 1975 ... good football and basketball player until a knee injury ended his playing career ... then he went off to San Diego State University, where he majored in political science ... had hopes of being a lawyer one day, but his plans were sidetracked when he became involved in a children's home just north of San Diego.

"Brian learned that he loved working with children more than anything. He loved their enthusiasm and their unbridled potential," Reverend Dawes said. "He loved it so much that he started his own mission. He raised some money and opened up a children's home that had a goal of not only housing children, but investing in them and building them up. Through the years more than 30,000 kids have gone through the doors of his home, and all of them have graduated from high school. Most of them have gone on to lead productive lives, with good jobs, getting married and having children of their own. Many of those kids will point to Brian Keaton as their inspiration in life."

Brian's mother started to cry, as did his wife and children. From fifteen rows back, Brutey felt a tear in his eye, too. He always knew Brian was a special kid, but he was moved by what he had accomplished through the years.

"But do you know who Brian Keaton points to as an inspiration in his life?" Reverend Dawes let the words hang for several moments, for emphasis.

"Well, there were several. First, thankfully, he stayed faithful in his walk with God. And second, there was, of course, his parents. And like so many people I talk to, he was inspired by many teachers and coaches from his younger days when he was growing up here in Springboro.

"But there was one very special person, and he talked about this person many times over the years. There was a time in Brian's life when he was at an awkward age, and he felt a little disconnected from his parents. It was the sixties, and many of you know that was a time when many of the young people were rebelling against authority. Brian wanted to wear his hair longer, and he wanted to listen to that rock and roll music that was becoming so popular back then. And there were days, as Brian's parents will tell you, that life in their home wasn't so happy because of it.

"But Brian was motivated throughout his life by what he learned growing up in Springboro. He loved this small town and the people in it. He loved the varsity games on Friday night, and the way the players on those teams motivated him, even after he left here. And he especially loved his many coaches. Mr. E.B. Smith was his football coach one year, and Bill McGraw was his baseball coach. He looked up to the varsity coaches like Don Ross and Harry Hall and Larry Hefflin, and his dream was to play for them one day. And there was another coach he admired, a man sitting back there in the back of this church, who loved Brian and worked with him, and molded him into not only a fine athlete, but also a fine person. And Brian never forgot Brutey Baker because of it."

CHAPTER 43

Norma felt chills go down her back. Brutey couldn't believe what he was hearing. He barely remembered doing anything special for Brian.

Unless that meant he did something special for all of his players.

"Brian learned from this town, its people, and his coaches that if you will take the time to invest in a child's life, and be there for them, and really believe in them, then that child can someday move mountains. That child will go off and do more than you may even imagine they are capable of. That's what Brian has done. And he has consistently given a lot of the credit for that to the lessons he learned from little Springboro, Ohio."

Reverend Dawes pulled out a piece of paper and adjusted his glasses so he could read it. The people he was talking to were spellbound, hanging on his ever word.

"In The Life Project headquarters in California, this plaque is near the front door, and this is what it says: 'The heart of a child is the heart of our world. Nurture it, feed it, and care for it, and then watch it grow. My hometown did that for me at a time I needed it most. Now you go and be that inspiration to some other child. People were the heart of my hometown, and they were the heart of my school. The town, its people, the players and their coaches, they were the heart of the Panthers.' Signed, Brian Keaton."

Norma put her hand on Brutey's, and together they cried. For the first time in years, Brutey remembered the value he had. His head was spinning, with so many thoughts spiraling through his head – like how often he thought he was worthless, and yet how many people loved and believed in him, and how he had made his life miserable in believing the worst about himself. He was nearly seventy now, thirty-five years removed from coaching. But was it possible he had been wrong about himself? Is it possible that Norma was right about him all along?

They mingled with the crowd once the service was over, and later they joined in the lunch. Afterward, Brutey told Norma he needed to go for a walk, and that she could go ahead and go on home.

He walked across the street to the school that used to be the Springboro High School and now is the intermediate school for sixth graders. Behind it was the field that used to be Springboro's football field, and now is the soccer field. He sat in the bleachers there reliving his wonderful memories, and thinking about what he could do with the rest of his life.

Was it possible at his age to still do something?

He asked the question over and over. He remained there for more than an hour, reminiscing about memories from long ago. He could see himself working with Coach Ross, Coach Hefflin and Coach Smith, discussing a change in an offensive scheme that would exploit a hole in an opponent's defense. Behind him were the outside basketball courts where he had spent many hot summer night watching the best players Springboro had work on their game.

Was it possible to still do something?

Was it really possible?

The answers in the air were loud and clear.

CHAPTER 44

Life is all about second chances. The trick is learning from the mistakes we made the first time around, and enjoying the happy ending that's waiting for all of us.
-- The good news

FOOTBALL PRACTICE AT THE FIELD

PRESENT DAY

The first team meeting of the new football season was thirty minutes away, and Brutey stood at midfield, soaking in the warmth of the hot July sun. The meeting would take place at the new football field, the one on top of the hill by the high school that replaced the older, original field from years earlier. At the moment, Brutey thought it was the most spectacular place on Earth. He wondered how he could have ever criticized such an amazing place.

He held in his hands his trusty clipboard, the one that had the list of practices and games and, most importantly, the sixty kids who would play football for the Springboro sixth grade traveling team. The players and their parents would arrive any minute now, and he would lay out the ground rules for the season ahead – positive attitudes, hard work, and all-out effort. At age sixty-nine, after more than thirty-five years away from coaching, he was back where he always knew he belonged.

He was home.

Brutey took a deep breath and looked around at the field, the goal posts, and the massive bleachers that lined both sides of the field. He could practically hear the call of a quarterback's cadence, and feel the pounding of linebackers crunching a running back. On the very spot he stood, his team would one day face a fourth-and goal and he would have to call the right play. Do it right, and the Panthers scored a touchdown. Do it wrong, and he'd hear about it from the bleachers. Truth be known, he was as nervous as he was excited.

"Do you smell that? Football is in the air. I'm going to meet some great kids and hopefully build a good rapport with their parents right from the start, because that can be the whole key to the season. The kids are always great, but the parents … that's the only part that can be a headache. Plus I have to do is figure out what a 'Team Mom' is. I got a call from a woman the other night telling that's who she was. Did they have that back in your day?"

"Not a chance," I responded.

"I didn't think so."

Brutey checked his notes and sat quietly in the bleachers, waiting for the SUVs and mini-vans to pull into the parking lot.

"Years ago, kids just rode to the practice field on their bikes. I didn't have to deal with parents," he said.

Brutey warmly greeted each of the players and their parents as they arrived. He had chairs positioned throughout the north end zone for them to sit in. Some of the boys waltzed in with a confident swagger, wearing jerseys from the season before. Their fathers wore Bengal hats and Springboro football T-shirts, clear statements they knew football. Other players were more tentative. Some wore glasses and others had Space Invader T-shirts, which indicated they didn't have much experience, and they weren't sure they belonged. Little did they know that they were kind of kids Brutey most loved to coach. He knew full well that sometimes the studs from fifth grade were nowhere to be found when high school ball started.

"Pleasure to meet you, Coach," one father said. "This here's Tyler. We lived in Cincinnati last year, and just moved in. We're looking forward to playing this year."

"Good to have you. Nice to meet you. Tyler, are you ready to go to work?"

He tasseled the boy's hair and told him to take a seat. Then he gathered everyone together.

"Everyone take a seat, please." They assembled in quick fashion, adjusting their chairs and personal items, before finally looking up at the man in front of them.

CHAPTER 44

Brutey was tanned, a little thinner around the waist, and dressed in gray coaching shorts, white socks, tennis shoes and a Panther blue sport shirt.

He paused for a second to look over the parents and players in front of them.

A smile never left his face.

"For you young fellas, today begins a journey that can last your entire life. When you put on a blue and white jersey, you become a Panther. And as a Panther you become part of an exclusive fraternity. You will become connected with so many great guys and girls who have been Panthers through the years.

"I've seen all the good ones in my day. I coached many of them. They all started like you do today, and you can grow up and work hard and someday be the captain of a very good football team, just like they did. That's my hope for all of you. I can assure you, there will be few things in life that will stay with you like being a Panther."

Brutey spoke like a skilled attorney making his case. He had undivided eye contact from every player and every parent. He had a few more things to say, so he went right to it.

"So I have several goals this year. First, I want us to learn some of the history of Springboro football. When you see Ed Wade in the bleachers, I want you to see him as someone more than just an insurance agent. I want you to see him as one of you, as a kid who was once the varsity quarterback. Bob Fares is more than just a guy who works the chains. He played on the '82 undefeated team and was one of their most valuable linemen. Bobby Anderson is more than just a freshmen coach. He played on the '91 team that almost made the playoffs and made second-team all-Ohio.

"These guys are Panthers. They have different jobs now, but they carry that Panther blood in them, and they watch and follow you because the current Panthers are like extensions of themselves. If you do well, they're happy for you. They can feel like their lasting legacy was to leave a productive and successful football program for the kids who followed them."

Nearby, some of the old-timers had emerged from a meeting inside the school. They listened to Brutey for a little while. They nodded in agreement as he spoke.

"I'm putting together some booklets that give some of the history of Springboro football. We're going to review those every now and again, probably as much as we're going to review proper pass protection and good defense. By doing this, you're going to know who paved the way for each of you. And maybe you can thank them someday."

He paused momentarily, looking down at his clipboard. He knew his next statement was likely to ruffle some feathers.

"The other thing I want to do is make sure I give each of you a chance to show yourselves. Here's why I say that. Some of you have natural talent, even though you're only eleven or twelve years old, and in most situations you would be the starters who played most of every game. But others of you have to work at it, because you're just not there yet. It'll come if you're only given the chance. And I've seen so many potentially good players just give up because they grow tired of practicing all week and never getting to play. And then what happens? By the time everyone gets to high school, the natural athletes quit because they're tired of playing all the time, and the potentially better players have all quit and are instead walking the halls -- because no one gave them a chance. My goal is to keep a proper focus for all of you, regardless of where you are on the talent scale right now.

"So here's what I'm going to do. We play our games on Saturdays. That's when I'll have starters and I'll try to get as many of you in as I can. It's hard to do with sixty players, though. I'd say it's probably impossible. But we'll have our games in our nice blue uniforms, just like you did in third, fourth and fifth grade and like you'll do in the years to come.

"But, in addition to that, Wednesdays will be a night we have our own intra-team league. This group will be broken down into four separate teams, and we'll have two games going every Wednesday. We'll have a black team, a red team, a green team and a yellow team. And each of you will be starters on those teams and you'll play the whole game, both ways. That's the way a lot of peewee programs used to do it; some still do. By doing this, those of you who may not get a lot of playing time on the Saturday games, you can look forward to your Wednesday games."

Brutey still found undivided eye contact. He didn't see any grimaces on the faces of the parents. In fact it was just the opposite. There seemed to be a sense of relief. Nobody liked practicing all the time. The fun part was game action.

"Here's what I think will happen if we do that. One of you kids who isn't quite sure of himself, you'll get the chance to play and work on your game. You'll mess up a time or two, but you won't have to wait a week or two for your next chance to play. You'll have another chance in just a few minutes. And then, by the end of the season, we have a bunch of even better football players. The naturally talented athletes will still be good, but also we'll have a whole crop of guys who improved tremendously over the year. As a result, the Panther mystique gets wider. The Panther tradition grows.

"And that's the heart of the Panthers."

He waited for any additional reaction. He was prepared to say if anybody had a problem with that approach, they could go ahead and leave now. But he never had to say it. For the parents, there would be no additional game time or practice time. And they're kids would be happier.

He talked about working hard and having fun. He never once indicated that they had to win games to be successful.

* * *

Later, after the meeting ended, he stopped at the K & W for old time's sake. All he could purchase was a Diet Pepsi, but it was the sweetest drink he'd ever had. He sat on a park bench near Mr. Chenault's house and watched all the traffic go by. The sun was setting in the distance.

One brand new car after another passed by him. It was so busy that a left turn onto Mill Street required a five-minute wait. The price of gas had increased again that day to a staggering $3.07 per gallon. A brand-new Suburban passed by with four teenagers inside, with all four of them on their cell phones.

Brutey barely noticed. He was lost in his players and the plans he had for the upcoming season. The images from long ago had passed. He no longer saw Bill Crocker, Jr. rolling our right looking to pass. And he didn't see Dick Mahan making a crunching tackle. Instead, he had images of today's Panthers. He could see them dressed up in their Springboro blue, with their white helmets and with blue and white streamers hanging from the antennas on their parents' cars.

He had fond memories of yesterday. But he now loved today.

He was a Panther again.

POST-GAME WRAP-UP

I was born in a small town
And I can breathe in a small town
I'll probably die in a small town
Ah, that's probably where they'll bury me.
-- John Mellencamp

A SUMMER FRIDAY NIGHT

Present Day

"Jeff!"

I could feel someone shaking my shoulder. Now who would be doing that? Couldn't they see I was in the middle of a big game? I was doing something awesome. Newspapers were going to put my picture in the paper. The town was going to have a parade in my –

"Honey! Jeff!"

I slowly opened my eyes to see my wife Kim standing over me. Where was I? What day was it? Could it be that I was no longer a kid, playing games all day? I'm sure I looked at her like she had three eyes.

What the –?

"Jim needs you next door. The guys are over there and he wants to show you something."

My body creaked as I tried getting off the sofa. "How long have I been asleep?" I asked. I looked at the clock over the television and it said 8:45. What I wasn't sure about was whether it was a.m. or p.m.

"A long time. I've already pulled all the weeds in the front flower bed. When you're over at Jim's make sure you get the hedge trimmers. We have to get that bush out front under control before Friday."

Uh, huh. Clearly I was back to reality now. But the time with Lance and Mitch and Brutey Baker had all seemed so real! I had been twelve again, laughing and living without a worry in the world. That had been fun, but I realized something that I'm not sure I comprehended before: Life is all about getting older and embracing the new challenges we must confront. There is no getting around that. Our bodies may grow older, and our circumstances change, but the key to life is keeping that childlike perspective – by creating happiness in any situation, and retaining a joyful innocence about the world around us, instead of dwelling on the negative.

And Brutey! Thank goodness my problems weren't as bad as his. I began to reflect on the mistakes of my life, the things that will weigh me down if I dwell on them, and came to only one conclusion, that we all have made mistakes and the key to life is to move on in spite of them. We can't spend our days reliving our mistakes in our minds. That serves no purpose. Instead, we should move forward and go after what is good in life.

We all have passions in life, and life is not complete until we pursue them. For Brutey, he needed to get back to coaching. For me, I was motivated to begin writing this book. Suddenly I was more at peace with being forty-something, with a mortgage and a stressful job. I was alive and problems like that are just part of being human.

I trudged next door to our neighbors, Jim and Jill Anderson's, trying to wipe the sleep from my eyes. There was a lot to do before Friday's graduation party, so I knew I couldn't stay long. We had invited only two hundred of our closest friends to celebrate it. So our house had to be in perfect shape for the party. Along the way, I saw five things I would have to do in the next few days.

"That's okay," I thought to myself. At least we had a reason to celebrate something. My family was safe, we lived in a nice neighborhood, and I was able to provide for them the way I need to.

I found Jim behind his house at his pool, sitting with Gene Simone, Dave Stuckey and Dave Ramig, all of whom had kids who had previously graduated from Springboro. They were drinking beer and laughing and smoking cigars – living life. I loved that about these guys, always celebrating life. Jim told me to sit down. "Here, let me tell you a joke," he said. And he let loose with an off-color joke with the same enthusiasm he had had moments before when he told it to the other guys.

It was a good joke all right. And the three of them laughed like it was the first time they heard it.

We had had many backyard discussions over the years. Invariably, our discussions would turn to the current state of Springboro athletics. Rodney Roberts was doing an excellent job as new coach of the football team, though he left soon after to go back to Franklin, and Troy Holtrey was firmly entrenched as one of the best coaches the basketball program had ever seen. But, more than that, there were questions to debate. Who were some of the best players over the years? Where are they now? How would history view their place within the program? We could debate this for hours.

We would do all of that again some other time. At the moment, I needed to go. I grabbed an extension cord, listened to one more joke, and then I returned home to keep up with Kim and the work she was doing around the house.

At least I had a house to take care of, I thought. And that was something good.

* * *

Rod Dillon left Springboro after high school and went to Kalamazoo College in Michigan, where he played quarterback on the football team until an injury sent him to the sideline. He coached briefly at Springboro for several years under head coach Bruce Smith before leaving teaching to go into the corporate world. He married **Pam Hepp** a few years out of high school, and they have two children. Rod has returned to teaching at Little Miami High School, and he is the scorekeeper for Springboro basketball games. Pam is a writer for *The Dayton Daily News*.

Coach Don Ross retired from coaching football after the '73 season and later went on to coach the girls basketball team, which, in the 1977-78 season, advanced to the state Class AA finals before losing. He later became the school's athletic director at a time his son Steve played basketball and daughter Jody ran track. He retired from the school district in 1993 and became a city councilman and an active member of the Springboro historical society. He now lives near Columbus.

Coach Harry Hall retired from coaching in 1977 and became, of all things, a basketball official, an ironic twist given the grief he always gave officials when he was a coach. **Coach Larry Hefflin** retired in 1988 after dominating the FAVC track scene for nineteen seasons. And **Coach Bruce Smith**, another assistant coach on the '72 team, became head coach after Coach Ross resigned. He went on to became the winningest head football coach in Springboro history, coaching from 1973 to 1986 and then again in 1988 before becoming athletic director. His dad, **E.B. Smith**, continued to dominate the peewee league until the influx of soccer decimated the program in the early 80s. Mr. Smith also worked the first-down markers on the sidelines during home games, something he did for thirty years.

Ed Wade joined his father's insurance agency right after graduation from Ohio State. **Ralph Wade** died in 1979 of a heart attack at the age of 51, and now the field that was once the varsity football field and is now the high school soccer field is named after him. The six-foot slope that was so evident in the late sixties is no longer there. Ralph's daughter **Sandy Wray** is principal of the Dennis Elementary School.

Jim Hough, Jr. played basketball at Wright State University and then returned to Springboro. His mother was a Wade -- Ralph Wade's sister -- so he went to work at Wade Insurance selling health insurance after graduation. Jim is now remarried and has a grown son, Brandon, and another son, Corey, who is a senior at Springboro and also universally recognized as one of the finer pitchers in the area. His father, **Jim Hough, Sr**., the former Springboro coach and principal, a man who in college played for University of Dayton teams that excelled in the NIT, died in 2003.

John "Hog" Mockabee opened a lawn care business known as The Master's Touch, which services many of the homes in and around Springboro. His younger brother **Chuck Mockabee** used to be in the same business, but has since moved on and continues to live in the area. **Gary Patton** became principal at the Warren County Career Center, where **Gordy Gregg**, who is now married to Kim Leisz, Mitch's older sister, also is a teacher. And **Dave Collins**, who received a scholarship after high school to the Naval Academy, has two children and lives in Washington Court House.

Jeff Howard enjoyed more basketball stardom after high school than he did during it. He went to Eastern Kentucky University, where he roomed with Dan Patrick Pugh, who now uses his abbreviated name of Dan Patrick on ESPN. He left school after a year and returned to Springboro where he worked for Mr. Nordheim's (our seventh grade math teacher) Sohio station in the center of town earning $1.65 an hour. To say that that's not what he wanted to do the rest of his life would be an understatement. Then one day Mike Flynn, who was a year younger than Jeff, suggested that Jeff join him at a college in Arizona. They were in need of good basketball players, Mike said. So Jeff went.

He had a standout career at Mesa College. What's more, with his scoring and leaping ability, he earned a try-out with the Los Angeles Lakers, and later tried out for the Indiana Pacers. He then had a good opportunity with the Milwaukee Bucks, but that was the year Sidney Moncrief left college early to turn pro, ruining Jeff's opportunity with them. "Obviously I wasn't a Sidney Moncrief fan for a while after that," he said. He married **Cindy Jozwiak**, who played on Coach Ross' 1977-78 girls basketball team that went all the way to the Ohio Class AA finals before losing, and they have three children; middle child Tyler transferred to Springboro for the 2004-05 basketball season, helping the Panthers to another brilliant season and a Mid-Miami League championship.

My buddy **Donny Wilburn** later became an all-star player for the varsity basketball team, then married **Karen Dalton** and moved with his family to Kentucky, where he took over his uncle's vending business. His father died years ago but his mom still lives in the house Donny grew up in on Maple Drive. **Mitch Leisz**, who also went on to play varsity basketball, is a chef and **Lance Penwell** works in the leather business and **Danny Kruer** is an excavator. **Roger Woolery** has done very well for himself, and he owns a home in Springboro and has two children. Chris Hill, "**Turkey**," lives in Florida, and the last I heard **Shane Hatfield**, who was a star running back for the Springboro varsity while in high school, was driving a truck along the eastern seaboard. I suspect he's somehow competitive in how he does that, too.

The Reverend Delbert Dawes was minister of the Springboro Christian Church until he retired a few years ago at eighty years old, but he continues to visit people in the hospital and in their homes. When my neighbor Jim Anderson's mother became ill in the spring of 2001, Reverend Dawes met with her many times a week and talked about life and family and the good old days, then preached a beautiful service at her funeral. He did the same thing when Jim's dad died a few years later. As always, Reverend Dawes projected an image that by being with him and talking to him, it was like being in the presence of God himself. He has always been God's special messenger.

But he suffered a terrible loss in 2005 when his beloved wife Omalee died suddenly.

Charlie Reedy and **Jimmy Beavers** both worked with the Springboro Police Department until the mid-1990s, when they each retired. Charlie remarried later in life to his wife Fran, and after retirement he became my first bailiff in the Springboro Court, where I am a magistrate. He never brought up publicly his suspicion that I set fire to the grass behind the Jonathan Wright Elementary School back when I was a kid, but he knew I'd done it. It remained our little secret. Charlie died suddenly in early 1996 from complications from surgery.

POST-GAME WRAP UP

Jimmy took over for Charlie as my bailiff and we worked together for six years until he retired to the solitude of country life and the sweet cooking of his wife Gladys. I enjoyed those years with Jimmy.

As for **The Kirby Family**, oddly enough, I never did become a varsity Panther, as I had dreamed about so many times when I was a kid. In the summer between seventh and eighth grade, my dad announced that we were moving to Franklin. When I told some of the kids at school, they were instantly devastated. One girl worried that I'd be killed within a week.

We moved to Franklin in late 1973 primarily because there was not a house big enough to house five fledging teenagers in Springboro. In today's world of one big house after another, that seems incredible. But I indeed went to Franklin, became a Wildcat, and actually enjoyed my time there. My next project will be titled, *Once A Wildcat, Always A Wildcat*, and I intend to tell the story of a somewhat misunderstood town.

I'm now a lawyer and magistrate in Springboro, and I did finally kiss a girl one day, and later even got married. My wife Kim is beautiful, and Adam and Chloe are the joy that all children should bring to their parents.

My youngest brother Joey is also a lawyer, plus he is judge of the Warren County Court in Lebanon. He's married and has three children, Connor, Chase and Sophie. My brother John, who still has his red hair, is a stand-up comedian and manager of Tri-City Title Agency. My sister Jenny is a teacher in Franklin, married, and she too has three children, Sara, Alison and Kevin. My other sister Julie is a flight attendant with American Airlines, for whom she flies international, going to London and Paris several times each month. Meanwhile, Mom and Dad live in a house across from the newest Springboro High School and specialize in being doting grandparents.

I am thankful to many people and their cooperation in writing this book. I've talked to Eleanor Cushman, Dick Chenault, Betty Reedy, Fran Reedy, John Mockabee, Jeff Howard, Gordy Gregg, Rod Dillon, Pam Dillon, Jim Hough, Coach Harry Hall, Mitch Leisz, Gary Powers, Linda Fish Oda, Dr. Scott Swope and Lance Penwell. I am especially thankful to Coach Don Ross, who was not only valuable because of his insight, but also because of his editing abilities. He was an English teacher for thirty years, and a former *Star Free Press* sports editor, just like me, and without his assistance this book would not have been possible.

* * *

Adam's graduation party was fabulous. The house looked great and everyone had a great time socializing and listening to the live band. At nine o'clock we circled everyone around a movie screen and showed them a ten-minute tribute to Adam, which was a wonderful moment. Kim cried, as did Adam's dad. It was hard to believe that this kid who's now six-two had ever been so little. But now he's all grown up, which is a reminder again that time passes and things change.

And life is good. Adam smiled the whole night, and then gave his mom a kiss and a hug. He appreciated the party and thanked us many times over – right up until the time he got in his car and drove away. There's always someplace else to be, you know.

The next day, I drove to the grocery to pick up some lunch items for the next work day. I turned left onto Sycamore Trails and made my way out of our subdivision. As I drove, I saw Jeremiah and Elijiah playing basketball with Barrett and Ben and all their buddies in the cul-de-sac to my right.

And then on down the street, to my left, there was Austin once again, shooting outside jumpers in the din of the evening light at the house that had the fantastic basketball court. In a few years, some seventh-grade kid was going to look up at him the way he looked up at Chip James and Seth Daliboa. And thirty years from now, they would all look back and call these the good old days.

I returned home to find Kim on the phone to her mother. Chloe was next door playing with Jill Anderson and their dog Jake. It was a beautiful summer night, with a cool breeze coming from the north.

I went into the garage and found my basketball. I laced up some tennis shoes and took a spot near my make-believe free throw line. I took three dribbles and let the ball spin in my hands. There were two seconds left in Springboro's big game against Mason. We were down by one point. The standing room only crowd was on its feet, screaming at the game's every move.

I let fire the first of the two free throws…

I had the heart of a Panther again.

AUTHOR'S NOTE

One of my favorite movies was *Forrest Gump*. I enjoyed its imagery and its reflection of our American culture. Perhaps more than anything, I was moved by Forrest's unending love for people – his mama, Bubba and Lt. Dan, and especially Jenny. And when Forrest finished a particular subject, he didn't have a complicated and flowery ending to it. Instead, he'd say, "That's all I have to say about that."

Because I have loved that movie so much, I have seen it no less than a hundred times. Maybe twice that.

While watching that movie, I have never been tempted to wonder if Forrest was a real person. I have also never been tempted to wonder who he personifies. That is, was his creator actually telling someone else's story in Forrest's name?

This book is a true account of life in Springboro in 1972 and 1973, and in the years thereafter. Many of the characters in it are real, for they embody the very fabric of the town. But other characters are fictional, utilized to help tell its story.

That's all I have to say about that.

-- Jeff

Jeff Kirby was sports editor of the Springboro Star Free Press from 1981 through 1987. He then became a lawyer in the Springboro law firm of Kirby & Kirby, where he practices with his father, Thomas Kirby, and his youngest brother, Joseph Kirby. He is magistrate in the Springboro court on Wednesdays.

He lives in Springboro with his wife Kim and their two children, Adam and Chloe.

www.jeffkirbybooks.com